T0291334

THE STRUGGLE FOR DEVELOPMENT IN IRAN

THE STRUGGLE FOR DEVELOPMENT IN IRAN

The Evolution of Governance, Economy, and Society

Pooya Azadi, Mohsen B. Mesgaran, and Matin Mirramezani

STANFORD UNIVERSITY PRESS
Stanford, California

STANFORD UNIVERSITY PRESS

Stanford, California

©2022 by Pooya Azadi, Mohsen B. Mesgaran, and Matin Mirramezani.
All rights reserved.

No part of this book may be reproduced or transmitted in any form or
by any means, electronic or mechanical, including photocopying and
recording, or in any information storage or retrieval system without the
prior written permission of Stanford University Press.

Printed in the United States of America on acid-free, archival-quality paper

Library of Congress Cataloging-in-Publication Data

Names: Azadi, Pooya, author. | Mesgaran, Mohsen B., author. |
    Mirramezani, Matin, author.
Title: The struggle for development in Iran : the evolution of governance,
    economy, and society / Pooya Azadi, Mohsen B. Mesgaran, and Matin
    Mirramezani.
Description: Stanford, California : Stanford University Press, 2022. |
    Includes index.
Identifiers: LCCN 2021048614 (print) | LCCN 2021048615 (ebook) |
    ISBN 9781503630468 (cloth) | ISBN 9781503631540 (ebook)
Subjects: LCSH: Economic development—Iran. | Iran—Economic
    conditions—1945–1979. | Iran—Economic conditions—1979–1997. |
    Iran—Economic conditions—1997– | Iran—Economic policy.
Classification: LCC HC475 .A934 2022 (print) | LCC HC475 (ebook) |
    DDC 338.955—dc23/eng/20211029
LC record available at https://lccn.loc.gov/2021048614
LC ebook record available at https://lccn.loc.gov/2021048615

Cover photo: Tehran, Walter Bibikow, Getty Images

Typeset by Newgen in Minion Pro 11/14

بر زمستان صبر باید طالب نوروز را

CONTENTS

Preface   ix

Acknowledgments   xiii

	Introduction	1
1	Governance	5
2	Demographic Trends	58
3	Labor Force and Human Capital	76
4	The Economy	96
5	The Financial Sector	123
6	The Energy Sector	142
7	The Agriculture Sector	166
8	Migration and Brain Drain	189
9	Research and Development Policy	206
	Conclusion: The Path Forward	223

Appendix A: Governance Indicators   229

Appendix B: Water Balance Data   231

Appendix C: Migration Data   232

Appendix D: Scientific Output Data   237

Notes   241

Index   257

PREFACE

Writing about Iran and its complex history of development in the modern era is a difficult task. Much of the serious literature on modern Iran focuses on politics, political history, geopolitical affairs, or narrow economic or technical subjects. The intellectual discourse about the impediments of growth in Iran is dominated by an exaggerated notion of the role of ideology, class struggles, imperialism, and historical contingencies while overlooking the profound impacts of institutions and fundamental socioeconomic trends. In this environment, ironically, stating the truth based on undeniable facts and data is often deemed as a political act. Furthermore, there are issues with the availability and quality of data which render broad data-driven studies of Iran a tedious undertaking. The primary sources of data on Iran are sparse, nonhomogeneous, and often not available in a format that can be readily used. Secondary datasets, such as those compiled by international organizations, are limited in temporal coverage and scope, and in some cases, are inconsistent with the underlying primary source. These are the reasons, despite the great deal of attention that Iran receives from scholars and the media, there is still a lack of understanding of the fundamental forces and trends in its economy and society. Without deciphering Iran's current issues by looking at the facts and data, predicting how the future of the country will unfold, both in domestic and international contexts, will remain guesswork. To address this issue, the Hamid and Christina Moghadam Program in Iranian Studies at Stanford University launched an initiative, the Stanford Iran 2040 Project, in 2016 to conduct data-driven research on key strategic areas relating to long-term development in Iran. The project has also been supported by the Freeman Spogli Institute at Stanford from the early stages of planning and development. The content of this book is based on the research conducted under this initiative.

In this book, we offer a multidimensional analysis of Iran's struggle for development over half a century between 1970 and 2020. Iran in this period witnessed one king, two supreme leaders, over a dozen prime ministers and presidents, a revolution, a long war, numerous episodes of economic crises, international sanctions, and political turmoil, as well as profound social changes toward more modern ways of life. The book consists of a short introduction, nine chapters on different subjects pertinent to development, and a final reflection of what the future may entail for Iran. We hope we have constructed a fair and somewhat holistic picture of some of the complex issues of development in Iran's modern history. The text has been written in clear and concise language which makes it accessible to a broad readership. The audience of the book encompasses researchers of a variety of disciplines, policymakers, journalists, and the business community. It can also be used as a textbook for a wide range of topics including Iranian studies, Middle Eastern studies, international development, political economy, and comparative politics.

Much of the content of this book is positive economics and data-driven analysis with a focus on fundamentals, institutions, and long-term trends. However, we have not been reluctant to criticize policies and policymakers if evidence and data warrant it. This approach distinguishes the present study from that of some other diaspora scholars whose work on Iran is, sadly, driven by their ideologies which can be anywhere across the political spectrum. For example, there has emerged a group of Islamic Republic apologists among the Iranian diaspora scholars with powerful roots in every domain of Iranian studies who are willing to openly or discreetly defend the regime under any circumstances using transparently fraudulent data and purposefully misleading arguments. On the opposite end, there are scholars who glorify the Pahlavi era with no regard for its shortcomings and the widespread dissatisfaction across large segments of Iranian society which ultimately led to the overthrow of the Shah and ended Iran's dynastic era. We strived to produce an unbiased account of the developments in Iran's troubled history of the past half century by drawing on evidence and citing data for every argument made throughout the book.

We welcome comments from scholars and experts and hope that this book contributes to professional and honest discourse among those who genuinely care about Iran and its future.

Pooya Azadi
California
June 2021

ACKNOWLEDGMENTS

Over the past five years, many colleagues and friends helped with the research presented in this book. We are greatly indebted to Abbas Milani, the director of the Hamid and Christina Moghadam Program in Iranian Studies at Stanford, not only for making the Iran 2040 initiative possible but also for generously sharing his vision and providing unconditional support. We are also thankful to Hamid Moghadam for his insightful and constructive comments on our research throughout these years. Our appreciation is also extended to Roma Parhad and Franco Errico for their invaluable help with every aspect of the Stanford Iran 2040 Project. We are grateful to Farzaneh Roudi, Razieh Zahedi, Sadra Sadeh, and Amin Feizpour who contributed to earlier versions of the work presented in chapters 2, 5, and 9. We would also like to thank Francis Fukuyama, Michael McFaul, and Behdad Aminzadeh for helpful comments and discussions on some of the working papers published by the Stanford Iran 2040 Project. We are grateful to the editorial and production teams at Stanford University Press, especially to Steve Catalano for his editorial guidance, encouragement, and thoughtful comments. Finally, we would like to thank our families for their support throughout the writing of this book.

The publication of this book was supported by the Hamid and Christina Moghadam Program in Iranian Studies at Stanford University.

THE STRUGGLE FOR DEVELOPMENT IN IRAN

INTRODUCTION

AT THE TIME OF THIS writing in 2021, Iran is facing a major crisis which, in terms of depth and scope, is unprecedented even by the Islamic Republic's own standards. The economy is spiraling downward, social crises are omnipresent, political and petty corruption are spreading like wildfire, political institutions are in decay and unable to function properly, and the legitimacy of the regime in the eyes of Iranians as well as the international community is at its lowest point in history. For decades, the Islamic Republic has responded to the challenges facing the country and the demands for change with irresponsible policies and brutal repression, which—although sometimes successfully eliminating the symptoms—have never properly addressed the underlying problems. As a result of this approach, as will be discussed in this book, the past few decades in Iran have been a period of sluggish and noninclusive economic growth, ill-fated social engineering with an Islamic template, political repression, and extensive environmental degradation. The compounding effects of these structural crises have brought Iran to the verge of a historic crossroad. While the continuation of business as usual will inevitably lead to a dire future, nothing is yet predetermined as the current crisis may in fact unite large segments of society to take collective action to bring about a positive paradigm shift. After all, difficult decisions and painful changes are often facilitated by deep crises, and in that spirit, the current crisis facing Iran need not beget a catastrophe and can in fact give rise to substantive changes in a desirable direction.

The literature on Iran over the past few decades has mostly focused on its ideological and political landscape, and geopolitical issues, sometimes with an obsession for the role of imperialism, while largely overlooking the role of the fundamental forces of the economy and social undercurrents that shape the development of the country. The aim of this book is to help fill this gap by presenting a multidimensional and critical analysis of Iran's path of development over its troubled history of the past half century. The book has an ambitious scope—to cover a wide array of subjects including governance, political economy, macroeconomy, demography, education, energy, food, and the environment. The content of the book is organized such that it helps readers gain a better understanding of the complex interactions among different dimensions of development.

Our analysis framework to decipher complex issues discussed in this book is based on a bottom-up approach where granular-level data are collected and analyzed to depict a more holistic picture with important policy implications. The data used throughout this manuscript were meticulously collected from hundreds of sources over several years. The data contain official statistics reported by national and international organizations and the authors' own estimates and calculations based on data extraction from online resources, which in some cases required applying innovative data-mining techniques.

The chapters of this book are organized as follows. In chapter 1, we discuss the evolution of Iran's political institutions and explain how they interacted with the economy in Iran's rapidly changing society. To this end, we focus on the evolution of three sets of political institutions, namely state, rule of law, and democratic accountability during four distinct periods: prerevolution (1970–1978), the early stage of the revolutionary state (1979–1988), reconstruction and reforms (1989–2004), and the period of governance deadlock and political decay (2005–2020). Chapter 2 provides an in-depth account of Iran's demographic dynamics by analyzing trends in population growth, fertility, marriage, age structure, life expectancy, urbanization, and population geographical distribution. Chapter 3 presents major trends in the labor market and human capital formation. In the first part, we describe the developments in Iran's labor force with a focus on the employment ratio in order to present the combined effects of unemployment and economic participation. We then discuss trends in Iran's labor productivity and wages. We also put the issue of the gender gap in Iran's labor market—which has remained unresolved despite the closure of the educational gap a long time ago—into a broader context using data from other countries. In the second part of chapter 3, we discuss Iran's progress and shortcomings in its century-long quest to improve literacy and human capital. The analysis covers both quantitative and qualitative aspects of human capital formation and their impacts on economic performance.

Chapter 4 provides an overview of the main trends in the economy using the same periods outlined in chapter 1. To delineate the overall economic performance of each period, we explore several important economic indicators such as real GDP growth, sectoral contributions, employment, inflation, trade, and capital formation. The last part of this chapter evaluates some of Iran's formidable economic challenges—namely, rising public debt, low tax extraction capacity, insufficient investments, imbalances in the financial sector, and water scarcity. We conclude this chapter by discussing the compounding effects of the above issues on the future trajectory of the economy.

In the next chapters of the book, we delve into several more specific but hugely consequential topics. Chapter 5 provides an account of developments in the financial sector with a focus on the performance of the banking system. It begins by evaluating the outcomes of Iran's Central Bank's monetary policy and the underlying institutional causes for its poor performance in controlling inflation. We then discuss trends in Iran's financial depth and the amount and distribution of credits allocated to different sectors. We end the chapter with a discussion on the challenges of the banking system using indicators that measure the soundness of the financial sector as a system. Chapter 6 provides an overview of Iran's energy landscape, starting with the trends in oil and gas production, domestic consumption, and exports. We also evaluate the historical role that oil revenue has played in financing public expenditures and discuss its future potential in light of the shifting paradigm of the global oil markets from scarcity to abundance. We will then explain how Iran's sheer volume of produced natural gas is allocated to different uses and discuss the inefficiencies associated with its misallocations. Finally, we will delineate trends in demand and supply sides of the electricity market and analyze Iran's controversial nuclear program from an economic standpoint. Chapter 7 is concerned with Iran's water crisis which is one of the most consequential issues that current and future generations of Iranians must deal with. This chapter begins with historical trends in Iran's domestic food supply focusing on agricultural water consumption, cultivated area, patterns of irrigation, and the amount and composition of agricultural output. We then show how historical demand for food has been affected by changes in population and the per capita income. The chapter ends with an analysis of future food demand and the increasing need for the import of foodstuff warranted by the need to reduce water consumption.

Chapter 8 takes a close look at the issue of migration and brain drain from Iran. The first part of the chapter presents new sets of data compiled from various sources to shed light on how the number of Iranian emigrants, international students, scholars, and asylum seekers have changed over the past half century. We then explain the drivers of migration and discuss the obstacles that prevented Iran's highly successful diaspora from taking part in the development of their homeland.

Chapter 9 provides a critical analysis of the Islamic Republic's claim of miraculous achievements in the realm of science and technology. This claim plays a central role in the regime's broader propaganda to create the impression that under its jihadi-style approach to development, Iran has joined the club of the most technologically advanced countries of the world. We, however, argue that the drastic increase in the quantity of Iran's scientific publications stem from the state's productionist research policies which consider publication as an end in itself with no implications for technological advancement and the economic well-being of the nation. In fact, this publication bubble can be regarded as a perfect manifestation of what some development scholars call *isomorphic mimicry*, that is, when policymakers in a developing country adopt the outward appearance of a successful process from advanced countries while hiding or overlooking the lack of its real function.

The final chapter of this book discusses the trajectory of development in Iran based on insights and data presented throughout the rest of the book under three different scenarios of business as usual, reforms within the Islamic Republic, and a more optimistic paradigm triggered initially by transformation of political institutions to improve the rule of law and democratic accountability as an entry point to future development.

1

GOVERNANCE

BETWEEN THE INCEPTION of the Islamic Republic in 1979 and 2020, Iran has collected $1.5 trillion (constant 2020$) in oil export proceeds.[1] In the meantime, the country has entered—and already passed about half of—its one-time demographic window of opportunity in which the favorable age structure of the population is conducive to rapid economic growth. Yet the growth of average per capita income in real terms during this prolonged period has been almost zero[2] while the country also suffered from a loss of social capital, human capital flight, endemic corruption, and environmental deterioration. As the state struggles to reform itself, the intensification of these economic and social crises is now leading Iran to an important turning point in its history.

As we will discuss throughout this chapter, Iran's major challenges and shortcomings are deeply rooted in a lack of effective governance. To put this claim into a broader context, we first briefly compare Iran's key governance indicators with selected peer countries: China, India, Malaysia, Turkey, Pakistan, and the United Arab Emirates. While half a century ago Iran was perceived to be on a comparable or better trajectory of development than these countries, today it is behind them in virtually all major aspects of governance and development (as shown in Figure 1.1). Since 1980, the average annual GDP growth in Iran has been below 2%, which is low compared to the performance of the above peer

FIGURE 1.1. Comparison of Iran and select peer countries along key governance indicators.

Sources: International Monetary Fund, World Economic Outlook; Worldwide Governance Indicators (WGI) Project. World Bank, Washington DC; Corruption Perception Index: Global Scores, Transparency International, Berlin; Freedom in the World, Freedom House, Washington DC.

countries whose GDPs have expanded at an average rate of 4–10% per year. Compounded over forty years, these seemingly small differences in annual output growth have given rise to an enormous gap between the extent of improvements in the economic well-being of Iranians and the citizens of these peer countries.

Based on the quantitative measures provided by international institutions, Iran's comparative performance with regard to the political aspects of development such as rule of law, freedom (political rights and civil liberties), and control of corruption is also extremely poor (Figure 1.1). In the following sections, we first discuss the theoretical background for measuring the quality of governance in general and then apply the described framework to evaluate the quality of governance in contemporary Iran.

INTRODUCTION

Effective governance plays a decisive role in the social and economic development of nations. In fact, it is differences in the scope, capacity, and legitimacy of different states that bring about significant disparities in their policy outcomes. Governance can be defined as "a government's ability to make and enforce rules, and to deliver services, regardless of whether that government is democratic or not."[3] According to this definition, the quality of a nation's governance should be evaluated based on the performance of its political agents in fulfilling their given tasks, without a priori value-based judgments about the democratic nature of its institutions (norms of good governance versus norms of good democracy).[4] In other words, institutions should be evaluated in this view based on how their nature, dynamics, and interactions enable governments to achieve their goals. For instance, in order to describe the quality of governance in an authoritarian regime, one needs to assess the quality of decisions made by its leaders rather than conveniently recognizing the authoritarianism as the cause for certain outcomes.[5]

The institutions[6] that constitute modern political systems can be grouped into those that concentrate and use power[7] (i.e., the state which is the executive branch of government and its associated bureaucracies) and those that act as constraints on power, namely the institutions of rule of law and accountability (Figure 1.2).[8] Our assessment of the quality of governance in Iran is based primarily on the framework developed by Fukuyama[9] and Huntington[10] in which nations' development paths are explained through an analysis of the extent of institutionalization with regard to the abovementioned three pillars of governance as well as on the sequence in which their different institutions have been built and have evolved. Therefore, disaggregating the realm of political development into these three sets of institutions as the first step of the analysis allows for a more precise and dynamic assessment of the interaction between different dimensions of development by avoiding the limitations caused by the standard static and dichotomic views of economic versus political development.

One of the key determinants of the quality of governance is the capacity of the state. In general, the chief aims of benevolent modern states can be described as addressing market failures and protecting the poor and vulnerable.[11] Market failure occurs when the market economy, due to a variety of reasons, fails to allocate optimal amounts of resources to provide particular goods or services. Among the main forms of market failure in which state intervention finds a rational economic basis are providing public goods (e.g., defense), curbing negative externalities (e.g., pollution), promoting positive externalities[12] (e.g., education), and addressing monopolies in the economy and asymmetric information (e.g., moral hazard[13] and adverse selection[14] issues in health insurance).[15] States should prioritize among these functions by taking into account

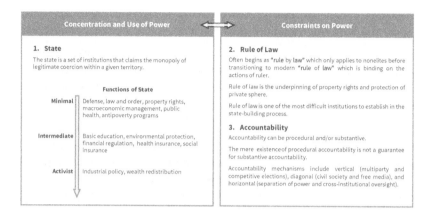

FIGURE 1.2. A conceptual framework for the analysis of governance based on three sets of institutions: state, rule of law, and accountability.

Sources: F. Fukuyama, "The Patterns of History," *Journal of Democracy*, 23 (2012); F. Fukuyama, *The Origins of Political Order: From Prehuman Times to the French Revolution* (Farrar, Straus and Giroux, 2011); F. Fukuyama, *Political Order and Political Decay: From the Industrial Revolution to the Globalization of Democracy* (Farrar, Straus and Giroux, 2014); "World Development Report: The State in a Changing World," Washington, DC: World Bank, 1997.

their potential impacts on the well-being of citizens as well as their own capacity and the resources required to fulfill them successfully. Based on their perceived suitability for different levels of state capacity, the World Bank classifies state functions into three groups: minimal, intermediate, and activist, although in reality some degree of overlap exists among these functions.[16] Figure 1.2 provides some examples for these three broad groups of state functions.

The higher the capacity of the state, the wider the range of functions it can successfully perform. In fact, many states in the developing world, including Iran, are expected to do too much with their limited capacity and, as such, end up playing a negative rather than a positive role. It is therefore suggested that states with low capacity focus on the provision of pure public goods in the early stages of the prolonged period of state-building,[17] as the pursuit of activist functions (Figure 1.2) by low-capacity and incompetent states often proves to be counterproductive. The industrial policy implemented by the state in Iran—which for decades has overridden market price signals through subsidized credit and import control measures—is a prime example of such policy mistakes as it failed to take into account Iran's low state capacity. In the subsequent sections, we will discuss how such ill-fated state interventions, in conjunction with the nontransparent and poorly managed process of privatization of state-owned enterprises, have become a major source for creation and extraction of rent and an important factor for the establishment of patronage relationships in Iran.

Another essential component for a functional governing system is the rule of law, which can be defined as "the impersonal and systematic application of known rules to government actors and citizens alike."[18] Central to the principles of good governance is a set of defined and fair rules and regulations that control the actors in the state, the market, and society in general. The main function of such a system thus comprises political actions (restricting the power of government) and economic actions (protecting property rights and enforcement of contracts). Moreover, and more fundamentally, the rule of law has an important societal impact by providing a basic form of a "social contract" which organizes the expectations and behaviors of different parts of society. Achieving a fully developed legal system spanning all those aspects is a complex and long-term process. Empirical data suggest that the rule of law may not be a necessary precondition for economic growth at early stages of development but becomes more important at later stages when the economy gradually becomes more complex. Development of the rule of law is a slow process which happens as a result of the interactions between political and economic institutions over long periods of time.[19] In fact, there are different stages of legality, whereby rule by law—that is, using laws as an instrument of domination by the rulers—typically precedes rule of law which emerges at a later stage when those rules apply not only to citizens but also to rulers and political elites.[20]

How exactly such a transition to the rule of law happens, including how the rulers stop using their power to violate those rules and respect an independent judiciary system, is not completely clear and there seem to be different paths in each country's case.[21] Different types of transitions have been identified historically, ranging from transition from an informal and highly pluralistic system of law to a successful adaptation of foreign legal systems.[22] In Iran's case, different components seem to be involved in the making of the current legal system. Sharia and tradition have historically been the main sources and origins of the legal system, but modern democratic components were also added to the law at different stages, including the constitutional revolution, the Pahlavi era, and even in the current constitution of the country written after the Islamic Revolution. However, Iranian society currently appears to be undergoing a transitionary period, whereby the legitimacy of the traditional sources of laws and order is declining due to rapidly changing values and the shortcomings of the religion-based rules to address the complex needs of a more modern society. As a result, a state of legal anarchy is emerging where the previous sources of traditional order and rules are not as legitimate and overarching as before, while a new, modern system of regulations has not yet developed. As will be discussed later, this decline in legitimacy of the law can be an important factor contributing to a drastic increase in the crime and corruption of the past decade.

Accountability constitutes another important element of modern governance. One of the main channels through which accountability contributes to the quality of governance is by making recruitments and promotions in the bureaucracy more meritocratic, thus enhancing the quality of decisions and their outcomes. Through periodic multiparty elections, procedural democratic accountability can potentially improve governance by providing the principals (the people) with a way to purge corrupt and incompetent agents (the officials), although in reality procedural accountability does not always lead to substantive accountability. In the modern era, authoritarian and even totalitarian regimes often feel the need to stage elections to legitimize their power. However, in the absence of real multiparty competition, such elections can never really challenge the monolithic power structure. In such regimes, existing and emerging cleavages are deactivated before reaching the stage of crystallization to form issue-oriented parties.[23] In any case, lack of substantive accountability can jeopardize the government's ability to embark on serious reforms, especially when those entail austerity measures such as reducing subsidies or increasing taxes.

Accountability has commonly been ascribed to the democratic elements of governance such as multiparty elections and free media. For instance, the relevant index in World Governance Indicators combines "Voice and Accountability," defined as the perception of "the extent to which a country's citizens are able to participate in selecting their government, as well as freedom of expression, freedom of association, and a free media."[24] It can be argued, however, that accountability might not be formally present in the form of procedures and institutions but may instead function in other forms, like moral accountability, in other political cultures.[25] Although democracy is an end in itself, it cannot be assumed a priori that procedural democratic accountability would necessarily give rise to improvement in substantive accountability and its subsequent effect on state capacity.[26]

Accountability can be divided into de jure (procedural) and de facto (substantive) forms in terms of the structure of institutionalization, and can be divided into vertical, horizontal, and diagonal in terms of the type of interactions between citizens and officials that it affects.[27] Vertical accountability is related to the mechanisms outside the state institutions and concerns the relationship between the citizens and the elected bodies (e.g., multiparty elections), horizontal accountability highlights the separation of power in the state and manifests in terms of the oversight exercised between different institutions (e.g., questioning government officials by legislative committees).[28] Diagonal accountability, which is also called social accountability, highlights the role of citizens, civil society, and independent media in holding the state accountable beyond participation in elections.[29] All three mechanisms can be present to various degrees, in either de jure (procedural) or de facto (substantive) forms. De jure accountability is related to the presence of formal institutions that make accountability possible (e.g., constitutional provisions for multiparty elections; legal provisions for extensive suffrage; statutes providing for formal independence of the judiciary). De facto accountability refers to the extent to which accountability mechanisms are realized in practice (e.g., free and fair elections without vote buying or systematic fraud; effective oversight by the judiciary).

Although the idea of popular sovereignty has had a strong presence in the political discourse of Iranians since the late nineteenth century,[30] in terms of the actual governance structure, the state in Iran has revolved around a single person—the king or the supreme leader—who has been beyond the rule of law, accountable only to the divine rather than the public or other parts of the government. The main tenet of this structure has persisted in contemporary Iran, both during the Pahlavi dynasty and after the Islamic Revolution, although in different forms and by alluding to different grounds for legitimacies. Iran's current constitution gives an almost unconstrained power to the supreme leader as the head of the state. His supervision and control span over all major aspects of governance institutions, including direct control over the judiciary, armed forces, state media, and foundations (*bonyads*), plus indirect control over the central government and parliament (primarily through the role of the Guardian Council in elections and decrees). Nevertheless, even in a system with such a high level of concentration of power in a single person, the quality of governance is influenced by complex and dynamic interactions between the institutions and more fundamental trends in society.

The rest of this chapter thus discusses the quality of governance in Iran based on the broad conceptual framework that explains the three sets of governance institutions with minimal reference to decisions at the personal level. This approach allows for a better understanding of the role of institutions and fundamental forces which underpin governance in Iran rather than being trapped in daily politics and historical contingencies. In other words, detailed historical information is distilled to elucidate the major patterns and underlying forces driving a complex phenomenon such as a social movement or a chronic economic issue. In contrast with the historical accounts that focus mainly on specific events that unfolded in the past, this analysis seeks to shed light on fundamental forces and deeper trends. These forces are behind the evolution of society and governance while the actual historical events, which may appear to be haphazard, ride on top of these more fundamental trends and are modulated by them. In other words, the characteristics of the institutions play a subliminal role in driving the events, although the exact time and appearance of events depend on individuals and microfactors. Overall, this chapter should be seen as an attempt to discuss the gap between what constitutes "good governance" (normative view) and the general patterns of governance in contemporary Iran (empirical account).

Finally, we note that this chapter primarily presents a qualitative account of governance although it frequently refers to empirical data to advance its arguments. Readers interested in direct quantitative measures of governance are referred to Appendix A, which provides a discussion of the merits and limitations of quantitative approaches for evaluating the quality of governance, particularly those related to Iran.

GOVERNANCE AND DEVELOPMENT

In this section, we attempt to evaluate the quality of governance in Iran through the conceptual framework described in the previous section. To this end, we look at how the three sets of political institutions (state, rule of law, and accountability) evolved and interact with each other, with dominant ideas and demands of the nation, and with economic factors.

As mentioned earlier, the advantage of this framework is that it does not reduce development to a single dimension (e.g., economic or political), nor does it reduce the evolution of governance to isolated factors in a static manner. Instead, it takes into account the dynamic interactions among multiple dimensions.

The analysis presented here divides Iran's past half-century into four distinct periods: the prerevolution period (1970–1978); the early years of the establishment of the Islamic Republic up to the end of the Iran-Iraq War and appointment of the new supreme leader (1979–1988); the postwar period commonly referred to as reconstruction and reforms (1989–2004); and, finally, the postreform period of governance deadlock and economic stagnation (2005–2020) (Figure 1.3). Major developments within each period are explained by specific dynamics of interaction between the components mentioned earlier, as we briefly outline in the following.

Prerevolution (1970–1978): The dominant process in this period was acceleration of the previous top-down efforts by the state for modernization and industrialization, which were enabled to a large extent by the massive oil revenues of the 1970s. Perceptions of injustice and exclusion in the fast-growing economy, combined with the natural resistance of a traditional society against a top-down modernization agenda, gradually gave rise to social mobilization which, through multiple complex channels, brought about a huge increase in demands for fundamental changes and eventually toppled the Pahlavi dynasty. In a way, the revolution of 1979 was a replay of the constitutional revolution about seven decades earlier where secular and modern forces among the intellectuals, along with parts of the clergy, *bazaar* (the traditional merchant class), and the then-emerging working class, joined forces to replace the patrimonial Qajar rule with a liberal-democratic system of governance based on limited constitutional monarchy.[31] The dynamics and sequence of interactions between institutions in this stage are in fact very similar to the classical scenario of political decay in quickly modernizing countries as described originally by Samuel Huntington.[32]

Early Stage of Revolutionary State (1979–1988): This period encompasses the transition from a state with a modernization and westernization agenda to a revolutionary state with Islamic ideology and cadre organizations. The new state was based on completely different grounds for legitimacy: independence, freedom, and a return to Islamic values[33] as opposed to modernization; and redistribution of resources and egalitarian rhetoric as opposed to industrialization and growth. Spearheaded by a charismatic leader whose personality initially overshadowed all formal institutions, the revolutionary state increased the political participation of the public, especially the poor and underrepresented classes, but at the same time undermined the institutions of rule of law and never improved substantive accountability. Economic conditions started to deteriorate soon after the revolution due to political turmoil and the dire consequences of the eight-year Iran-Iraq War. Despite its negative impact on the economy, the war and, for that matter, the hostage-taking of US diplomats, paradoxically helped the establishment of the revolutionary state by creating an environment where any form of suppression of the opposing political groups and civil society could be justified.[34] The contraction of the economy, at least for some years, did not significantly delegitimize the state since economic growth was never the primary goal of the revolution's ideology.

Reconstruction and Reforms (1989–2004): This period starts with the appointment of Khamenei as the supreme leader and Rafsanjani as the president. The main feature of this period was an attempt to introduce development-oriented policies to the revolutionary state in order to reconstruct a shattered economy while being cautious about not destabilizing the political structure. This period marks the beginning of the pursuit of industrial policy by the Islamic Republic and renewed public investments made according to the country's first five-year development plan after the revolution. These state-dominated economic activities, along with the lack of transparency and weak institutions of rule of law, gradually created large rent-seeking opportunities, which can be seen as the beginning of a new era in the public perception of corruption. Later in this period, demand for accountability and formation of a more structured civil society increased, which then manifested itself in the election of Khatami and the emergence and partial bureaucratization of the Iranian reform movement. Lack of a viable path for the implementation of meaningful reforms within the current constitutional framework and lack of incentives for the reformists to push for more serious reform agenda were among the main causes of the failure of the reform movement. Before reformist attempts were fully blocked and eventually dismantled by the unelected part of the state, this period arguably represented the peak of the state's legitimacy and, in hindsight, the best window of opportunity for meaningful reforms in governance institutions.

Governance Deadlock and Economic Stagnation (2005–2020): The start of this period coincides with the election of Ahmadinejad when progress toward reforms had already come to a halt a few years earlier. The reversal in the development of political institutions was amplified by Ahmadinejad's anti-institution and populist policies, which intentionally undermined or bypassed bureaucracy to achieve his goals. By the end of Ahmadinejad's first term, a combination of failures in different arenas (political, economic, and social) had already created a significant demand for change in the way that the country was governed. This pressure culminated in the controversial presidential election of 2009 which ultimately caused a major blow to the legitimacy and political stability of the state. Since then, Iran has consistently struggled with serious internal issues (including economic stagnation, escalation of crime and violence, and entrenchment of corruption) and external challenges (most notably, surrounding its nuclear program and regional behavior). Following his election in 2013 as the next president, Rouhani attempted to depict a more rational, internationally cooperative, and even—in some cases—socially liberal picture of the state. In reality, however, Rouhani's only major achievement was the nuclear deal which temporarily restored Iran's oil exports to their full capacity before the United States' unilateral withdrawal from the agreement in 2018. Today, after decades of the state's resistance to political and economic reforms, Iran is facing the most severe and extensive economic, social, and environmental crises in the history of the Islamic Revolution. The cumulative impacts of the past irresponsible policies and economic mismanagement, along with the entrenchment of corruption at all levels, have eroded the state's ability to address the crises that are gradually causing the country to fall into a path of political instability and decay.

Note that, in the conceptual model depicted in Figure 1.3, we mainly focus on major drivers and their interrelations to highlight the principal patterns in governance, without delving too much into the second-order details. As such, different periods and the distinctions between them should be considered as ideal types, in the Weberian sense, to facilitate understanding and analysis. In reality, it is more likely that the idealized dynamics of each period exist to various degrees in other periods as well. For example, the period of governance deadlock and economic stagnation comprises two distinct periods of Ahmadinejad's and Rouhani's presidency. During each, the government tried to revive certain dynamics of the previous periods, namely the egalitarian rhetoric of the

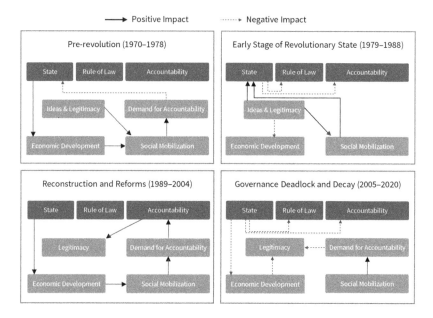

FIGURE 1.3. Interactions among various components of economic, social, and political development in Iran during four time periods spanning the past half-century. Different arrows show the transmission channel and *sign* of impact (positive versus negative) between different elements in the model. The framework was adapted from Fukuyama, 2014.

Source: F. Fukuyama, *Political Order and Political Decay: From the Industrial Revolution to the Globalization of Democracy* (Farrar, Straus and Giroux, 2014).

early stages of the revolutionary state period and the postwar pragmatism in the use of technocratic tools for public management, respectively. In the remainder of this section, a more detailed account of the evolution of the aforementioned components (legitimacy, state, rule of law, accountability, economic development, and social mobilization) is provided to illustrate the patterns of governance and development in Iran over the past half-century.

Legitimacy

Authoritarian regimes can often stay in power insofar as they preserve a minimum level of legitimacy, particularly among the elites tied to them and when a robust civil society does not exist. In such regimes, erosion of one source of legitimacy, if not replaced by a new source, leads to loss of capability for effective action. Throughout the decade leading up to the revolution and amid a period of unprecedented economic growth, paradoxically, the underpinning legitimacy of the Pahlavi regime declined to an extent that ultimately led to its collapse in 1979. In addition to motivations that were purely ideological, the causes that contributed to such a counterintuitive phenomenon can be grouped into three broad categories. First was the perception held by members of the low- and middle-income classes that they were being deprived of their fair share of the economic windfalls amid the oil boom of the 1970s. Second was social mobilization stemming from an improvement in literacy and increased urbanization—both catalyzed by the shift from an agrarian to a modern economy—which failed to be properly accommodated by the existing political institutions. Third was the coalescence of the traditional institutions of clergy and *bazaar* whose socioeconomic status was at risk due to the emergence of the modern institutions of education, the judiciary, and industrial manufacturing. Overall, the revolution of 1979 can be seen as a classic example of what Huntington labeled the political decay that happens at the early stages of the state-building process when the political system fails to accommodate its consequential social mobilization (Figure 1.3).[35] During the ensuing decade of the revolution (1979–1988), the relationship between the prevailing collective ideas of the people and changes in political and economic institutions was sharply different from what occurred in the last decade of the Pahlavi dynasty. During this period, the newly established regime consolidated power by purging previous top managers, cracking down on political opponents and civil society, and providing funds and human resources for a prolonged and devastating war with Iraq. As a result of these developments, the revolutionary state consolidated its power while the economy gradually contracted to about half the size it had been at the onset of the revolution.

The constitution of the Islamic Republic is composed of democratic, theocratic, and autocratic elements, where the democratic and theocratic elements serve as the de jure sources of legitimacy. The Islamic Republic's de facto sources of legitimacy in early stages, however, revolved around the twin principles of socioeconomic equality and independence—contrary to the Pahlavi dynasty that was seeking to legitimize its authority on the basis of modernization and nationalism (e.g., by referring to the idea of a Great Civilization and alluding to the golden era of the Persian empire). The two regimes also relied on different sources of traditional legitimacy, namely kingship and religion. Despite their tremendously different ideas and economic interests, different classes of society rallied behind the promises of equality and independence to address the historical quest of the nation for recognition: equality as being recognized by their own state to have the same value and rights, and independence as being recognized by other states to have the same value and rights. The evolution of governance in the postrevolution era can be analyzed in light of the ramifications and culmination of these new pillars of legitimacy.

The interpretation of the concepts of equality and independence that ultimately prevailed in the new regime was not only inefficient from an economic standpoint but also contained various forms of important internal contradictions. Reducing poverty to a mere issue of economic inequality paved the way for the implementation of various forms of ineffective redistributive measures such as heavy subsidies on energy carriers with far-reaching implications for the economic growth and patterns of institutional development throughout the history of the Islamic Republic. This naive interpretation of the concept of equality was to some extent attributable to the lack of a clear understanding of economic principles among the elites of the Islamic Republic and their unrealistic view of Iran's overall economic standing in the world. This exaggerated view of Iran's economic importance in the world was also shared by the Shah, with the difference that in the Islamic ideology of the revolution, the economy was secondary from the beginning. Regardless of their original intentions, the seemingly pro-poor policies of the revolution formed a lasting ground for a new form of clientelism at the national and subnational levels with implications clearly reflected in the country's chronic fiscal deficit and low productivity. High inflation throughout the life of the Islamic Republic has consistently imposed a hidden tax on those with fixed incomes (e.g., rank-and-file employees) and those who do not know how to invest their money. High and volatile inflation has also significantly damaged the Iranian economy by making long-term planning impossible.

Parallel to the idea of equality, the Islamic Republic's leaders pursued the image of an ideal independent state as another cornerstone of their legitimacy—although, in reality, the Islamic Republic has increasingly tilted toward the east in later stages: China for finance and Russia for military and intelligence. The concept of independence proved effective in buying popular support in the early stage of the Islamic Republic, but it has had enduring consequences for the quality of governance and development in the entire postrevolution era. Anti-imperialist rhetoric increased the isolation that Iran faced after the Islamic Revolution, and this isolation in turn fueled the same anti-imperialism rhetoric. This vicious cycle has severely affected Iran in multiple ways, for example:

- Declining productivity due to lack of access to international financial markets and new technologies
- Missing the opportunities created by globalization
- Unsustainable population expansion due in part to pronatalist policies (from the early days of the revolution to the mid-1980s and again from 2014 until the present) as a large population has been perceived as strengthening and stabilizing the revolution against foreign interventions
- Unsustainable exploitation of the country's water and land endowments to achieve food self-sufficiency and hence reduce vulnerability against potential international embargoes rather than focusing on the long-term food security of the nation
- Poor quality higher education and research, due in part to an intentional disconnect between Iran and the modern world aiming to curb what is frequently labeled as cultural diffusion

Noticing the practical shortcomings of the original grounds for legitimacy in the ideology of the revolution, the Islamic Republic inclined to somewhat more developmental and modern behavior in the postwar period commonly referred to as "reconstruction and reforms" (1989–2004). The period started with the presidency of Rafsanjani, who, through the following decades, tried to depict himself as a pragmatic and technocratic state builder by alluding to the image of Amir Kabir as one of the first state builders in Iran. In reality, however, it seems that Rafsanjani was more influenced by Deng Xiaoping, who had just successfully led China out of the inefficiencies of its centrally planned economy without mass privatization or structural reforms in the political realm. Rafsanjani's economic liberalization reforms, unlike their counterparts in China, failed to buy much new popular support. Nevertheless, some elements in these reforms, such as the improvements of technocratic capacity at high managerial positions, persuaded a significant portion of the middle class that development and modernization could still be achieved through gradual reforms of the current regime. It was, in fact, such hopes working in tandem with demographic factors that led to a landslide victory for Khatami, then a relatively unknown politician. He galvanized people's demand for better governance in general and for more social and political freedom in particular. The social mobilization that resulted in Khatami's election soon resulted in the victory of his close supporters and allies in parliamentary and city council elections. These in turn created the impression that the Islamic Republic could be made more accountable through available constitutional mechanisms. These developments temporarily boosted the legitimacy of the regime before disappointment in reforms became dominant yet again in its ensuing years.

The failure of Khatami's political reforms despite their wide popular support can be attributed to two distinct factors. First was the inherent limitation of elected officials' power due to the coercion of legal and quasi-legal power by the nonelected parts of the state (e.g., the Guardian Council). Second was the occurrence of a classic principal-agent problem where the elected reformist politicians (i.e., the agents) did not act in the interest of their constituencies (i.e., the people who wanted change) simply because these politicians knew their future success in politics would depend primarily on satisfying the nonelected institutions of the state. These politicians viewed competition for people's votes as an easy win due to the lack of strong alternative opponents. After a few rounds of trial and error, the nonelected part of the state also realized the rules of the game and started to disqualify any politicians who had the political will to pursue genuine reformist agendas, based on an underlying assumption that people always participate in elections regardless of the candidacy of a particular group or individual.

The next period in the evolution of governance during the Islamic Republic started with the presidency of Ahmadinejad, who possessed all the main characteristics of a populist politician: implementing unsustainable but popular economic policies for short-term political gain, trying to weaken formal institutions and fill the void with a direct connection with the people, and narrowing the definition of *the people* to only those who were supportive of him. The widespread belief that the state rigged both presidential elections of 2005 and 2009 in favor of Ahmadinejad was arguably the first major blow to the legitimacy of the state in the eyes of the educated middle class which, until then, was seeking change primarily through the ballot box. Ahmadinejad's policies or, more accurately, the policies of the state during the period in which he was president, had lasting and multifaceted impacts on the regime's legitimacy. First, like many other populist politicians, he leveraged the resentment that existed among the poor and marginalized classes to justify his anti-elite and anti-institutional actions. He in fact tried to present his plans as the resurgence of the revolution's original ideals and ideas, especially equality and independence. For some years, close ties to religious leaders and the deep state helped him push many controversial policies whose implementations were otherwise impossible. On the economic front, Ahmadinejad embarked on a number of major populist programs, similar to Venezuela's former president Hugo Chavez, whose costs exceeded even the country's enormous oil revenue at the time. Despite their inefficiencies, these policies strengthened the position of the state among the targeted classes for some years. Furthermore, as will be discussed later, a significant part of privatization and associated misconduct occurred when Ahmadinejad was in office. During his second term, the economic pressures of some of the state's poorly designed megaprojects, such as affordable housing (*Maskan-e-Mehr*), intensified by the effects of oil sanctions, resulted in another bout of very high inflation and a wide dissatisfaction among the very constituencies who were the beneficiaries of Ahmadinejad's populist policies in the first place. Besides the economic direction of the country, the aftermath of the highly controversial presidential election of 2009 and wide and intensive attacks on civil society can be viewed as a turning point in the perception of a large part of the middle class with regard to the workability of reforms advocated by the former president, Khatami, and his political allies.

Like the Soviet regime, the Islamic Republic has made sporadic attempts to make up for its troubled economy and justify sociopolitical repression by claiming technological achievements perceived by the public as associated with superpower status. The most notable example of these legitimacy-boosting strategies has been the country's highly controversial and expensive nuclear program. Besides its obvious strategic regional purposes, the program has been presented to the public as a technological leapfrog whose economic, environmental, and even medical benefits would change the course of history for the nation. In fact, for more than a decade, the rhetoric of irreversible progress toward the edge of nuclear technology was the state's most glorious message sent to its core supporters. However, just within a year after the start of the 2012 oil sanctions, Iran's fragile economy underwent such a significant contraction that continuation of the nuclear program could have imposed existential risks to the regime. It was under these circumstances that the presidential election of 2013 was held, leading to Rouhani's election. His main promise was to solve the complicated nuclear deadlock, which eventually led to the Joint Comprehensive Plan of Action (JCPOA) in 2015. But contrary to his previous views and track record, Rouhani also augmented his message with promises for more social and political freedom to appeal to members of the educated middle class who were disappointed by the regime's crackdown after the 2009 presidential election.

In addition to the effects of sanctions that reduced the amount of Iran's oil exports to half their presanctions level, the sudden drop in the price of oil between July 2014 and July 2015 (when Iran signed the JCPOA) resulted in Iran's oil revenue being cut by another half. Following the implementation of the JCPOA in January 2016, and thanks to the increase in oil exports, economic growth started to improve from deep negative rates. However, being aware of the existential threat to his position from both top-down and bottom-up pressures, Rouhani avoided reforms, as they would have provoked the people, the regime's elites, or both. Besides lacking political will for embarking on economic reforms, Rouhani's administration was mostly comprised of the top managers of the previous governments who did not have many new ideas for policy improvement anyway. He instead almost entirely relied on the impacts of the nuclear deal for fostering economic growth and encouraging investments. Since mid-2018, the unilateral US withdrawal from the JCPOA, which immediately eliminated all the economic benefits for Iran from the deal, severely undermined hopes to salvage the economy. All in all, the fate of the nuclear program and its economic consequences resulted in a major blow to the regime's legitimacy. The former undermined the regime's legitimacy among core supporters and elites, and the latter created a wide sense of dissatisfaction and even agony among all economic classes.

One of the most important impediments to economic reforms in Iran is the role of the Islamic Revolutionary Guard Corps (IRGC) in the economy. Soon after the end of the Iran-Iraq War and during Rafsanjani's presidency, the IRGC embraced for-profit economic activities as a contractor in infrastructural projects (e.g., building highways and dams). Over time, however, the IRGC expanded to all other possible sectors of the economy, including oil and gas, banking, agriculture, telecommunication, and car manufacturing. Today, the nature of the IRGC's economic activities has somewhat changed from the original contributions, which were based on engineering capacities, to a middle-man position, taking public contracts and distributing different parts of the project among domestic (including the IRGC's own subsidiaries) and even foreign companies. Given the amount of profit the IRGC makes in this process, and its essentially unsupervised military power, it comes as no surprise that the IRGC resists any structural changes, especially with regard to increasing the role of the real private sector in the economy.

Despite the failure of economic and political reforms, the strong loss aversion and status quo bias of Iranians—which presumably has roots in the events of the revolution and war—continued to inhibit demands for radical change until recently. Today, with unprecedented levels of socio-economic dissatisfaction, the regime's remaining legitimacy is plummeting among a wide range of social and economic classes. The regime has tried to avoid the fate of Mikhail Gorbachev's Soviet Union by postponing any form of structural reforms, failing to realize that the window of opportunity for meaningful reform will not be open forever. In hindsight, during the now more than four-decade history of the Islamic Republic, Khatami's first term in office, about twenty years ago, was arguably the best time to address institutional problems in governance, as the state's legitimacy and social capital were both at their peak.

State

To provide an overview of the evolution of the state in Iran, we use a two-dimensional framework that considers scope and capacity as the principal components of statehood—the former to capture the extent of functions that the state seeks to fulfill and the latter to capture the extent to which the state properly performs these functions.[36]

Scope and Capacity

While states with high capacity can be found across almost the entire range of government sizes, states with a wide scope and low capacity, such as Iran, represent the least desirable combination (Figure 1.4). As will be discussed shortly, there is a significant difference between the size of the central government in Iran and the actual size and interventions of the public sector (i.e., state's effective size, see Figure 1.4). The difficulty of reforms for the countries in this position arises from the need to simultaneously reduce the state's size and enhance its capacity.

Similar to global trends from the beginning of the twentieth century to the 1980s, the relative size of the government in Iran, as measured

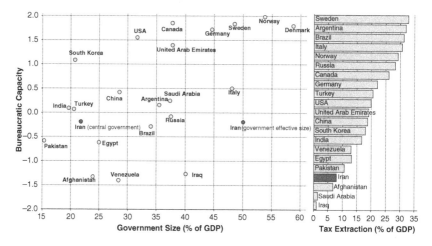

FIGURE 1.4. Bureaucratic quality vs. scope (left) and tax extraction (right) for select countries.

Source: Worldwide Governance Indicators (WGI) Project and World Bank Open Data, World Bank, Washington DC.

by the ratio of government expenditure to GDP, increased gradually to reach about 50% in the years before the 1979 revolution. However, in drastic contrast with Western countries, the expansion of the government in Iran was driven by the windfalls from oil exports rather than an increase in the capacity of the state for tax extraction. In fact, the amount of tax collected in Iran (Figure 1.5) has never even reached 10% of the country's GDP.

Given the radical promises made during the revolution for a complete change of the governance system to align it with Islamic principles and pro-poor policies, the Islamic Revolution started with a heavy footprint on the state institutions from its early days. The leaders began changes immediately by creating parallel institutions to some of the existing ones, nationalizing large private enterprises and banks, and purging the top- and mid-level managers of the just-toppled regime, replacing them with young, inexperienced, idealistic, and ideologic revolutionary members who, before long, took the lead in most aspects of governance. As such, part of the institutional capacity of the country was lost while the new institutions struggled to deliver when faced with the realities of governance, especially in the chaotic conditions after the revolution, exacerbated by the emergence of the Iran-Iraq War and the consequences of the hostage-taking of

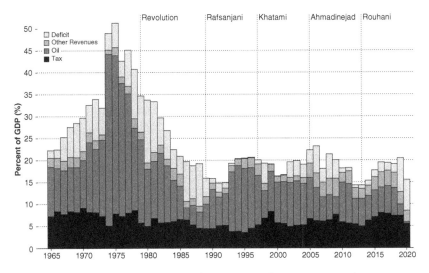

FIGURE 1.5. Government revenue relative to GDP between 1965 and 2020.
Source: Economic Time Series Database, Central Bank of Iran (cbi.ir).

the US diplomats by Muslim Student Followers of the Imam's Line (*daneshjouyan-e-peyro-khat-e-imam*).

In addition to an extensive and excessive scope, the Iranian state has also suffered from limited strength and capacity. For example, as described above, the state has historically had a limited capacity for tax collection. The modernization of the state which started early in the twentieth century could in principle have enhanced the state's capacity, but two factors hindered this process. First, oil revenue windfalls in the 1970s undermined the importance of bureaucratic institutions and made them secondary in decision-making. This started the process of capacity destruction, which notoriously happens in natural resource–driven booms,[37] especially in countries with weak political institutions. This was then continued and intensified by the revolution in 1979, which reversed the process of modernization of the state, not only by purging the previous high-level bureaucrats but, more fundamentally, by undermining the very structure of the previous bureaucratic institutions. In fact, revolutionaries tried their best to replace—or, in cases where not possible, to supplement—any previous structure with a new revolutionary one, such as the IRGC positioning itself as a parallel institution to the modern army.

Such parallel structures and institutions have persisted to the present, adversely affecting the capacity of the state for making decisions and implementing its policies. This has contributed to the constant tension between the elected part of the governance system (e.g., the central government and the parliament) and the unelected parts (e.g., the judiciary or the Guardian Council, revolutionary foundations, and the IRGC). The presence of such factionalism has contributed to the short-sightedness of the elected governments and their inability to embark on serious reforms and long-term planning. They are only able—or willing—to address immediate issues with short-term results, postponing the confrontation with the challenges and their associated risks to the next administration. This short-sightedness is exacerbated by two more contributing factors: the weakness of political parties (or lack thereof) and the demise of social capital and accountability (for more discussion, see the section on Accountability in this chapter).

In addition to the general problem of the state's excessive scope which broadly affects its performance, there are two other important factors, namely the difficulty of reform and the degree of institutional autonomy, that impact the performance of each institution separately. The difficulty of improving the performance of different institutions through reforms can be broadly estimated by considering two factors: their number and scatteredness of their transactions, and the extent to which their outputs can be readily measured.[38] It is often difficult and more time-consuming to improve the performance of institutions with a high number of transactions and low specificity, such as primary education and institutions of the rule of law, because their functions are inherently harder to codify and outcomes are harder to judge objectively. In contrast, the small variance in the form and functions of high-specificity institutions with low numbers of transactions and the ease of measuring the quality of performance, such as central banks (whose primary goal is to control inflation which can be measured directly), allows for the use of best practices from other countries, making them more susceptible to reforms. Against this backdrop, and considering the fact that economists have known both the causes of inflation and practical solutions to control it within a healthy range (typically 2–4%) since the 1980s, one may conclude that the extremely poor performance of the easy-to-reform institution of the Central Bank during the Islamic Republic should be attributed to the regime's dysfunctional political system rather than the bank's low technocratic capacity.

This brings us to another factor that adversely affects the quality of governance in Iran, that is, large mismatches between the optimum and the actual degrees of autonomy given to each state institution. The Central Bank and the IRGC, as institutions which, respectively, have too little and too much autonomy, can be used as examples to explain this point. In the case of the Central Bank, this means lack of autonomy to set inflation goals and, more importantly, to use means and procedures to shield itself from political pressures which are almost always in favor of short-term political (and even in some cases, personal) gains. As will be discussed in greater length in chapter 5, for over four decades, the Central Bank has directly and indirectly financed the government's large fiscal deficits which were a product of the regime's undemocratic source of legitimacy and prevented it from collecting any meaningful amount of tax to supplement oil revenues in the budget. On the opposite side of the spectrum, the institutions of the rule of law and accountability have failed miserably to put any form of constraints on a number of powerful institutions, chief among them being the IRGC which has extended the scope of its activities far beyond the realm of military and security to virtually any field that could be economically profitable for the institution itself and its surrogates in the pseudo- and real private sector.

Privatization

During the 1980s and 1990s, Western countries reversed the trend of government expansion and reduced the size of their governments by implementing policies that are today commonly referred to as Reaganism and Thatcherism. In the meantime, the International Monetary Fund and the World Bank were encouraging developing countries to rapidly liberalize their economies and privatize state enterprises by pushing a policy package known as the Washington Consensus.[39] During the 1980s, in another unintended development caused by massive changes in oil revenue, the size of Iran's central government contracted substantially before stabilizing at nearly 20% of GDP in the following decades (Figure 1.5). A decade past the revolution and after the economic contraction of wartime, the Iranian state found itself with no choice but to make an economic U-turn and half-heartedly take some steps toward price liberalization and privatization. Since then, the Islamic Republic's economic policy has been a realm of trial and error at the fundamental level. There is no clear underlying strategy despite the official long-term economic plans that are frequently published by the state, but which are of little value due to their unrealistic mandates. While a more detailed analysis of the macroeconomic policies of the state will be provided later in this section, we here focus on the state's path toward privatization as an effort to directly adjust the scope of its functions.

By the end of the 1980s and after a decade of statism, the idea of privatizing state-owned enterprises emerged among the regime's elites. The end of war had created public anticipation for improvement in the disastrous economic situation. Since 2001, approximately $130 billion (in constant 2020$) worth of state-owned enterprises have been sold off, $120 billion of that during Ahmadinejad's presidency.[40] Also, given that only a small proportion of state assets and enterprises were actually sold off to the real private sector,[41] the de facto outcome of privatization was the transfer of public enterprises from the central government to parastatal organizations such as pension funds, *bonyads (revolutionary foundations)*, IRGC-affiliated corporations, and banks. In terms of the ultimate beneficiaries of privatization, about 20% was given to the poor and lower-middle income class through the Justice Shares scheme (*Saham-e-Edalat*), 20% to the working middle class (through debt cancellation agreements between the government and major pension funds), 20% to business elites in the private sector with close ties to the state, and the remaining 40% to revolutionary foundations and IRGC-linked business entities. As such, the economy has not made a meaningful move toward liberal capitalism, nor can it be controlled by the central government anymore.[42]

In hindsight, while there was nothing wrong with the idea of privatization per se, lack of state capacity and the corruption and misconduct that occurred throughout the process resulted in its failure, evidenced by the country's stagnant, if not declining, capital productivity.[43] In 2021, after about three decades, privatization in Iran seems to be approaching an end as the majority of the remaining state-owned enterprises and assets to be sold are loss-making or small in value. As a result, selling off the remaining state-owned enterprises can no longer be used for paying the government's large and growing debt to government bondholders, pension funds, banks, and contractors, which in total are estimated to be at least 40% of GDP. The transfer of ownership of state enterprises from the central government to the nongovernment public sector allowed the regime's elites to tap into a huge opportunity, as the transferred companies have remained under various forms of governmental support such as directed credit and import licenses (which discourage them from making efforts to improve productivity) while now being able to generate lucrative salaries and bonuses for their managers. All in all, Iran has joined the club of countries where, due to low state capacity and lack of a proper rule of law, the outcome of the privatization process was disastrous for development.

Public Management Style

Another important feature of public administration in Iran over the past four decades has been its revolutionary-style approach (colloquially called *jihadi*). This was best exemplified during the war period and especially highlighted in the different style and approach of the IRGC to war compared to the classic army, namely reliance on motivated volunteers rather than formal order and training. This approach was later institutionalized in the form of Jihad of Construction (involved in activities like road building, electrification, and irrigation canals in rural areas) and formation of an independent ministry which was subsequently merged with the ministry of agriculture to form the current Ministry of Agriculture Jihad. Revolutionary public management, which was the dominant operational tool during the first decade after the revolution, played a central role in mitigating the delegation problem and somewhat compensated for the state's low capacity amid the turmoil of the 1980s. The revolutionary-style type of public management, which shares some similarities with the Chinese cadre organization model,[44] is based on the ideological commitment of the personnel to the policy doctrine of the state. In this model of public management, in any specific situation, instead of making decisions based on a detailed set of rules, agents would do what the top managers would have done in that situation. This is why ideological training is of absolute importance in the revolutionary type of organization. A comparison of the main characteristics of the Weberian type of bureaucracy and the revolutionary type of public management is provided in Table 1.1.

Rule of Law

The institution of rule of law is an important cornerstone of good governance. This section discusses how different aspects of rule of law, including its roots and functions (political, economic, and societal), have evolved in Iran over the past decades. It is important to note that rather than being a binary characteristic of the governance that either exists or

TABLE 1.1. A comparison between the characteristics of Weberian bureaucracy and revolutionary-style public management. Partially adapted from Rothstein, 2013.

Characteristics	Bureaucracy	Revolutionary Public Management
Recruitment	Merit	Commitment
Basis of decisions	Detailed rules	Policy doctrine
Motivations	Incentives	Ideology
Group cohesiveness	Weak	Strong
Predictability	Strong	Weak
Tools	Routine	Ad hoc
Knowledge accumulation	Possible	Low
Position on transparency	Neutral	Uncooperative

Source: B. Rothstein, "Understanding the Quality of Government in China: The Cadre Administration Hypothesis," CDDRL Working Paper 133, 2013.

not, the rule of law is the result of a complex and long-term process, often entwined with other aspects of political and economic development.

Rule of Law versus Rule by Law

One of the main functions of the rule of law is its political role in containing and controlling the concentration of power in the state. This aspect is best highlighted in the distinction between rule *of* law and rule *by* law. The transition to rule of law typically starts with institutionalization of rule by law, where laws are used by rulers to enforce their domination. Rule of law emerges at later stages when rulers and elites themselves are willing to, or are forced to, accept the constraints of law on their decisions and actions. Despite top-down efforts to establish rule by law and prolonged bottom-up pressures to make the rulers subject to the laws, rule of law is still in primitive stages in Iran. In spite of efforts toward top-down modernization of the state and the legal system during the Pahlavi era, in reality, whenever the king (be it Reza Shah or Mohammad Reza Shah) was in a strong position, he ignored the constraints of law on his absolute power and acted independently according to his personal desires. This was the case during the peak of Reza Shah's power but also resurfaced during the oil boom of the 1970s as, for example, documented by the Shah's notorious rejection of advice from experts in the bureaucracy.[45]

This tendency did not change for the better after the bottom-up revolution of 1979, despite its anti-dictatorship sentiments. Several factors contributed to this. First, the charismatic legitimacy of Khomeini as the revolutionary leader gave him a special position above and beyond rules. This charismatic legitimacy, which had the effect of legitimizing the rules rather than being bound by them, was further substantiated by the general tendency to return to religion (in effect, authority of the clerical establishment and the jurists) as the source of law. Apart from his revolutionary stance, Khomeini's legitimacy was rooted in his position as a religious and legal authority in Shia's clergy system, as the highest ranking authority of the Twelver Shia community (*Marja al-Taqlid*, the authority to be followed by the public in religious matters). As such, he was in essence representing the traditional source of rules and regulations (*Fiqh*, or Sharia) as opposed to modern Western laws, in a society which was increasingly feeling alienated through a rapid process of top-down modernization (westernization) and hence demanding the "return" to its roots.

This could have potentially led to the confinement of the (Islamic) ruler by the (religious) law, and hence establishment of an indigenous route to a rule *of* law. However, Khomeini's theory for Islamic governance, namely the theory of Governance of the Islamic Jurist (*Velayat-e Faqih*), and later the Absolute Governance of the Islamic Jurist, effectively gave primacy to the jurist-ruler and hence defined the ruler as the key religiopolitical figure above the rules. Although this has been seen as a solution to give the jurists the flexibility to interpret (*Ijtihad*) the traditional texts in a way which is compatible with the needs of modern times, in practice it has led to a situation where the religious ruler has the absolute, unchecked power to interpret the religious rules in the interest of survival and expediency of the Islamic state. This tendency to override the rule of law has been continued and further institutionalized during Khamenei's period as the supreme leader, as manifested in numerous decrees and unofficial orders that have been issued by him. As a result, the postrevolution system of governance reinforced the position of the ruler above the rules and thus hindered the realization of the political functions of the rule *of* law.

The most prominent manifestation of this can be observed in the judicial system, which notably lacks the necessary political independence from other parts of the state, especially the supreme leader who directly appoints its head. Since its inception, the postrevolutionary system of governance has used the judiciary as a political tool to suppress the opposition. This was, maybe not surprisingly, the case in the chaotic situation immediately after the revolution, when "revolutionary courts" formed to rapidly prosecute and execute former officials or confiscate properties without proper legal procedures. But, surprisingly, the essence of the legal system in the Islamic Republic regime has changed very little forty years after the revolution. The lack of rule of law manifests itself more clearly whenever critical conditions like social turmoil or political unrest appear in the country (e.g., in the aftermath of the presidential election in 2009 and brutal repression of the 2017–2018 and 2019 bloody protests) or when the unelected faction of the government wants to undermine the elected parts (as when this faction cracked down on the reform movement during Khatami's period or suppressed the free press). The function of the judiciary in contemporary Iran can thus be best described as a process of "judicialization" in autocratic regimes,[46] whereby the judicial system is functioning as an instrumental tool to "resolve" the controversial issues arising from political tension between different political and special interest groups, rather than representing an independent institution guaranteeing fair and impartial implementation of the laws across parties and citizens alike.

Such a structure has also seriously limited the economic function of the rule of law. The problem started with the original wave of confiscation and nationalization right after the revolution, which at the time had strong popular support due to the dominance of leftist rhetoric and the anti-aristocratic tones of the revolution. This initial trend was further consolidated and institutionalized in the next years by the formation of unelected, and mostly unmonitored, revolutionary foundations (*bonyads*). They took control of major industries and enterprises, public or private, as well as national resources in the name of the public and with the apparent goal of egalitarian redistribution. Tightly linked to one of the main pillars of the regime's legitimacy, equality, these "pseudo-public" institutions acted as another wing, next to the judiciary, to enable the political aspirations of the state.

The judicial system became, therefore, politically subordinate and systematically incapable of preserving the property rights of individuals and private companies, especially when in conflict with the state or its political elites. It also proved unable to enforce contracts and rules effectively and predictably, as legally vague and undefined terms like "spreading corruption on Earth" (*fesad fel'arz*) or "war against God and the state" (*moharebeh*) could be invoked whenever the state wished to suppress any individual or organization. This could happen even in purely financial scenarios, since the state might see certain financial activities as threatening its stability or general interest, making in turn the distinction between the political and financial sectors more obscure. Such unpredictable enforcement of the law, heavily reliant on the political conditions and interests of the state, has not only halted the transition to the rule *of* law but has undermined even the credibility of the system in ruling *by* law. This problem has been exacerbated by the presence of multiple sources of rules and regulations, where several bodies of law are present and often in conflict with each other. Unlike negative implications for the establishment of the rule of law, the ambiguity and disarray in the legal system provide a means for the government to interpret the law as it sees fit depending on the situation.

The dominance of state political interests over legal and financial dimensions meant that even later changes in government policies toward economic liberalization were ineffective in bringing about any structural change. A case in point is the large-scale privatization effort which culminated during Ahmadinejad's administration, with close to one-third of government assets and shares of firms covered by Article 44 being sold to the "private" sector from 2006 to 2009. However, even such large-scale privatization programs did not stimulate or protect the private sector. In fact, they strengthened the unofficial and unregulated part of the state and its oligarchs (e.g., elites tied to the IRGC and *bonyads*), with inevitable deeper corruption and nontransparency in this process.

The combination of these deficiencies in the rule of law has seriously affected its legitimacy and hence its social function. As a result, the public has lost faith not only in the institutions of rule of law but also in the necessity or benefit of adhering to the law in general. This is specifically problematic as the Islamic Republic's system of governance has utilized the traditional sources of religious rules and regulations as the foundation of the legitimacy of its laws. Lack of proper function of these laws in practice has, therefore, left the public psyche in a state of legal anarchy, whereby the traditional foundations of laws have lost their ground for legitimacy, while a new, modern regime of the rule of law has not yet emerged. Thus, a system of governance which emerged as the result of a revolution opposing modern laws and advocating a return to traditional laws at its heart has, through its own evolution, ruined the legitimacy of those norms and regulations in the public mind.

Perhaps the most obvious point where the dysfunction of the rule of law and its different economic, political, and societal aspects manifest themselves is corruption. Corruption in its basic form is defined as misusing public resources for private gain, and it is known to significantly reduce the capacity of state.[47] It damages both the economy and the political order by decreasing the capacity of the state to recruit the most competent people and to utilize the full potential of its human capital, while depriving the state of its legitimacy and public trust. As a result, corruption could also significantly affect social capital.

Although fighting corruption has been one of the main slogans of the Islamic Republic since its inception, four decades after the revolution, corruption has reached a level that is widely accepted to be systemic. That is, corruption is present among high-ranking officials, and fighting corruption has become increasingly more difficult. More fundamentally, the culture, the expectations, and the rules of the game have changed, as the state and its citizens are both accepting new norms of lawlessness and corruption as the common—if not the only—means to reach their goals and obtain short-term benefits. This has, in turn, severely limited the bureaucratic capacity and quality of governance. The most fundamental consequence of such endemic corruption has been its adverse effect on social capital, as it has seriously damaged the trust between the public and the state. The chasm between the people and the government has especially widened, as such pervasive corruption at the level of officials is at odds with one of the major pillars of the legitimacy of the postrevolution government, namely equality.

It is helpful to study which factors have contributed to the emergence and sustenance of corruption in its evolution to a systemic level in today's Iran. As we discussed, failure to establish the rule of law and its different functions (political, economic, and social) has contributed significantly to this process, with the judiciary's lack of political independence being the most crucial impediment to any serious reform. This deficiency has been exacerbated by factors such as the growth and dominance of the unofficial and unregulated part of the state and the state's lack of accountability and transparency. Since the beginning of the revolution, the unofficial, unregulated part of the state has constantly increased its presence and influence, thanks to the nation's constant state of crisis. This started with the chaos resulting from conflicts between different revolutionary factions in the political void after the revolution and culminated in the eight-year war between Iran and Iraq. It is still present, especially when international conflicts are heightened, and manifests itself the most when sanctions are imposed, compromising the normal operation of the state. The constant crisis in the political arena has nourished an abnormal regime of governance, whereby the official part of the political order remained smaller than—and secondary if not subordinate to—the unofficial part. In fact, aware of the necessity of the state of crisis and emergency for its existence and proliferation, the unofficial part of the government has actively tried to disturb the normalcy of the political arena with every tool at hand, especially in the international domain. This has therefore kept a large part of the state out of the scope of transparency and regulation and has created a political and financial system which is inherently prone to corruption.

The second contributing factor to the genesis and entrenchment of systemic corruption is a constant crackdown on parties and civil organizations in the past four decades along with suppression of free media and the press, which inevitably limits the transparency and accountability of governance. As we mentioned in the State section and will discuss in more detail in the Accountability section, this has led to the formation of a circle of "insiders" which simultaneously reinforces the circulation of power and rent within a limited body of loyal supporters and blocks a meaningful competitive rotation of political groups in power. See the next section of this chapter for an elaborated discussion of corruption in the Islamic Republic.

The spread of corruption is mirrored in the number of crimes occurring as well. As shown in Figure 1.6, there has been a dramatic rise in the number of robberies and lawsuit cases in Iran in the past decade (note that the values are normalized by population). Although economic factors have played a role in this phenomenon, the rather sharp rise in the number of robberies that started around the 2009 presidential election implies that the change that occurred in the public perception of the law and legitimacy of the state has significantly contributed to this social issue.

Accountability

Accountability, the process of holding power accountable to external authorities, can affect the quality of governance in different ways. It can improve the responsiveness of the government to economic and social demands of the citizens, hence boosting the state's legitimacy and creating

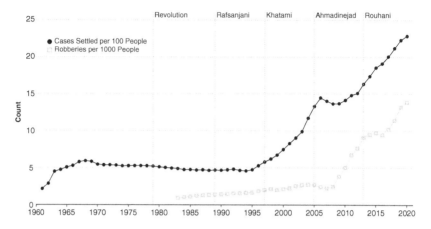

FIGURE 1.6. Number of lawsuits closed (per 100 people) and number of robberies (per 1,000 people).
Source: Iran's Statistical Yearbooks, Iran's Statistical Center, 1966–2019; Iran's Judiciary Statistics, Ministry of Justice.

a productive social environment which can foster growth. Moreover, transparency and accountability institutions can help create strong institutions of rule of law and control various forms of corruption including patronage, clientelism, rent-seeking, and prebendalism. In particular, accountability can reduce patronage appointments by incentivizing meritocratic recruitment, which can in turn improve the state's capacity.

This section evaluates the status of accountability institutions in Iran using the vocabulary and definitions provided in the introduction. In brief, vertical accountability is concerned with the relationship between citizens and elected officials, diagonal accountability is related to active civil society and independent media, and horizontal accountability is concerned with the separation of power and the oversight of different political institutions on each other.[48] All three mechanisms of accountability can be evaluated on the basis of their procedural (de jure) and substantive (de facto) dimensions which can be subsequently used to gauge the *implementation gap* that may exist between the constitutional provisions and the reality of the accountability institutions in a country.[49]

De Jure and De Facto Accountability

Table 1.2 summarizes the overall status of the accountability institutions in Iran, de jure and de facto, and across the vertical, diagonal,

TABLE 1.2. Status of procedural (de jure) and substantive (de facto) accountability in Iran by mechanism (vertical, diagonal, horizontal). The framework was adapted from Lindberg, Lührmann, and Mechkova, 2017.

Mechanism	Indicator	Procedural	Substantive Outcome
Vertical	Universal suffrage	✓	✓
	No vote buying, clean elections	✓	Weak
	Existence of programmatic parties	Limited	✗
	Multiparty election for the head of state	✗	✗
	Limits on term of office for the head of state	✗	✗
Diagonal	Freedom of assembly	Limited	✗
	Freedom of press and expression	Limited	✗
	Freedom of civil society	Limited	✗
Horizontal	Legislature investigates executive	✓	Weak
	Legislature controls resources	✓	Weak
	Judiciary independence	Limited	✗
	Judiciary accountability and oversight	Limited	✗

Sources: S. I. Lindberg. A. Lührmann, V. Mechkova, "From De-Jure to De-Facto: Mapping Dimensions and Sequences of Accountability," World Development Report Background Paper, World Bank, 2017.

and horizontal mechanisms. Although Iran's current constitution is endowed with some elements of accountability spanning across all three mechanisms, these provisions are woefully inadequate to establish a meaningful level of procedural accountability. First and foremost, the idea of *Velayat-e Faqih*, governance of Islamic jurist, is fundamentally irreconcilable with democratic governance.[50] Furthermore, except for the universal suffrage—which was granted during the Pahlavi era in 1963—the government, in reality, is far more unaccountable in all other major aspects compared to the de jure institutional framework. A recent empirical study by the World Bank has shown that a common historical pattern in the development of de facto accountability often starts with creation of vertical accountability institutions which is then followed by development of diagonal accountability, which itself precedes the creation of de facto horizontal accountability.[51] This would imply that, unless Iran can create meaningful de facto electoral accountability institutions, one cannot expect the diagonal and horizontal institutions of accountability to hold the government more accountable in the foreseeable future.

Concerning the vertical mechanism of accountability, freedom of political parties, albeit with some serious preconditions, are recognized in the constitution. However, in reality, there has been a great implementation gap between de jure and de facto dimensions of electoral accountability in Iran. Dominant clientelistic relationships and insufficient social demand for accountability institutions, at least until recently, are among the contributing factors to creation of this gap. As a result of this actual chasm, the scope and structure of substantive elements of vertical accountability do not lend themselves to meeting conventional minimum standards for democracy and fail to provide any meaningful mechanism to remove incompetent and corrupt officials. The potential benefits of real competitive elections are thus never really materialized due to shortcomings in both procedural (constitutional) and substantive (implementational) factors. Therefore, the Islamic Republic should be recognized as an electoral autocracy or competitive autocracy and should not be placed in the same basket of countries known as transitional democracies.[52]

Accountability institutions in Iran suffer from the lack of established programmatic political parties. An important component of accountability, whether downward (democratic multiparty system) or upward (within a centralized autocratic party), is the presence of enduring structured political institutions which shape the collective decision-making process in the political arena, provide feedback to political actors, and substantiate the long-term stability of the political system. Analysis of the political landscape in contemporary Iran reveals the absence of stable programmatic political parties with long-term principles and visions. Even the Tudeh Party, which seemed to be an organized and stable party for decades, was not an independent party formed inside Iran and had clear affiliations with the Soviet Union. One of the most notable examples was the main party of the Islamist wing of the revolution, the Islamic Republican Party, which had the endorsement of the charismatic Khomeini and survived through postrevolutionary conflicts by sidelining all other organized rivals. Yet, it did not last for even a decade (1979–1987) and was dissolved due to "internal conflicts" before the end of the Iran-Iraq War. This is in stark contrast with authoritarian countries like China (compare the Communist Party of China, 1921–present), where a centralized party provides some stability and continuity and ensures a minimum level of accountability, first to the party bosses, but ultimately, to some extent, to the people. After the revolution in Iran, the major ideological cleavages (e.g., secularism versus religious fundamentalism) were

deactivated and demobilized,[53] and the cleavages over which the parties were constructed were limited to the Islamic bloc's intra-elite issues
(modernizing Islamist versus conservatives). Over the past two decades,
parties are mainly reactivated or newly formed transiently near the time
of elections to win short-term political gains, without providing a ground
for long-term planning and accountability. Such shallow and short-term
political structures have, therefore, not been functioning properly to
make the elected bodies more responsible and competent nor to shape
their decision-making process to be less short-sighted. Hence, they have
failed to help the government increase its capacity in a meaningful way.
For example, besides their lack of any economic plans during the election campaigns, none of Iran's presidents and prime ministers of the
past four decades had a basic understanding of economic principles at
the time they assumed office.

In the absence of programmatic parties and strong civil society and
given the near-monopoly of state over media, social media has emerged
recently as a powerful platform for grassroots anticorruption efforts in
the country. Large-scale expansion of communication technologies in
recent years, combined with the constant censorship and suppression
of free expression in official media, has made the internet and social
media the major arena for criticizing the policies of the government
and its officials. In fact, the officials are ironically very conscious of their
"image" in social media, to the extent that they typically respond—either as individuals or as institutions—very rapidly to critical comments
that go viral in social platforms. Given the paucity of other means of
accountability, the process of consolidation and expression of public
opinion in social media has provided the only mechanism to ensure a
minimum level of transparency, responsibility, and accountability. However, it is not entirely clear if the result of such an "institution" would be
more than its short-term yields. Although officials' sensitivity leads to
their rapid responses to the "highlights" of social media, this response is
typically quite superficial. It primarily aims to alleviate public concerns
with the most ostensible and populist moves—and not necessarily the
most relevant or fundamental measures needed to solve the problem
in the long term, as the latter does not appeal to the very mechanism
of accountability embodied in the short-term attention span of social
media. Thus, although social platforms provide some scarce and short-
term mechanisms of accountability, they are not likely to significantly

increase the capacity of the state to address its fundamental challenges in the long-term.

Like many other autocratic regimes, in the absence of a free press and multiparty system, and even lack of effective upward accountability in the hierarchy, corruption in Iran has intensified. Over time, more opportunities for rent-seeking and corrupt activities have become available for the elites tied to the regime. But a more fundamental problem seems to be the natural decline in the supply of benevolent officials who would be able to climb the power ladder to reach high-ranking positions. This is, in turn, a natural consequence of the weakness of various mechanisms of accountability, as the lack of meaningful competition and of rotation of officials severely limits the potential human capital and hence adversely affects the capacity of the state. On the other hand, the political structure (e.g., in the form of an organized party) lacks the right feedback mechanisms to regulate and filter out corrupt and incompetent officials. This means that the recruitment process is devoid of the meritocratic elements necessary for preserving a reasonable level of effectiveness. The result is a situation where the state in Iran may in reality prefer not to embark on a genuine campaign to address corruption, since regardless of the severity of the punishment imposed on the identified corrupt officials, such anticorruption campaigns would ultimately do more harm to the legitimacy of the state by eroding public trust in the entirety of the system, compared to the small gains in public support by signaling good faith. In fact, in order to avoid the buildup of bottom-up anticorruption pressure against the vested interests of powerful rent-seeking groups and corrupt officials, the state in Iran has never been transparent about the activities of its main economic institutions such as the national development fund, the privatization organization, *bonyads*, IRGC-affiliated corporations, the Central Bank, and the state-owned banks.

The state's capacity for implementation of radical reforms has also been heavily compromised by the decline of social capital. Lack of trust between the state and the people, along with the fear of further social turmoil given the fragile conditions, has resulted in a situation where the government increasingly deviates from prudent long-term policies which inevitably entail short-term austerity for the people and hence may exacerbate public discontent (e.g., the 2019 protests which were caused by a spike in gasoline prices). Desperate attempts at "responding" to any apparent sign of social dissatisfaction, as exemplified in the case of social media outlined above, highlight the severity of this deadlock. The state is therefore trapped in a situation whereby the combination of political (horizontal) and social (bottom-up) pressures does not allow it to undertake the critical long-term reforms necessary to deal with fundamental challenges. On the one hand, the state does not have the uniformity and political will needed to decide independently in order to act upon major problems, as the government needs to constantly compromise and accommodate other factions (often unofficial and existing in the shadows) to survive. The result of this political disarray and social fragility is that the fundamental challenges of the country are inevitably piling up and solutions are being deferred to the future.

Recruitment

The lack of accountability has also affected the state's capacity in a more direct manner, namely via recruitment. One of the key dichotomies introduced from the early days of the revolution was the distinction between being committed (*mote'ahed*) and being qualified (*motekhases*) with the former distinctively prioritized and valued over the latter. Originally, this was used to distinguish the revolutionaries, who were mostly of low capacity and inexperienced, from the old executives and bureaucrats of the past regime, who were not aligned with the ideology and principles of the revolution. Forty years later, this demarcation persists to filter outsiders from insiders. In fact, the dichotomy has been continuously employed in past decades to serve ideological filtering (e.g., cultural revolution), effectively turning to an instrumental tool to protect the closed circle of insiders in recent years. One way this works is by blocking political rivals from strategic positions or by biasing the appointment of faculty toward those with "proper" affiliations in universities. This has added a new dimension of patronage appointments and promotions to nepotism and kinship that were historically prevalent in the Iranian bureaucracy.

The problem of recruitment in the Islamic Republic goes beyond the quality of individuals who are appointed to managerial positions. For example, in recent years, some of the state's high-level officials have offered mid-level technocratic positions to young Iranian academics at Western universities. Although the primary motivation was the officials' hope that such moves can help depict a progressive and open-minded picture of themselves to the public, the outcome could have been productive regardless of the disingenuous intention. However, due to the following reasons, this has not been the case so far. First, given the historical sensitivity of the Islamic Republic to collaboration with the Iranian diaspora (and foreigners), only those academics are invited who have not been seriously critical of its policies in the past, and hence most likely lack the aspiration to fight for significant reforms. Moreover, given the situation of Iran in past years, in most cases, invitees who respond positively to such offers not only have a great appetite for a political career but also feel comfortable defending the past and future policies of the bosses who hire them. As a result, even employing highly educated and talented individuals does not endow the system with any significant capacity for real reform through this type of recruitment, as the faulty system dominates the potential merits of such individuals and even takes advantage of their presence by aligning them with the needs of the system.

Another way to look at the problematic link between accountability and recruitment is by highlighting the faulty system of rewards and feedback in bureaucracy, whereby the rewards are not distributed, and hence the incentives are not shaped, in proportion to the efficiency of units and agents. In fact, instead of promoting and encouraging the most efficient and creative individuals and structures, there seems to be a consistent tendency in recent years to suppress any emerging potential in different social, political, and cultural arenas that passes a certain threshold. The most likely explanation for such a counterintuitive attitude seems to be the dominance of a paranoid mindset which sees anything too powerful as a potential threat to its security and stability. Such a mindset leads to a vicious cycle of insecurity and lack of capacity. The state finds itself in a weak and insecure position, and as a result it perceives any powerful individual or organized structure as a serious threat to its integrity. By suppressing such capacities as potential threats, the state eventually becomes even weaker and more paranoid. Such a vicious cycle, therefore, inherently represses the potential and limits the capacity of governance by favoring a perceived notion of stability and security over capacity-building and growth. In summary, the capacity of the state has been heavily compromised, as factors other than efficiency and functionality (e.g., loyalty, subservience, security, and stability) played the main role in the recruitment process. Needless to say, such a faulty system fuels the vicious cycle of corruption and trust,[54] which in turn makes the state less efficient in undertaking any fundamental reform.

The exclusion of a large part of society as "noncommitted outsiders" has resulted in the state's inability to exploit the huge capacity of the new generation, particularly at the peak of the golden demographic window of opportunity. Instead of tapping into this huge potential, Iran's undemocratic and unmeritocratic purge has deprived society and the economy of some of its best talents, as manifested in its massive brain drain in recent decades. Despite the sporadic mention of the issue by top officials, it seems that, in reality, the state is indifferent to human capital flight or even favors the process, as many of the emigrants are deemed critical of its major policies. Perceptions of exclusion and disparity have also exacerbated the issue of trust between the public and the state and have further undermined social capital. In conclusion, it appears that had the state been more politically inclusive and not been too worried about preserving its existing structure, it could have obtained the support of more social actors to help persuade the public to accommodate the kind of painful reforms necessary for long-term gains.

Economic Development

Economic growth and macroeconomic stability, as the ultimate goals of a state's economic policy, constitute important objective measures correlated with the state's capacity when considered over prolonged periods of time. While trends in economic development of Iran will be discussed at great length in subsequent chapters, here we focus on the interplay between economic growth (or contraction) and other dimensions of development. We note that major inflection points in patterns of economic growth in Iran almost perfectly match the onsets of paradigm change in the form and quality of governance (see Figure 1.3). The corresponding real GDP growth rate for each of these periods in both absolute and per capita terms are listed in Table 1.3. At a high level of abstraction, the interaction between the economic development and other dimensions of development can be summarized as follows.

1970–1978: The rapid economic growth, which averaged 6.5% per year (8.9% until 1977), resulted in the creation of two new and highly mobilized social groups, namely an educated urban middle class and migrant peasants who were marginalized in cities. Both of these social groups were far more politically active compared to their previous status, particularly the latter group who were politically inert prior to migration to the cities. These social groups were also joined by members of the working class who perceived that they did not receive their fair share of the rapidly expanding economic pie, and by traditional merchants of the bazaar whose institution was losing ground against industrial manufacturing and modern retailers. Later in this period and in the last two years prior to the revolution, the economic slowdown further exacerbated the grievances and anxiety among these groups. Therefore, the rapid economic growth of this period and its subsequent slowdown contributed to political activation of a wide range of social classes and played a central role in delegitimization of the Shah's regime.

1979–1988: In this period, the economy contracted at an average rate of 2.6% per year (6.1% on a per capita basis). This occurred during a period of coercive demobilization of social groups in the realm of politics by the then newly formed revolutionary state which was consolidating its grip on power by a brutal and bloody suppression of nearly all other political players and mobilization of society as a whole behind the national cause of the war. As a result, the dire state of the economy in this period did not yield any major changes in other dimensions of development, with the only exception being its role in persuading Khomeini to finally accept the ceasefire in 1988 due to lack of resources to continue the war, both materially and in terms of people's support.

1989–2004: The economy of Iran expanded in this period at an average rate of 4.8% per year (3.1% on a per capita basis). Although the postwar recovery was slow and associated with sporadic bouts of instability due to lack of a coherent and practical plan, it nevertheless created the notion for many people that the Islamic Republic regime could, at least to some extent, behave like a normal state. The economic growth of this period created a modest upward social mobility for lower social classes and enabled the middle class to partially reconnect with the rest of the world, first through satellite TV and video tapes and later through computers and the internet. These developments fundamentally changed the underpinnings of the then conservative society by shaping the aspirations of the younger generation and helped restore the demand for an accountable government. The conservatism and risk-averse attitude of the people at that time was due to the fact that, over the course of a mere decade, Iranian society had experienced three historic events: the end of the dynastic era, a long and devastating war with Iraq, and suppression

TABLE 1.3. Real GDP, non-oil real GDP, and GDP per capita growth rates during the time periods corresponding to different governance regimes.

Average Growth	1970–78	1979–88	1989–2004	2005–20
Real GDP	6.5	–2.6	4.8	1.9
Non-oil real GDP	5.9	–0.6	3.6	3.1
Real GDP per capita	3.5	–6.1	3.1	0.5

Source: Economic Time Series Database, Central Bank of Iran (cbi.ir).

by the new totalitarian regime which replaced the autocratic regime they had just managed to topple down.

2005–2020: In this period, the Iranian economy expanded at an average annual rate of a mere 1.9% which corresponds to 0.5% growth on a per capita basis. This low and noninclusive growth has had a profound detrimental impact on the legitimacy of the state. The economic hardships of the lower and middle classes have coincided with the emergence of a new class of elites closely tied to the state who, in sharp contrast with society's past norms and the revolution's egalitarian rhetoric, make little effort to hide their wealth, as money is increasingly becoming the determinant of social status. This recent phenomenon has done much to delegitimize the Islamic Republic regime in recent years. The longer the current situation persists, the less likely the state will be able to regain its vanishing grounds for legitimacy. Any meaningful economic reforms in Iran will inevitably entail severe austerity, job cuts, and elimination of subsidies on consumer goods which in the short term will contradict the goals of the reform and fuel public grievances. Such reforms will result in further delegitimization of the regime and destabilization of the political order. The consequences of previous irresponsible actions and economic misconduct by the state, which have thus far been limited to low output growth, are now morphing into a full-fledged crisis that may result in generations of economic growth loss.

Social Mobilization

Social mobilization is a term that refers to a cluster of changes that often occur together in a large part of a society that is moving from a traditional to a modern way of life.[55] During the modernization process, the rates of urbanization, literacy, and political participation increase while the fertility rate and agriculture's share of the economy decrease. Also, as the size of the market increases with economic development, labor becomes more specialized and mobile, and as workers move to seek better jobs, economic productivity improves. In the meantime, social relationships shift away from ascriptive (based on kinship, social class, and gender) to voluntary (based on shared interests). In democratic countries, civil society and political parties are the two channels through which these social developments can influence governance.

A common problem that many modernizing countries encounter is that the development of their weak political institutions lags behind the rapid evolution of their societies. According to Huntington's gap hypothesis,[56] by increasing aspirations and expectations, rapid social mobilization can turn into social frustration, particularly when coinciding with unfavorable economic conditions. Social frustration, in turn, translates into higher levels of political participation, as society demands that the government address new expectations. However, due to the lack of a sufficient degree of political institutionalization and capacity in modernizing countries such as Iran, political institutions often fail to fulfill the new, heightened demands. As a result, under certain conditions, social mobilization in modernizing countries can lead to political instability and decay rather than political development. This is particularly the case for the authoritarian regimes that succeed in educating their people and creating a middle class, as in such cases the population will sooner or later demand better institutions of rule of law and accountability.[57]

Table 1.4 provides a summary of the changes in selected indicators of social mobilization as mentioned above. The rapid demographic changes toward lower fertility and smaller families, the rise in the level of education, along with an increasing exposure to the elements of Western lifestyle, have led to gradual secularization and growth of individualism in society, particularly over the past two decades. These developments have also caused an ever-increasing divergence between the preferences and expectations of the people and the realities of their lives—both at the level of ideas (e.g., delegitimization of Sharia as a source of law) and at the level of performance (e.g., higher economic expectations and a lower tendency for sacrificing welfare at the individual level for a promise of greater public achievement). In the meantime, the diminishing power of the institutions of family, religion, and law has destabilized the traditional social order which, in tandem with governance deadlock and dire

TABLE 1.4. Changes in selected elements of social mobilization in Iran over three generations. See relevant chapters for sources of data and detailed discussion.

Indicator	1970	1995	2020
Urban population (%)	42	64	77
Internal migration (% population per year)	~1.0	1.9	1.1
Total fertility rate (births per woman)	6.4	2.9	1.9
Household size (persons)	5.0	4.8	3.1
Literacy rate (%)	36	80	88
Mean years of schooling	0.5	5.3	10
Employment in nonagricultural sectors (%)	53	74	82
Roads (m/capita)	1.4	1.3	2.7
Air passengers (per capita)	0.03	0.31	0.59

economic conditions, has resulted in a state of anarchy as, for example, manifested in rising crime rates (Figure 1.6).

The results of the above changes have culminated in a number of social movements and protests in the past two decades, most notably the reform movement, the Green Movement, the women's rights movement, and the economic protests of 2017–2018 and 2019. Among them, only the reform movement, which started with Khatami's election, underwent all four typical stages of a social movement: emergence, coalescence, bureaucratization, and decline (which can occur with success or failure).[58] The common denominator of all these movements is the regime's effort to suppress them at all costs. The most full-fledged one—the reform movement—ended and brought about further frustrations because all avenues for effective reform were blocked. The Green Movement was repressed by the state before even reaching the bureaucratization stage. More recently, Iran has seen two major episodes of mass protests due to its rapidly deteriorating economic conditions and the spread of poverty to a much larger share of the population. The first episode which occurred in late 2017 and early 2018, started in the city of Mashhad during what was apparently a staged protest by local hardliners against the government which soon got out of control and spread to some one hundred cities in just a few days. The second episode was triggered by a sudden rise in the price of gasoline by the government in 2019 (see chapter 6). As the legitimacy of the regime has diminished over the past decades, its reaction to the protests has become increasingly harsher and more reliant on the direct use of force. This is clearly reflected in the nearly exponential rise in the number of casualties as a result of protests (Kouy-e-Daneshgah in 1999, the Green Movement 2009, and the protests of 2017–2018 and 2019).

Finally, the women's rights movement is at the stage of coalescence and, despite repressions, seems to have a viable path for success, particularly given the expected increasing economic pressure on the state, which would most likely reduce the capacity for, and intention to, confront the public on nonexistential matters in the long term.

CORRUPTION

Iran is currently amid its deepest economic and legitimacy crisis since the inception of the Islamic Republic about four decades ago. At the root of these twin crises is a long period of political decay which has slowly but consistently eroded all three institutions that constitute modern governance: namely the state, rule of law, and accountability. Political decay occurs when governmental institutions which were created in the past under different circumstances fail to adjust to underlying changes in society and the economy.[59] Corruption is known to accelerate political decay by distorting resource allocation and incentivizing powerful players to block reforms to protect their vested interests. Figure 1.7 demonstrates the mechanism by which corruption and political decay have formed a vicious cycle in Iran. The aim of this section is to describe the structure

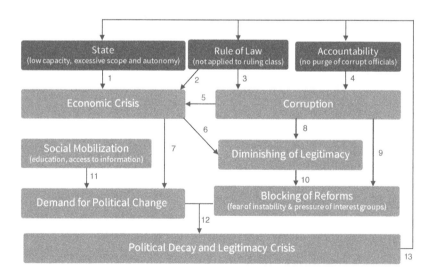

FIGURE 1.7. The vicious cycle of corruption and political decay.

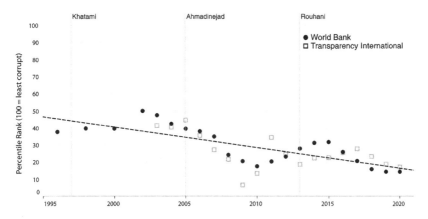

FIGURE 1.8. Iran's percentile rank in perception of corruption (100 = least corrupt country).

Source: World Bank, Worldwide Governance Indicators (WGI) Project; Transparency International, Corruption Perception Index: Global Scores.

and extent of corruption in Iran and discuss its dominant types and manifestations in recent years.

Transparency International defines corruption as: "The abuse of entrusted power for private gain. Corruption can be classified as grand, petty and political, depending on the amounts of money lost and the sector where it occurs." According to the World Bank and Transparency International,[60] Iran consistently ranks among the top third of countries for having the highest perception of corruption (Figure 1.8). Indeed, Iran's latest rank in Transparency International's corruption perception index is somewhere between Russia and Iraq and much worse than China and India, which are themselves notorious for having high levels of corruption. Yet, the picture depicted by these agencies likely understates the spread of corruption in Iran, given the harsh repression of the media and civil society which are essential elements in identification of corrupt activities. (According to Freedom House, Iran ranks near the bottom 10% of the countries in terms of political freedom and civil liberty.[61]) Therefore, it seems logical to assume that by lifting pressure on the media and civil society, not only will the number of corruption scandals in Iran rise drastically, but also Iran's position in terms of corruption perception relative to other countries will further deteriorate and could even become on par with countries such as Afghanistan and Somalia. In fact, it is an established practice in the Iranian judiciary to punish the whistleblowers and journalists who reveal cases of corruption rather than the officials who committed the corrupt actions. In any case, regardless of where Iran stands on the global corruption ladder, it is certain that the corruption in Iran has become systemic; that is, corruption is deeply embedded in political and administrative systems and can no longer be attributed only to the rogue behavior of a limited number of bureaucrats.

Corruption is broadly defined as the use of public office for direct or indirect personal gain. Rent seeking, which is a different concept from corruption, but closely related to it, is when a person gains added wealth without increasing productivity or benefiting society. Corrupt governments can distribute rents to their patronage networks by creating artificial scarcity and semi-monopoly markets. Although there is a vast body of literature on corruption, there is still no universally accepted framework and vocabulary to describe various forms of corruption.[62] Here, in order to discuss the structure of corruption in Iran, we categorize corrupt actions into the following major groups while acknowledging that, in some cases, there could be some degree of overlap among them: political corruption, administrative corruption, corruption that involves parties from the nongovernmental sector, favoritism, and coercive corruption. A list of specific corrupt actions that fall into each of these categories along with a few examples for each type are provided in Figure 1.9.

Among the above five broad groups of corruption that are prevalent in Iran today, political corruption—which is also referred to as "grand corruption" or "state capture"[63]—is by far the most consequential type. Political corruption in Iran entails a wide array of activities including clientelism, patronage appointments, corruption in elections, smuggling and money laundering by the state, and manipulation of statistics.

Since its early days, clientelism has been embedded in the political machinery of the Islamic Republic in a number of different ways, but all with a common denominator of distributing goods and jobs in exchange for political support through hierarchical organizations which can in turn mobilize people when needed. Examples of such organizations include the Basij, pro-poor bonyads (e.g., Mostazafan Foundation, Imam Khomeini Relief Committee), and the Islamic Advertisement Organization. The task of monitoring the client side of the contract to ensure their loyalty to the regime is performed by Jihadi-type, highly autonomous local institutions such as *Herasat*, which carry the DNA of the Islamic Republic at a microlevel. Although clientelism is among the chief reasons why Iran has been stuck in a low equilibrium for so long, it can also be viewed as an initial phase of transition to democratic accountability.

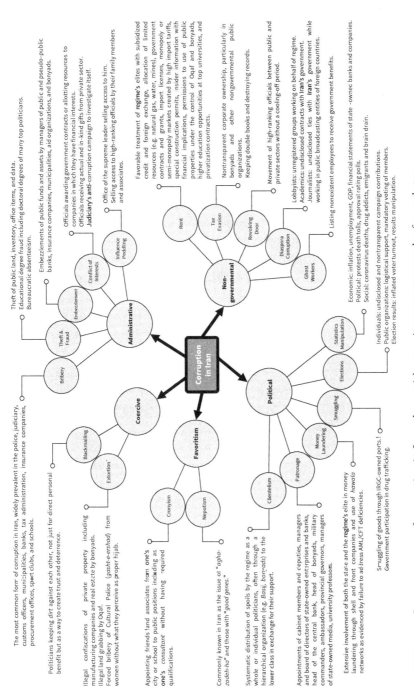

The most common form of corruption in Iran, widely prevalent in the police, judiciary, customs officers, municipalities, banks, tax administration, insurance companies, procurement offices, sport clubs, and schools.

Theft of public land, inventory, office items, and data.
Educational degree fraud including doctoral degrees of many top politicians.
Bureaucratic absenteeism.

Politicians keeping *dirt* against each other, not just for direct personal benefit but as a way to create trust and deterrence.

Embezzlements of public funds and assets by managers of public and pseudo-public banks, insurance companies, municipalities, aid organizations, and bonyads.

Officials awarding government contracts or allotting resources to companies in which they have financial interests.
Officials receiving actual and in-kind gifts from private sector.
Judiciary's anti-corruption campaign to investigate itself.

Illegal confiscations of private property including manufacturing companies and real estate by bonyads.
Illegal land grabbing by Oqaf.
Forced bribery of Cultural Police (*gasht-e-ershad*) from women without what they perceive as proper hijab.

Office of the supreme leader selling access to him.
Selling access to high-ranking officials by their family members and associates.

Favorable treatment of **regime's** elites with subsidized credit and foreign exchange, allocation of limited resources (e.g. natural gas, water, mines), government contracts and grants, import licenses, monopoly or semi-monopoly markets created by high import tariffs, special construction permits, insider information with financial implications, permissions to use of public properties under the control of Oqaf and bonyads, higher education opportunities at top universities, and privatization contracts.

Appointing friends land associates from **one's** city or school to public positions including as **one's** *consultant* without having required qualifications.

Nontransparent corporate ownership, particularly in bonyads and other nongovernmental public organizations.
Keeping double books and destroying records.

Commonly known in Iran as the issue of "*agha-zadeh-ha*" and those with "*good genes.*"

Movement of high-ranking officials between public and private sectors without a cooling-off period.

Systematic distribution of spoils by the regime as a whole or individual politicians, often through a hierarchical organization (e.g. Basij, *bonyads*) to the lower class in exchange for their support.

Lobbyists: unregistered groups working on behalf of regime.
Academics: undisclosed contracts with **Iran's** government.
Journalists: undisclosed ties with **Iran's** government while working in public broadcasting entities of foreign countries.

Listing nonexistent employees to receive government benefits.

Appointments of cabinet members and deputies, managers and board of directors of state-owned enterprises and banks, head of the central bank, head of bonyads, military commanders, ambassadors, provincial governors, managers of state-owned media, university professors.

Economic: inflation, unemployment, GDP, financial statements of state-owned banks and companies.
Political: protests death tolls, approval rating polls.
Social: coronavirus deaths, drug addicts, emigrants and brain drain.

Extensive involvement of both the state and the **regime's** elite in money laundering through shell and front companies and use of *hawala* networks as evidenced by failure to address AML/CFT deficiencies.

Individuals: undisclosed and nontransparent campaign contributions.
Public organizations: logistical support, mandatory voting of members.
Election results: inflated voter turnout, results manipulation.

Smuggling of goods through IRGC-owned ports.!
Government participation in drug trafficking.

FIGURE 1.9. Common types of corruption in Iran along with some important examples for each type.

Patronage appointments are the second type of political corruption in Iran. In fact, virtually all high-level public officials are appointed to office by top political leaders based on patronage relationships with little or no regard for the appointee's qualifications for the job. In return for the favor, patronage appointees show political loyalty and pay lip service toward the patron. Some examples of patronage in Iran include appointments made by the supreme leader (e.g., military commanders and heads of state media and bonyads, cities' Imams of Friday Prayer, and members of the Expediency Discernment Council) and by the president or his appointees (e.g., ministers, provincial governors, ambassadors, and heads of the Central Bank, public banks, pension funds, and universities). Besides unmeritocratic recruitment of rank-and-file bureaucrats, patronage appointments are the primary cause of low state capacity in Iran.

For a long time, smuggling of goods from the IRGC's exclusive ports and government involvement in drug trafficking have been a source of funds for the state. According to the Basel AML index,[64] Iran's financial system tops the world in terms of money-laundering risk. In fact, Iran has committed to address its anti-money-laundering regulatory deficiencies since 2016 but has not done anything at the time of this writing. Considering the insurmountable consequences of Financial Action Task Force (FATF) countermeasures on Iran's already troubled economy, there is good reason to believe that high officials have significant interest in keeping the status quo and deferring regulatory reforms that can make the financial system more transparent.

In true democracies, elections play an important anti-corruption role by providing a peaceful way for people to purge corrupt officials. In Iran, however, not only would elections not play any such role, they are themselves associated with various forms of corruption, including nontransparent and illegal campaign contributions, inflation of voter turnout, and manipulation of the results. It is also highly likely that the state manipulates sensitive statistics (particularly in difficult times) such as inflation, unemployment, GDP, financial statements of state-owned enterprises, and the number of emigrants, protest casualties, political prisoners, drug addicts, and, more recently, coronavirus deaths.

The second most important group of corrupt activities are those known as administrative (or petty) corruption. Bribery (for legal and illegal actions), outright theft (e.g., from a government inventory or office supply), embezzlements (e.g., in banks), fraud (e.g., fake university degree), conflicts of interest (officials awarding government contracts to companies in which they have an interest), and influence peddling (public officials facilitating a meeting with political leaders in exchange for money or favor) constitute the dominant forms of petty corruption in Iran.

Another type of corruption related to the Islamic Republic is concerned with the professional activities of some among the diaspora community who fail to disclose their ties (or in some cases, official contracts) with the regime. This type of corruption exists among academics, journalists, and lobbyists in the Iranian diaspora community, particularly in the United States, United Kingdom, and Canada. Depending on their professions, they deliver various forms of favors to the regime such as more favorable media coverage, sugarcoated analysis of the state of the economy, and lobbying on behalf of the regime with governments of other countries. Figure 1.10 shows the geographical distribution of the regime apologists with large audiences on Twitter.

Favoritism based on family (nepotism) or other forms of personal relationships such as friendship is one of the most visible types of corruption in Iran. In fact, the widely used sarcastic terms of "Agha-zadeh" and children with "good genes" were invented to refer to the omnipresent nepotism of the Islamic Republic.

FIGURE 1.10. Map of the sympathizers and supporters of the Islamic Republic regime among the diaspora with high-follower Twitter accounts.

Source: P. Azadi, M. B. Mesgaran, "The Clash of Ideologies on Persian Twitter," Working Paper 10, Stanford Iran 2040 Project, Stanford University, June 2021.

Extortion, which is the extraction of bribes from victims by threat of violence, is a common form of corruption in Iran with greatest prevalence in the police and judiciary. For example, it is a fairly routine exercise for the cultural police (Gasht-e-Ershad) to ask a young woman who wears what they see as improper hijab to casually pay her "fine" on the spot. Otherwise, she will be held in custody and have to face trial as if she really had committed a crime. Another prevalent form of coercive corruption in Iran is blackmailing, which occurs after politicians and bureaucrats become blackmailable by another act such as receiving bribes. Besides its effects at the level of individuals, blackmailing plays an important role in creating trust among the players in Iran's political landscape, as every politician can blackmail other politicians and be blackmailed by them. This is one of the main reasons why broad coalitions against corruption never take root in the Islamic Republic.

The experience of other developing countries with high levels of corruption suggests that, at the level of corruption that is facing Iran, mere improvements in transparency and accountability are not sufficient to meaningfully reduce corruption. At the current stage, measures that aim to improve transparency can only increase the perception of corruption and intensify the sense of despair in people without enabling any specific collective action mechanism. The source of grand corruption in Iran is profoundly political, and it only has political solutions. This would mean that, regardless of the ruling regime, Iran needs a strong anti-corruption commission with the full political support and protection by the head of state and independence from corrupt institutions (e.g., judiciary and police) to investigate and prosecute corrupt officials and address loopholes. However, indirect strategies based on informal institutions (i.e., culture) will be needed in the long-term to fight the deeper causes and trends underlying systemic corruption.[65]

The end of the dynastic era in Iran in 1979 did not lead to a change from a patrimonial to an impersonal state along Weberian lines. Iran's revolutionary regime, similar to its communist counterparts in the Soviet Union and China, have gradually become more corrupt over time, partly due to the lack of a viable democratic way for people to purge the corrupt politicians and partly because more opportunities have become available for ambitious people to get rich by entering into politics and gaming the system rather than entrepreneurship. Combating corruption is a collective action problem, and it often takes a crisis to form the broad coalitions that are needed to break the political logjam created by the vested interests of powerful players. Whether the accumulated pressure in Iranian society today will lead to a meaningful change or the crisis will go to waste remains to be seen in the future.

SUMMARY

In this chapter, we evaluated the quality of governance in Iran and illustrated its effects on economic development over the past half-century. Given the inadequacy of the conventional output measures (e.g., GDP per capita) and synthetic quantitative metrics (e.g., World Bank governance indicators) for this matter, a multidimensional framework was utilized which takes into account the dynamic interactions among various components pertinent to governance and development (state, rule of law, accountability, legitimacy, social mobilization, and economic development). Looking through this lens, different periods with distinct patterns of interactions between these components were identified and discussed.

The impact of decades of poor governance can be seen in virtually all major challenges facing Iran: a sluggish economy, low employment ratio, chronic high inflation, water crisis, troubled pension system, human capital flight, and eroded social trust. Based on the analysis presented here, we conclude that the ineffectiveness of the governance system can be attributed to multiple factors:

- *State:* low capacity, large scope, parallel institutions, nonoptimal institutional autonomy
- *Rule of law:* decline in legitimacy of religion and tradition as a source of law, problem in transitioning from rule *by* law to the rule *of* law, systemic corruption, lack of independence of judiciary, unfavorable environment for private sector
- *Accountability:* lack of programmatic parties and continuous crackdown on civil society, state monopoly of media, non-meritocratic recruitment, clientelism, and populistic policies
- *Legitimacy:* international isolation, waste of public resources on social engineering efforts, impediment to economic reforms due to fear of social unrest
- *Economic situation:* problem in transitioning from a resource-based to a complex modern economy, unsustainable populist policies, low investment, declining productivity, favoring rent-secking activities over entrepreneurship, brain drain

In Iran's current situation, one-dimensional reforms that only focus on single problems like the economy or international relations can only provide short-term relief, and they are doomed to fail in mid- to long-term scenarios. Instead, what Iran urgently needs to stop the ongoing vicious cycle in political, social, and economic dimensions is an orchestrated transformational approach to governance that simultaneously addresses both internal and external challenges. However, a viable path for successful implementation of such reforms does not exist at the moment. First, there is no cohesive political will in the state to embark on these kinds of risky endeavors. Second, even if such political will emerges, it cannot be successful without the rule of law being applied to the ruling class. In the absence of the latter, corruption would continue to spread and further erode social trust—without which the reforms would potentially become even more destabilizing.

Besides domestic challenges, three looming global trends—beyond the control of the state and society—will have dramatic effects on Iran's future in the coming decades. First, climate change will likely have a broad range of impacts on Iran, such as extreme weather conditions and agricultural losses. Second, the new paradigm in the global energy markets will likely result in lower oil export proceeds for Iran in the coming decades. As the global economy gradually decouples from oil consumption, it is becoming increasingly more likely that a significant portion of Iran's proved oil reserves will never be produced. The amount of wealth that Iranians will lose due to stranded oil reserves could be in the order of ten to twenty times the current size of Iran's economy. Third, new trends in artificial intelligence and automation will make it increasingly difficult for countries like Iran to pursue labor-intensive, manufacturing-oriented growth in the future. In the long run, the combined effects of the above three external factors will by no means be less dramatic than the threats caused by Iran's internal challenges.

We would like to finish our concluding remarks by putting more emphasis on the urgency of deep reforms in governance institutions to be able to cope with the country's rather difficult challenges which will persist well into the future regardless of the prevailing political regime. The experience of the past decades has shown that a state-dominant development strategy in Iran does not yield satisfactory outcomes. In order to put an end to the current vicious cycle and improve the country's future trajectory, Iran should instead implement a transformational governance strategy to shift expectations to a positive direction, adjust the autonomy of political institutions, and allow for the creation of a strong civil society. To this end, the future development plans of the country should include a clear strategy for sequencing and pacing of structural reforms in both political and economic institutions rather than merely being numerical expressions of politicians' wish lists for the next five or twenty years. Finally, given the spread and depth of corruption in the country, in addition to measures aimed at improving transparency, Iran also needs a strong anti-corruption commission, independent from the judiciary and the police, to investigate and prosecute corrupt officials at any level.

2

DEMOGRAPHIC TRENDS

IN THE SECOND HALF of the twentieth century, Iran completed its demographic transition from high to low child mortality and, with a time lag, from high to low fertility. This transition first resulted in a high population growth rate which slowed later due to rapid fertility decline. The impact of this transition on population size and age structure is a two-edged sword. On the one hand, the explosive population growth of past decades has been, through different mechanisms, linked to nearly every problem confronting the nation: unemployment, poverty, water scarcity, undernourishment, urban pollution, the soaring domestic use of energy, and brain drain. On the other hand, the rise in the share of the working-age group in the population can potentially serve as a driver for economic growth and development.[1] The extent to which Iran can harness this transient opportunity primarily depends on development of human capital and institutional capacity to use it effectively.

Demographic trends will continue to play a central role in Iran's future trajectory of development. Therefore, a sound understanding of current demographic trends is of vital importance to policies and programs concerning Iran's development in the long run. In this chapter, we discuss

Based on Farzaneh Roudi, Pooya Azadi, and Mohsen Mesgaran, "Iran's Population Dynamics and Demographic Window of Opportunity," Working Paper 4, Stanford Iran 2040 Project, 2017.

the past trends and future projections of Iran's population dynamics, evaluate the contributions of its major determinants (fertility, mortality, and migration), and discuss trends in Iran's age composition. We then explore the distribution and select compositions of the population at a provincial level. Finally, we take a closer look at Iran's rapid fertility decline of the past decades and place it in an international context through a comparative analysis.

The analyses presented in this study are primarily based on the results of Iran's censuses and data from Iran's National Organization for Civil Registration, the Population Division of the United Nations Department of Economic and Social Affairs, and the World Bank.

POPULATION GROWTH

The latest Iranian census conducted in 2016 put Iran's population at 79,926,270 with a male to female ratio of 1.027 and urbanization rate of 74%. (The population of Iran at the time of this writing in 2021 is estimated at around 85 million people.) The census shows that the annual population growth rate of the country is currently 1.2%—a rate similar to the world average at the time but significantly lower than Iran's peak of population growth a few decades earlier.[2] The highest population growth rate in Iran occurred around 1980–1985, when the population grew by nearly 4% per year (Figure 2.1). As will be discussed later in more detail, due to large internal migration flows, the rural population of Iran has stayed almost flat over the past half century, and population growth has been almost entirely absorbed by urban areas.

According to Iran's birth registry, the annual number of births increased almost linearly from 0.9 million in 1960 to 1.4 million in 1978 but then sharply rose to about 2.5 million within the first few years after the Islamic Revolution. This was followed by a reverse trend that continued until 2000 when the annual number of births dropped to approximately 1.1 million (Figure 2.2). Since 2000, the number of births has increased again until a second peak in 2015, echoing the increase in the number of women of reproductive age. Since then, the number has plunged from 1.6 to 1.2 million births per year by 2020.

The UN data suggest that the number of deaths in Iran over the past several decades varied within a narrow range, with a hump occurring between 1975 and 1990 (Figure 2.2). Embraced within this period is the Iran-Iraq War (1980–1988), which claimed the lives of several hundred thousand

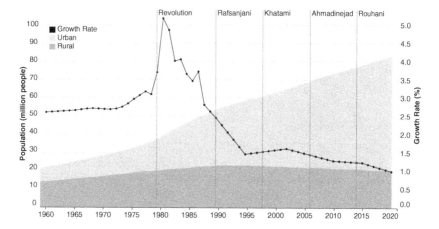

FIGURE 2.1. Iran's population size by urban and rural area and total growth rate.

Sources: Statistical Yearbooks (1966–2019) and Census Data (1956–2016), Statistical Center of Iran; UN Population Division, United Nations Department of Economic and Social Affairs.

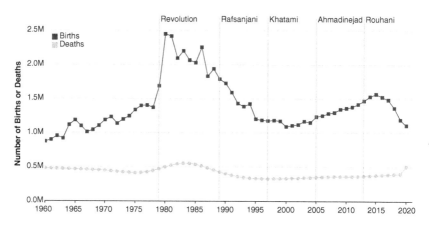

FIGURE 2.2. Number of births and deaths in Iran between 1960 and 2020.

Sources: Statistical Yearbooks (1966–2019) and Census Data (1956–2016), Statistical Center of Iran; UN Population Division, United Nations Department of Economic and Social Affairs; Iran's National Organization for Civil Registration (Sabt-e-Ahval).

Iranians. Furthermore, the high number of births during this period, in conjunction with the country's relatively high child mortality rate at the time, was another driver for the increased number of deaths in that period.

Improvements in health, which in turn resulted in higher life expectancy, have also contributed to Iran's population growth as, increasingly,

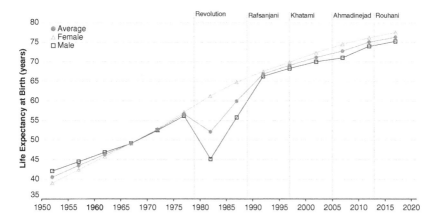

FIGURE 2.3. Trends in life expectancy at birth by sex.
Source: UN Population Division, United Nations Department of Economic and Social Affairs.

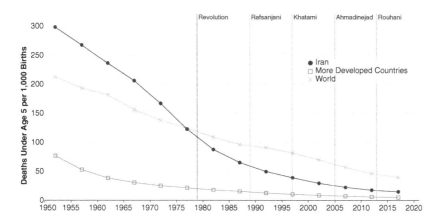

FIGURE 2.4. Trends in child mortality rate in Iran, developing countries, and the world.
Source: UN Population Division, United Nations Department of Economic and Social Affairs.

more infants survive to adulthood and have children of their own, and as adults live longer. The life expectancy at birth for males increased from 51 years in 1970 to 75 years in 2017, while that of females increased from 51 to 78 years (Figure 2.3). Such increases in average life expectancy at birth were largely due to rapid declines in infant and child mortality (Figure 2.4); Between 1970 and 2017, the under-five mortality rate dropped from 188 to 17 deaths per 1,000 live births. Improvements in health also increased survival rates of older age groups. During the same period, for example, the life expectancy of men and women at age 60 increased from 13 to 19 years, and from 15 to 20 years, respectively.[3]

Over the past decades, Iran has also experienced large inflows of immigrants and outflows of emigrants. The 2016 census shows that 2.2% of Iran's population (1.8 million people) are foreign nationals, of which 90% are from Afghanistan. However, the real figure is likely to be higher as censuses often tend to undercount foreign nationals. While some of the foreign nationals who came to Iran in previous decades have left the country, the numbers of those who stayed in Iran grew through natural increase. Provinces with the largest populations of foreign nationals are Tehran, followed by Razavi Khorasan, Esfahan, and Kerman. With over three million of its nationals living abroad (see chapter 8), Iran is also notorious for its brain drain, as those leaving the country are generally highly educated. Overall, migration as a whole has more significantly affected the stock of human capital in the country rather than the population size itself.

GEOGRAPHICAL DISTRIBUTION

The distribution of population and its rate of growth are significantly uneven among the Iranian provinces (Figure 2.5). The top five most populous provinces (Tehran, Razavi Khorasan, Esfahan, Fars, and Khuzestan)

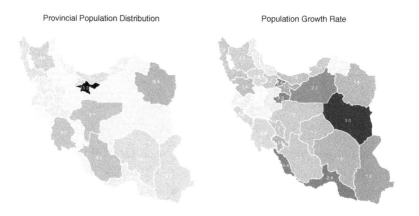

FIGURE 2.5. Provincial distribution of population (in million people) and average annual rate of population growth (%) between 2011 and 2016.
Source: Census Data (2016), Statistical Center of Iran.

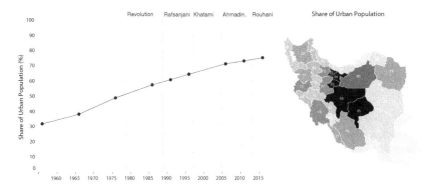

FIGURE 2.6. Share of urban population between 1956 and 2016 (left) and its provincial distribution in 2016 (right).

Sources: Statistical Yearbooks (1966–2019) and Census Data (1956–2016), Statistical Center of Iran.

contain 43% of the population while the five least populous provinces (Ilam, Semnan, Kohgiluyeh and Boyer-Ahmad, South Khorasan, and Chaharmahal and Bakhtiyari) are home to less than 5% of the population.[4] Through the five-year period leading to the 2016 census, the highest annual rate of population growth was registered in South Khorasan (3.0%), while Hamedan and North Khorasan lost population during that period.[5]

While the latest census shows that 74% of Iran's population reside in urban areas, the degree of urbanization among provinces varies within a range of 49% to 95% (Figure 2.6). Qom, Tehran, Alborz, and Esfahan provinces have the lowest shares of rural residents in their populations, while Sistan and Baluchestan, Golestan, and Hormozgan have the highest. Sistan and Baluchestan, with 1.4 million inhabitants, is one of the least developed provinces and is the only province in which the majority of the population still resides in the rural areas (Figure 2.6). About half of Iran's urban population (equal to 37% of the total population) lives in the country's top 20 largest cities while the remainder lives in over four hundred smaller cities. Based on the 2006 and 2016 censuses, the cumulative share of top 20 largest cities in the total population of the country has remained flat, indicating that the population growth rate in these cities (including the impact of internal migration) was similar to the overall population growth of the country. Figure 2.7 demonstrates how the distribution of the urban population among cities has changed over the past six decades.

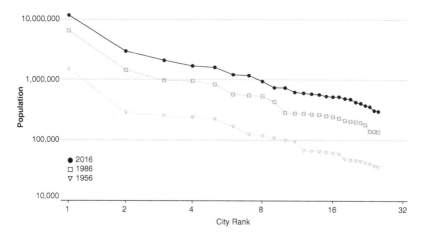

FIGURE 2.7. Distribution of Iran urban population across the top twenty-five cities in 1956, 1986, and 2016.

Sources: Statistical Yearbooks (1966–2019) and Census Data (1956–2016), Statistical Center of Iran.

In 2011, the total fertility rate of Iran's provinces ranged from 1.3 births per woman in Gilan to 3.5 births per woman in Sistan and Baluchestan.[6] It is important to note that Sistan and Baluchestan has the lowest economic participation rate and also the lowest literacy rate among all provinces.

FERTILITY AND AGE STRUCTURE

A multitude of socioeconomic factors have affected the reproductive behavior of Iranian women,[7] among which are the rise in urbanization, costs of raising a child, female education, age at first marriage, improvements in access to family planning services, and decreasing trends in child mortality. Marriage, a requirement for lawful reproduction in Iran, has undergone major changes in terms of the percentage of women ever married, the percentage of marriages that end with divorce, and the age of women at first marriage (Figures 2.8 and 2.9). According to Iran's censuses,[8] between 1976 and 2016, the average age at first marriage increased from 19 to 23 for females and from 23 to 27 for males. Also, during this period, the percentage of women ever married before the age of 35 decreased from 97% to 84%, while that of women below the age of 25 decreased by more than one-third.

As shown in Figure 2.10, in the late 1980s and early 1990s, fertility rates declined sharply for almost all age groups of women of reproductive age.

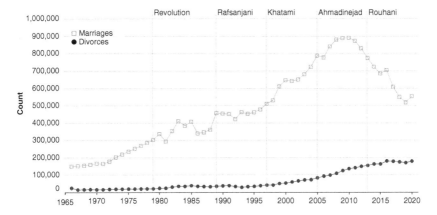

FIGURE 2.8. Number of registered marriages and divorces.

Sources: Statistical Yearbooks (1966–2019) and Census Data (1956–2016), Statistical Center of Iran; Iran's National Organization for Civil Registration (*Sabt-e-Ahval*).

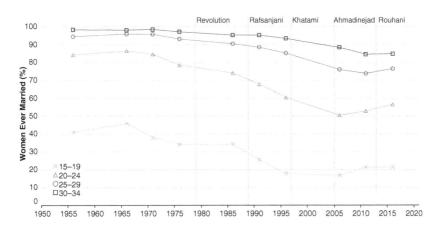

FIGURE 2.9. Trends in percentage of women ever married by selected age groups.

Sources: Statistical Yearbooks (1966–2019) and Census Data (1956–2016), Statistical Center of Iran.

A comparison of the changes in marriage and fertility of women in different age groups (Figures 2.9 and 2.10) reveals that, overall, the decline in fertility has been primarily caused by the desire of couples to limit the number of children, with smaller contributions from the changes in marriage patterns, except for the decline in fertility for younger age groups (i.e., women below the age of 25) which seems to be more closely

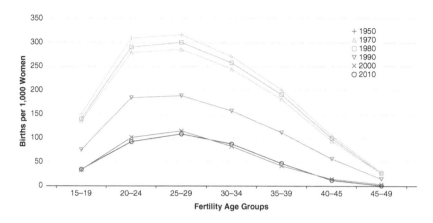

FIGURE 2.10. Changes in age-specific fertility rates based on UN Population Division and authors' calculations based on Iran's official statistics.

Sources: UN Population Division, United Nations Department of Economic and Social Affairs, accessed June 2019. Statistical Yearbooks (1966–2019) and Census Data (1956–2016), Statistical Center of Iran; Iran's National Organization for Civil Registration (*Sabt-e-Ahval*).

correlated with changes in their marriage status compared to that of older ages. For example, during the 1980s and 1990s, the percentage of women ever married and their corresponding fertility rate in the age group of 15–19 decreased by 48% and 40%, respectively. In contrast, the percentage of women ever married for the age group 25–29 in the same period decreased by 6%, while their corresponding fertility rates dropped by half. During 1996 to 2006, the same age group observed a further 10% reduction in marriage while the reduction in the fertility rate amounted to one-third.

Throughout the past five decades, Iran has seen four episodes of radical reversals in its government's fertility policies. First, a family planning program was rolled out in 1967 as part of the country's development plan to lower fertility and improve maternal and child health. According to estimates,[9] the program had limited impact on lowering fertility before being practically ended by the Islamic Revolution in 1979. Then, the new government implicitly adopted pronatalist policies that were implemented for about a decade through 1989 when, in yet another sharp turnaround, the government launched a national voluntary family planning program to lower fertility and control population growth. Lastly, claiming to be concerned about the country's low fertility and the aging problem it could cause in the very long run, the Iranian government once again has been taking a pronatalist stand since the early 2010s, encouraging couples to have more children.

The astonishing fertility decline in Iran began around 1985 in the midst of governmental advocacy for more children and four years before the inauguration of the national family planning program by the government.[10] When launched, the family planning program was effective in accelerating the fertility decline by removing social and economic barriers to contraceptive use through education and provision of modern contraceptives free of charge throughout the country. Family planning counseling and services were provided to rural couples through the country's rural health networks.[11] At the same time, the desire for smaller families was on the rise,[12] and therefore the program enjoyed a high level of social acceptance. The use of modern contraceptives increased from 27% to 57% between 1989 and 2004.[13] In all, the level and speed of the fertility decline went far beyond the government's original conservative targets.[14]

Around two decades later, claiming to be concerned about potential issues that might arise decades into the future caused by the country's low fertility (which was in fact near the replacement level), Khamenei issued a decree in 2014 to officially change the population policy of the country to a pronatalist position yet again. The directive called on all government agencies to implement direct and indirect measures to help raise the total fertility rate to, or above, the replacement level. Given the high number of births during the 2010s (i.e., 1.2–1.5 million per year), it is likely that some of the previous cross-sectional fertility rate analyses underestimated the tendency of the current generation for reproduction or were simply miscalculated. For example, the 2017 revision of the UN Population Division data mistakenly reported a total fertility rate (TFR) of 1.7 for the period of 2010–2015 but later corrected it in its 2019 revision to 1.9 for that period and also reported a TFR of 2.1 for 2015–2020.[15] Iran's TFR, calculated based on the 2011 census, was reported at 1.8[16] while our calculations and those reported in references[17] show values between 1.8 and 2.1 using alternative methods and data. Therefore, the decision to implement a pronatalist policy seems premature and would benefit from a more holistic analysis, particularly as more data will become available over time to allow for a longitudinal analysis of the fertility of the new generation. Also, the directive falls short of calling for universal access to family planning services. Lack of universal access to modern

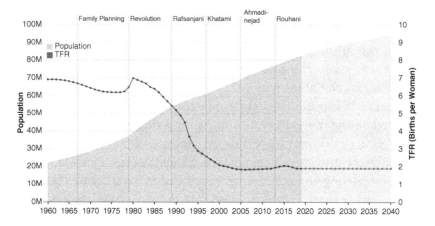

FIGURE 2.11. Trends in population growth and total fertility rate (TFR) based on raw official data and TFR values reported by Hosseini-Chavoshi et. al. Future population projection is based on the assumption that TFR remains unchanged after 2019.

Sources: Statistical Yearbooks (1966–2019) and Census Data (1956–2016), Statistical Center of Iran; UN Population Division, United Nations Department of Economic and Social Affairs, accessed June 2019; Iran's National Organization for Civil Registration (*Sabt-e-Ahval*). M. Hosseini-Chavoshi, M. J. Abbasi-Shavazi, and P. McDonald, "Fertility, Marriage, and Family Planning in Iran: Implications for Future Policy," *Population Horizon* 13 (2016).

contraception jeopardizes women's and children's health and can have costly and unintended consequences for the government (e.g., caring for a larger number of women suffering complications from unsafe abortions). Furthermore, imposing such limitations on access to contraceptives is a matter of social inequality affecting the less privileged segments of society more profoundly, especially in rural areas. More privileged residents are better equipped to meet their needs through the private health sector which is more readily available in urban areas.

Assuming that the total fertility rate remains in the range of 1.9–2.0 births per woman, the population of Iran will increase to 90 million by 2030 and then to around 95 million by 2040 (Figure 2.11). This estimate highlights the fact that Iran's high fertility of past decades could still give momentum to its population growth. If it materializes, the current pronatalist policy not only could boost Iran's population to 100 million before 2040 but could also create momentum for further population increases in the following decades. Although the aging of the population brought about by low fertility could have economic consequences for Iran in the long run (e.g., beyond 2040), a further increase in population will greatly exacerbate the existing challenges facing the nation, hence the pronatalist policies aimed at raising fertility will likely cause more damage than good. The economy has been unable to create enough employment for the country's expanding labor force, resulting in chronically high unemployment rates and fairly low economic participation rates, particularly for youth and the educated (see chapter 3). With current trends in the use of automation, it is likely that creation of routine jobs will become even more difficult in the future. Furthermore, a faster population growth, which can be the result of the new pronatalist policy, will inevitably add to the country's formidable water crisis, affecting the quality of life for tens of millions of people and the country's overall path of development. Iran's current per capita renewable water is estimated at 1,100 cubic meters per year, which is already one-third below the water stress threshold (i.e., 1,700 m3/y) as defined by the United Nations[18] (see chapter 7). Further population growth would inevitably reduce per capita freshwater availability, which could in turn cause serious food and national security challenges.

Iran surprised the world when the results of its 1996 census showed that its total fertility rate had declined by more than half in ten years, from an average of 6.2 births per woman in 1986 to 2.5 births per woman in 1996. Iran's fertility decline has been particularly impressive in rural areas. In only one generation, the total fertility rate in rural areas dropped by three-quarters, from 8.1 births per woman in the mid-1970s to 2.1 births per woman in 2006. To put this into perspective, it took around three hundred years for some European countries to experience a similar decline. In recent years, Iran's total fertility rate—which has been near the replacement level–was comparable to that of many Eurasian and European countries. Figure 2.12 shows the relationship between the GDP per capita and TFR for Iran and other countries. In 2020, more than eighty countries have fertility rates below 2.1 births per woman.[19]

The extraordinary rate of fertility decline in Iran becomes apparent when compared with those of select countries representing a wide range of economic development, religions, and cultural backgrounds (Figure 2.13). It is also worth mentioning that such rapid decline was achieved in the absence of a coercive government policy (e.g., China's one-child policy) or the legalization of abortion (e.g., Turkey).

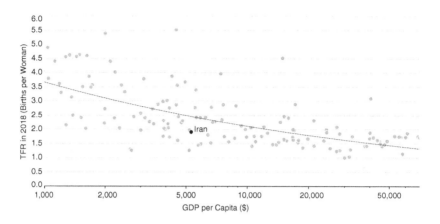

FIGURE 2.12. Total fertility rate (TFR) versus GDP per capita for Iran and select countries in 2018.

Sources: Statistical Yearbooks (1966–2019) and Census Data (1956–2016), Statistical Center of Iran; UN Population Division, United Nations Department of Economic and Social Affairs, accessed June 2019; Iran's National Organization for Civil Registration (*Sabt-e-Ahval*). World Bank Open Data, World Bank, Washington DC.

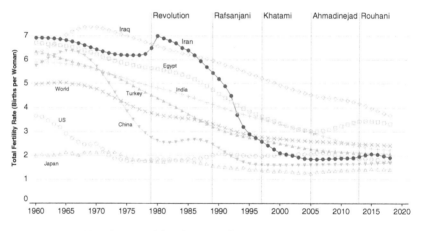

FIGURE 2.13. Trends in total fertility rates for Iran and select countries.
Sources: UN Population Division, United Nations Department of Economic and Social Affairs.

Iran's average household size has also undergone drastic changes stemming from lower fertility and other social trends such as the patterns of marriage and divorce. In 2016, there were 24.2 million households in Iran with an average size of 3.3 persons which is almost two persons smaller than what it was a generation ago in 1986 (Figure 2.14). The average size of

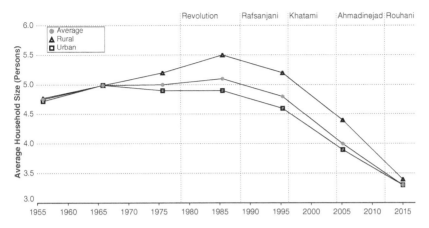

FIGURE 2.14. Changes in average number of people living in a household.
Sources: Statistical Yearbooks (1966–2019) and Census Data (1956–2016), Statistical Center of Iran.

rural households fell from its peak of 5.5 persons in 1986 to 3.4 persons in 2016, nearly closing the gap between rural and urban areas. The reductions in the average sizes of both urban and rural households are attributed to the decrease in the number of children, as the average number of adults per household (i.e., 2.5–2.8) has remained virtually constant over time.[20]

With a median age of 32 years, Iran is ranked 113th in the world for having a young population. For comparison, the median age at the onset of the 1979 revolution was only 18 years.[21] As shown in Figure 2.15, Iran's current population age structure is almost similar to that of Turkey, younger than those of Japan, China, and the United States, and older than those of Egypt and India. Shaped by changing mortality and fertility trends, the age composition of Iran's population has undergone marked changes over the past four decades (Figures 2.15 and 2.16). Before the dramatic reduction in fertility, which started in the mid-1980s, Iran's age structure resembled a pyramid with a wide base. However, in the 1990s and in the wake of rapid fertility decline, Iran's population pyramid became narrower at the bottom, giving rise to a youth bulge. With the largest cohorts in the population ascending the pyramid, in the 2010s, the distribution of younger age groups in the population is becoming more uniform over time. It should be noted that, in 2016, the two largest female cohorts (ages 25–29 and 30–34) constituted the age groups that also have the highest fertility rates (Figure 2.10). As a result, they gave

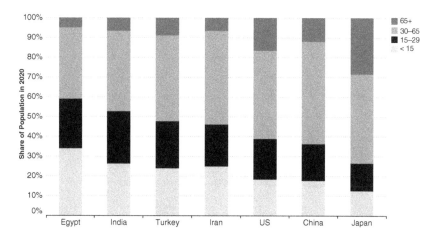

FIGURE 2.15. Comparison of Iran's population age distribution with those of selected countries in 2020.

Sources: UN Population Division, United Nations Department of Economic and Social Affairs.

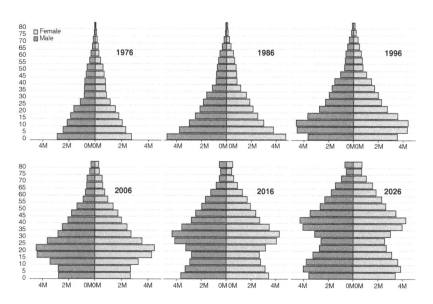

FIGURE 2.16. Iran's population age pyramids. The 2026 projection is based on the UN Population Division's constant fertility scenario.

Sources: Statistical Yearbooks (1966–2019) and Census Data (1956–2016), Statistical Center of Iran; UN Population Division, United Nations Department of Economic and Social Affairs.

rise to the annual number of births reflected in the 2016 age pyramid's slightly wider base (Figure 2.16).

The country's fertility decline has had a significant impact on its age composition. The percentage of children under age 15 in the population, which for a few decades had stayed above the 40% level, started to decline from its peak of 46% in 1986 to 24% in 2016 (Figure 2.15). The percentage of elderly (65 and older) decreased from 5% in 1950 to 3% around the mid-1980s but increased again to reach 7% in 2021. The share of the remainder of the population who are aged 15–64, commonly known as the working-age population, first decreased from about 60% in 1950 to 50% around the mid-1980s, but then sharply increased again to 70% in early 2000s and has more or less stayed the same until the time of this writing in 2021. The number of people in the working-age population is expected to reach its peak at about 65 million in the mid-2030s before starting to decline. As those born during Iran's baby boom of the 1970s and 1980s reach age 65, the elderly population will grow rapidly, from 5 million in 2020 to about 20 million in 2050. In the meantime, the number of children under age 15 is going to hover around 20 million. These changes in the age structure will cause Iran's population in 2050 (Figure 2.17) to become older than

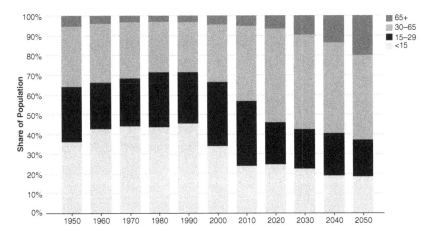

FIGURE 2.17. Changes in Iran's population distribution by broad age groups and future projections based on the UN Population Division's constant fertility scenario.

Sources: UN Population Division, United Nations Department of Economic and Social Affairs, accessed June 2019.

the current population of the United States and younger than the current population of Japan (Figure 2.15).

When a country's fertility rate falls, there is a period of typically five decades, known as the demographic window of opportunity, during which its labor force grows more rapidly than the rest of its population.[22] This situation is conducive for capital formation and rapid economic growth as each person in the working age population needs to support fewer dependents. The potential dividends from such growth-friendly demographic age composition have a transitory nature because the population grows older and eventually its share of working-age adults shrinks. As such, countries generally have only one chance to reap the benefits of their demographic window of opportunity. However, a second demographic dividend is also possible should the workers during the period of the demographic window save and invest for their retirement, thereby transforming the initial bonus into increased assets and economic development in the longer term.[23]

As a result of the changes in population dynamics explained above, Iran entered this one-time demographic opportunity in the early 2000s where the ratio of children and elderly (under 15 years old and above 65) to the working age population (15–64 years old) has fallen below 50%, a situation which will likely remain through the mid-2040s (Figure 2.18).

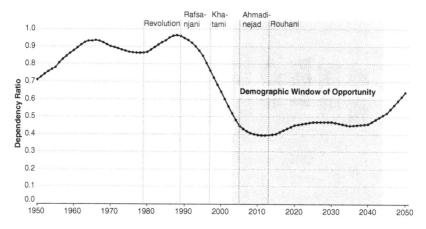

FIGURE 2.18. Trends in age dependency ratio of Iran. Future projections are based on constant TFR beyond 2019.

Sources: UN Population Division, United Nations Department of Economic and Social Affairs.

Having passed almost half of the demographic golden window without improvements in the nation's stock of capital (see chapter 4), the country must reap the benefits of this historic opportunity now before the share of the working-age population shrinks and the dependency ratio rises again.

SUMMARY

Iran's population size has increased from about 20 million in the middle of the twentieth century to 36 million at the onset of the 1979 revolution, and then to about 85 million in 2021. With annual growth rates upwards of 4%, the peak of population growth in Iran occurred in the first five years after the revolution. An important feature of Iran's demographic changes of the past decades is its record fertility decline which in a mere ten-year period between the mid-1980s to the mid-1990s decreased from 6.2 births per woman to 2.5. Iran's current TFR is estimated at nearly 2.0 births per woman, which is close to the replacement level and higher than the average TFR for the more developed countries. The life expectancy has increased from 41 years in 1950 to 76 years in 2019 (before the COVID-19 pandemic) due largely to improvements in child mortality which, in the same period, decreased from 300 per 1,000 births to 15.

The country's fertility decline has drastically changed the population's age composition. The ratio of children and elderly to the working-age population—which is known as the age dependency ratio—decreased from 0.95 in 1990 to 0.45 in 2005. With fewer dependents to support, Iran is currently in its demographic window of opportunity which is expected to last until the mid-2040s. The opportunity must be seized now before the share of the working-age population shrinks and the population grows older.

Fast-changing demographic dynamics have affected virtually all aspects of life in Iran including economic growth, labor force and unemployment, internal and external migration, depletion of water and other natural resources, environmental challenges, and even the country's oil and gas exports through the amount of fuel consumed domestically. Future chapters will discuss the link between population dynamics and some of the profound challenges facing the country including youth unemployment, the water crisis, and brain drain.

3

LABOR FORCE AND HUMAN CAPITAL

THE SIZE AND CHARACTERISTICS of the labor market in Iran have been affected by the interplay between demographic trends, the rise in the educational attainment, macroeconomic factors, flows of migration from rural to urban areas, as well as international migration to and from Iran. We discussed the effects of demographic trends on the size of the working-age population and on the population dependency ratio (the number of children and elderly relative to the working age population) in the previous chapter. In this chapter, we describe the main characteristics of the labor market in Iran and its evolution since 1960. We then provide an analysis of the major developments in the areas of education and human capital and evaluate their impact, or lack thereof, on economic growth in Iran. We will return to the subject of education in chapter 8 in the context of brain drain.

LABOR FORCE

Over the past half century, Iran's labor force has undergone profound changes in size and characteristics. The labor force is defined as the number of people who are employed or are unemployed and looking for a job, and the economically inactive population is defined as those in the working-age population but not in the labor force. Figure 3.1 shows how the sizes of the labor force and economically inactive population in Iran have changed since 1960. In this figure, the labor force is broken

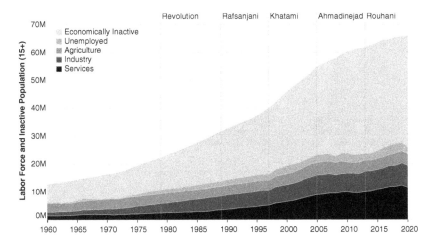

FIGURE 3.1. Working-age population in Iran between 1960 and 2020 by employment status.

Sources: Statistical Yearbooks (1966–2019), Census Data (1956–2016), and Labor Statistics, Statistical Center of Iran; Statistical Yearbooks of the Ministry of Labor and Social Welfare, www.amarkar.ir.

down by the number of jobs in broad economic sectors (i.e., services, industry, agriculture) and the number of unemployed people. A high-level summary of the main trends and characteristics of Iran's labor market is as follows:

- The working-age population increased from 13 million in 1960 to 66 million in 2020,[1] corresponding to an average growth of about 0.9 million people per year.
- The labor force participation rate, which had been hovering around 50% for two decades before the revolution, gradually declined to about 40% by 2020[2]—a level that is lower than most other countries in the world and only on par with countries such as Syria and Yemen[3] which are involved in civil wars.
- Despite the persistence of low economic participation, the unemployment rate has typically varied in the range of 10–15% for nearly half a century with an additional 10–15% of the labor force being underemployed.[4]
- A cross-country comparison of the labor force participation rate between Iran and other developing countries[5] with roughly similar levels of the per capita income suggests that discouraged workers are likely to constitute 15–20% of the inactive population. This would mean that at the time of this writing in 2021, some 25–30% of the working-age population (16–20 million people) are

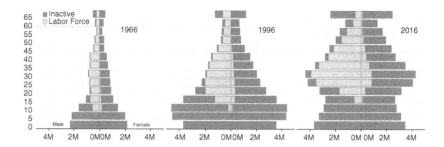

FIGURE 3.2. Iran's labor force and economically inactive population by gender and age in 1966, 1996, and 2016.
Sources: Statistical Yearbooks (1966–2019), Census Data (1956–2016), and Labor Statistics, Statistical Center of Iran; Statistical Yearbooks of the Ministry of Labor and Social Welfare, www .amarkar.ir; Statistics and Datasets, International Labor Organization (ILO).

unemployed, underemployed, or failed to find employment and stopped the job search (discouraged workers).

- The industry and service sectors were responsible for the largest number of jobs created before and after the 1979 revolution, respectively, while the number of jobs in agriculture has remained virtually constant for about half a century.[6] This sectoral shift has been part of the country's development from an agrarian economy (which was almost in a Malthusian equilibrium) toward a more urbanized population with a greater labor mobility (as discussed in chapter 1 under the topic of social mobilization). The existing paradigm in the labor force also indicates the country's failure to fully industrialize before shifting to a service-oriented economy. We will return to this subject later when we explain the contributions of different sectors to the economy in chapter 4.

Iran's rapidly growing population, and its subsequent effects on the population age structure, has been by far the most influential factor on labor force dynamics. The labor force in the 1960s was almost uniformly distributed among men aged 15–45 (Figure 3.2).[7] By the mid-1990s, in a mere three decades, both the total population and those in the labor force had more than doubled, but due to the faster growth of the working-age population compared to the labor force, the labor participation rate plunged by 10%.[8] Between 1995 and 2015, the labor force was heavily affected by the entrance of baby boomers born 1975–1995 to the job market. In 2020, the baby boomers constituted 60% of the labor force. Since the middle of the past century, the labor force has seen a gradual decrease in the economic participation rates of both teenagers and the elderly: the former due primarily to higher perceived value of secondary and tertiary education, and the latter due to expansion of social security and lack of low-skilled jobs for the elderly (which still had a large share of illiterates in 2020). The median age of workers in 1966, 1996, and 2016 were 27.2, 28.1, and 31.0 years, respectively.[9]

Another important characteristic of the labor force in Iran is the persistent dominance of men across all age groups. It has been generally observed that female labor force participation follows a U-shaped trend during the process of development.[10] That is, participation of women in the labor force is typically high prior to industrialization, which often marks the beginning of sustained economic growth in countries. The initial phase of industrialization and modernization typically involves a shift from traditional small-scale production in households and family farms to industrial and large-scale production, which often happens during the time when women are still poorly educated compared to men, hence leading to a reduction in the direct role of women in the economy. Later in the process, as educational gender gaps close and cultural barriers diminish, women become more active in the economy, and therefore their participation rate rises again.

In the case of Iran, there has been virtually no educational gender gap since the beginning of the twenty-first century (Figure 3.3)—implying that educational factors cannot be the cause for the significant disparities in labor force participation between men and women today. Besides the closure of the educational gender gap, growth of white-collar jobs after the revolution, both in absolute numbers and in terms of share in the job market, could in theory have helped boost the participation of women in the labor market. Further, as discussed in the previous chapter, compared to previous generations, today's young women in Iran more often remain single, have a higher median age at the time of first marriage and childbearing, and more often get divorced, all generating pressure and incentives for them to find paid jobs outside the household. Despite the aforementioned factors, which increased the potential for women to take part in the economy, the reality points to a different direction as shown in Figure 3.3.

Figure 3.4 compares the total and gender-specific labor force participation rates of Iran and selected economies in the developing and developed worlds. As can be seen in this figure, Iran's male labor force participation rate of 72% lies almost in the middle of the range of the

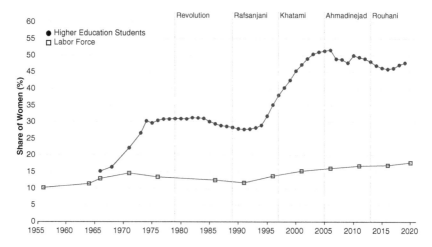

FIGURE 3.3. Shares of women among Iran's university students and labor force between 1955 and 2020

Sources: Statistical Yearbooks (1966–2019), Census Data (1956–2016), and Labor Statistics, Statistical Center of Iran; Statistical Yearbooks of the Ministry of Labor and Social Welfare, www .amarkar.ir; Institute for Research and Planning in Higher Education, Ministry of Science, Research, and Technology, irphe.ac.ir.

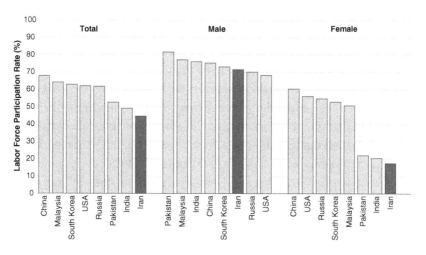

FIGURE 3.4. Labor force participation rates of Iran and select countries by gender.

Sources: Statistical Yearbooks (1966–2019), Census Data (1956–2016), and Labor Statistics, Statistical Center of Iran; Statistical Yearbooks of the Ministry of Labor and Social Welfare, www .amarkar.ir; Statistics and Datasets, International Labor Organization (ILO).

selected countries, while its female labor force participation rate of 18% is not only far below the rates of China, the United States, Russia, South Korea, and Malaysia but also below other traditional societies such as Pakistan and India.[11] In all likelihood, it will take several decades to reach a relatively balanced labor market for men and women in Iran. It is, for example, interesting to note that it took about thirty years (1950–1980) for the United States to see a rise in the female labor participation rate from about 20%—similar to Iran's level in 2020—to about 50%.[12]

Historically, due to large variations in oil revenue and its consequences for government expenditures and trade as well as the dominance of the public sector in the job market, Iran has seen multiple episodes of jobless economic growth (e.g., 2005–2013) and job creation during periods of economic slump (e.g., 1979–88) as shown in Figure 3.5. Despite improvements in education and widespread use of computers and communications technology, labor productivity (measured as the ratio of non-oil GDP to workers) has not increased since the early 1970s (Figure 3.5).

Over the past half century, Iran has persistently struggled with high rates of unemployment, typically in the range of 10 to 15% while almost

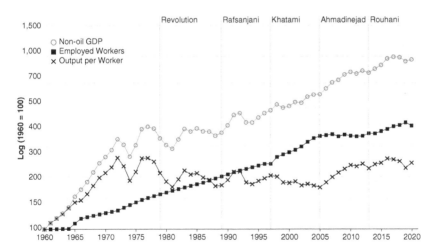

FIGURE 3.5. Iran's non-oil GDP, number of employed workers, and labor productivity measured as non-oil GDP per worker (1960 = 100).

Sources: Statistical Yearbooks (1966–2019), Census Data (1956–2016), and Labor Statistics, Statistical Center of Iran; Economic Time Series Database and Other Statistics, Central Bank of Iran (cbi.ir).

an equal percentage of the workforce has always been underemployed.[13] Discouraged workers are also likely to account for as much as 10% of the working-age population (i.e., nearly 20% of the labor force) based on a cross-country comparison with other developing countries.[14] Therefore, total unemployment, underemployment, and discouraged workers should be approximately 40–50% of the labor force (this is similar to the U-6 unemployment rate in the United States which accounts for discouraged and underemployed workers). The employment ratio, which measures the ratio of employed workers to working-age population, is another indicator that combines the effects of the participation rate and unemployment. Since the middle of the twentieth century, the size of the working-age group and the number of jobs have expanded at average rates of 2.75% and 2.47%, respectively, causing a secular decline in the employment ratio from 55% to about 42% in 2020. In the coming decades, the annual growth of the working-age population is expected to be around 1.2%, which is significantly lower than its historical average and would in turn somewhat alleviate the demographic pressure on the labor market. Furthermore, due primarily to the large and highly variable influx of new labor, the rate of unemployment has been essentially decoupled from inflation and short-term economic cycles.

The unemployment in Iran varies greatly across four dimensions, namely, age, gender, level of education, and geographical location. Unemployment among youth (aged 15–24) has typically been higher than the average unemployment by more than twofold—a ratio which is comparable to the world average.[15] In spite of women's low participation in the labor force, female unemployment has been about twice that of men,[16] suggesting that discouraged workers (i.e., those who have given up looking for a job) are likely to be more prevalent among women. There is almost the same level of gender disparity in youth unemployment (i.e., 23% and 39% for men and women in 2019, respectively). Given that no educational gap exists between men and women in the younger generation, the higher unemployment rate of women cannot be attributed to a gender skill gap but rather is rooted in the culture and various forms of discrimination. In addition to the large gaps in participation and unemployment rates of different age and gender groups, there are also large regional disparities in the labor market such that the employment ratio varies over a wide range of 28% to 43% across provinces (Figure 3.6).[17] Sistan and Baluchestan, Qom, Kohgiluyeh and Boyer-Ahmad, Markazi,

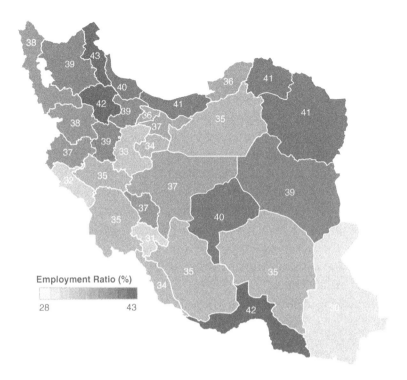

FIGURE 3.6. Geographical distribution of Iran's employment ratio in 2020.
Sources: Statistical Yearbooks of the Ministry of Labor and Social Welfare, www.amarkar.ir.

and Ilam have employment ratios below one-third. The primary driver for this regional disparity in the employment ratio is the labor force participation rate rather than the unemployment rate. In addition to large variations in the labor market across provinces, there are significant disparities within each province between its rural and urban areas. The unemployment rate in urban areas, on average, is twofold higher than that of rural areas.

Migrant workers play a sizable role in the Iranian labor market, especially for low-skilled jobs in the construction sector. According to the 2016 census, Iran hosts about 1.8 million foreign nationals, 90% of whom are from Afghanistan.[18] However, this number is likely to be an underestimation due to the presence of many undocumented migrants. Most of this population lacks adequate access to schooling or job training and are often deprived of protections provided by the labor laws. Aside from being a host to a large migrant population, Iran also experiences a large outflow of its population, particularly from the highly educated segments of society. This issue is further discussed in chapter 8.

The chronic shortage of jobs in the Iranian economy is attributable to a multitude of causes: demographic pressure resulting in rapid growth of the labor force; dominance of the public and pseudo-private sectors which inflate wage expectations; large foreign currency revenue from natural resources, which exerts negative pressure on the competitiveness of labor-intensive manufacturing; a large share of capital-intensive industries (e.g., oil, gas, and petrochemicals) in the economy; skill mismatches due to lack of a feedback mechanism between the labor market and the education system; and large internal migration flows from rural areas to cities. By 2020, Iran had already passed half of its golden demographic window without reaping any benefit from this one-time transitory opportunity due to the inability of the government and economy to create jobs at a desirable rate.

The prolonged period of chronic unemployment and low labor force participation is causing deep and enduring damage to Iranian society. The stock of human capital for millions of university graduates (who are even less likely to find a job compared to their counterparts without university degrees) continuously depreciates over time. The grim labor market for educated youth has, to some extent, decoupled economic growth from developments in human capital. Lack of job opportunities over prolonged periods is in fact transforming millions of university graduates of the past two decades from unemployed to unemployable—causing them to develop a sense of hopelessness and uselessness. The longer educated people stay unemployed or outside the workforce, the less prepared they become to find a highly skilled job.

Figure 3.7 shows long-term trends in real minimum wages in Iran, which can be seen as a proxy for trends in the living conditions of the lower economic class. In 2020, the minimum wage of Iranian workers was about $2.00 per day, implying that millions of families lived with a per capita income of less than a dollar per day—a level which is about half the commonly used $2.00 daily wage threshold for abject poverty. While wages in Iran were historically comparable to, or even higher than, wages in countries like Turkey and China, they shrunk to substantially lower than those countries over the past decades. Even more striking is that the real wage in 2021 for unskilled labor was comparable to its level back in the 1960s. The drastic slump in real income depicts only half

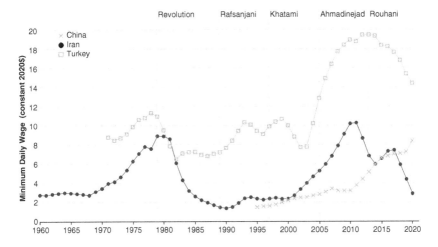

FIGURE 3.7. Comparison of Iran's minimum daily wage with that of China and Turkey (2020$). A two-year moving average is applied.

Sources: Statistics and Datasets, International Labor Organization (ILO); Economic Time Series Database and Other Statistics, Central Bank of Iran (cbi.ir); Various Iranian news archives; Center for Strategic Research, Expediency Discernment Council, Iran; Gross Domestic Product: Implicit Price Deflator, Federal Reserve Bank of St. Louis, US.

the story of the dire situation for the lower and middle classes as, in the meantime, inequality has also been on the rise.

Furthermore, Iran's baby boomers of 1975–1995 will start to reach retirement age by 2030 without having worked enough to accumulate sufficient savings to support themselves during their elderly years. These dynamics in the labor market are exacerbating Iran's pension crisis which is already approaching insolvency despite the favorable age structure of the population since the start of the twenty-first century. For decades, the state has implemented generous populist policies regarding retirement age and individual retirement contribution mandates while failing to pay its own share of contributions. Over time, the buildup of a large public debt to pension funds has triggered a systematic transfer of the central government's assets (state-owned enterprises) to pension funds, which are public but nongovernmental. As such, these pension funds, as the majority stakeholders of the transferred enterprises, have taken charge of the day-to-day operations of some of the country's largest industrial companies. In the new arrangement, while the firms still benefit from government support (e.g., in terms of regulations and licenses), they are now able to

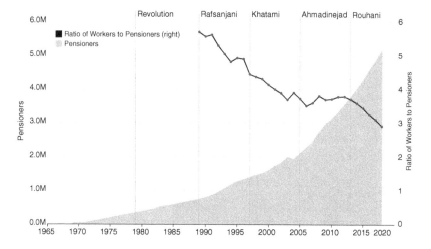

FIGURE 3.8. The number of pensioners (left axis) and the ratio of workers to pensioners (right axis). The values only include *Tamin-e-Ejtemaei* and *Sandoogh-e-Bazneshastegi Keshvari*.

Sources: Statistical Yearbooks (1966–2019), Census Data (1956–2016), and Labor Statistics, Statistical Center of Iran; Statistical Yearbooks of the Ministry of Labor and Social Welfare, www.amarkar.ir.

produce huge personal gains for their managers who are appointed by politicians often in a patronage relationship (see the discussion on corruption in chapter 1). Iran's pension time bomb will seriously damage the economic well-being of millions of vulnerable pensioners and their families and will also lead to an even smaller fiscal space for capital expenditure in the future. Figure 3.8 shows the trends in the number of pensioners and worker-to-pensioner ratio for two of the largest pension funds in the country (i.e., *Tamin-e-Ejtemaei* and *Sandoogh-e-Bazneshastegi Keshvari*).

EDUCATION

One of the most important and consequential contemporary developments in Iranian society has been the steady and relatively fast improvement in educational attainment (Figure 3.9). Before the mid-twentieth century, the literacy rate in Iran was considerably lower than in countries such as China, Turkey, and India. The backwardness of Iran in terms of literacy was partly due to the late arrival of the printing press, which was adopted only in the first half of the nineteenth century—three to four centuries after it found widespread use in Europe. Like many other modern institutions in the country, mass education in Iran was introduced

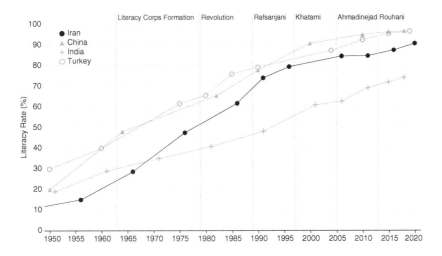

FIGURE 3.9. Changes in literacy rates in Iran, Turkey, China, and India.
Sources: Statistical Yearbooks (1966–2019), and Census Data (1956–2016); World Development Indicators, World Bank, Washington DC.

by Reza Shah in the 1930s as a part of his state-building project—about a century after the introduction of compulsory education in Europe. This process accelerated later due in part to the formation of the literacy corps by the Mohammad Reza Shah in 1963 as a cost-effective method for improving rural education[19] and in part by the gradual transformation of the economy from agrarian into a diverse mix that increased the demand for educated and skilled labor. At the onset of the revolution, about half the population and less than a quarter of adults were literate. Four decades after the revolution, the literacy rate has reached nearly 90%.

In comparison to other countries and on a quantitative basis, the development of Iran's human capital resources over the past few decades has been nothing short of remarkable. Iran tops global trends both in enhancing its mean years of schooling and in boosting the scientific output of its researchers: the mean years of schooling increased from 4.2 in 1990 to 10.0 years in 2018,[20] and the number of scientific papers published by Iranian scholars rose by about fiftyfold merely over the past two decades (see chapter 9).

The relationship between education and economic growth has been studied for many decades by researchers, with several cross-country analyses finding a strong positive association between the cognitive skills of nations and their rates of development in the very long run.[21]

At the macro level, education can improve the productivity of a nation as a whole and boost innovation and technology adoption. When controlled for other factors, both the quantity of education (commonly measured by mean years of schooling) and the quality of education were found to be associated with economic growth—although the quality of education was shown to be much more important than the quantity.[22] Figure 3.10 compares the changes in educational attainment (expressed in mean years of schooling) and the real GDP per capita of Iran and selected countries between 1990 and 2018. As illustrated, the marked improvement in the educational attainment of Iranians has not been accompanied by a parallel progress in economic output. As discussed in the previous chapter, since the early 2000s, the country has entered its one-time demographic window of opportunity during which the ratio of the working-age population to the children and elderly remains high for about half a century—a condition conducive to financial capital formation, hence economic growth. However, the country's output per capita has hovered around an unimpressive level of $4,000 per year for a prolonged period[23]—placing Iran among countries whose higher educational attainments have failed to boost economic output.

Besides other institutional impediments, the low economic growth of Iran is, in part, due to poor quality of the education system which is ineffective in fostering critical thinking and fails to provide students with the practical knowledge required to solve real-world problems. While an in-depth analysis of this issue falls beyond the scope of this book, the poor outcome of the education system in Iran can be broadly attributed to the bold presence of ideology in educational materials (which is aimed at producing the ideal man of the Islamic Republic), overemphasis on performance in national contests (*concours*) and dominance of the teach-to-the-test approach, ineffective curriculum design and top-down capacity planning for universities with no regard for the needs of the market, and setting aside a sizeable portion of university seats for the regime's elites and their relatives. As shown earlier in this chapter, formal and cultural discriminatory rules in the labor market against Iranian women—who have contributed to the overall enhancement of mean years of schooling more than men—is another cause of divergence between trends in educational attainment and economic productivity.

Concerning the quality of primary and secondary education, according to the results of major international student achievement tests in

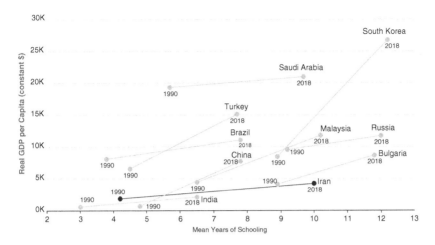

FIGURE 3.10. Changes in the mean years of schooling and real GDP per capita for selected countries between 1990 and 2018.

Sources: Economic Time Series Database and Other Statistics, Central Bank of Iran (cbi.ir); Human Development Data (1990–2018), United Nations Development Programme, and World Bank Open Data, World Bank, Washington DC.

mathematics and science,[24] Iran has consistently ranked at the bottom third among countries participating in these tests (Figure 3.11). Compared to Iran, the rapidly developing nations of East Asia have underperformed in terms of improving mean years of schooling but have likely benefited much more from their investments in education[25] thanks to the excellent quality of their educational systems.

One of the factors that contributed to Iran's improvement in the mean years of schooling has been the explosive population growth of the past few decades, which in turn increased the ratio of young and more educated cohorts to older and less educated ones. As discussed in chapter 2, Iran's fast population growth began in the 1970s and accelerated following the 1979 revolution before decelerating with a fertility decline which started around 1985. The baby boomers of the 1970s and 1980s put significant strain on primary and secondary education in the 1980s and 1990s. By the late 1990s, this cohort gradually reached adulthood, ready to enter the job market or continue education, which resulted in an explosive increase of university students.

Besides demographic factors, the huge demand for higher education in recent decades is attributable to cultural factors (e.g., parents'

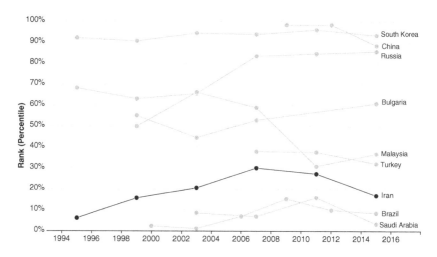

FIGURE 3.11. Ranks of Iran and select countries in quality of primary and secondary education based on average international test scores.

Sources: Trends in International Mathematics and Science Study (TIMSS), International Association for the Evaluation of Educational Achievement, 1995–2015; Programme for International Student Assessment (PISA), OECD, 2000–2018.

expectations and the role of a university degree in the marriage market), an education wage premium for jobs in the government and state-owned enterprises which essentially dominate the economy, and migration aspirations of youth which increase the expected return on higher education for them. Despite this growing demand, by the mid-2000s, universities only had the capacity to accommodate less than a fifth of the applicants (Figure 3.12). It was under such circumstances that the government—which viewed higher education as a means to postpone the introduction of this cohort into the country's distressed job market—widely expanded university capacities. Since the early 2010s, over 40% of the population cohort aged 19–25 were enrolled at a university at any point in time.

The expansion of higher education capacity was achieved by increasing the number of students in existing universities as well as increasing the number of new public and private institutions, which led to commodification of higher education across almost all social classes. College education has turned into a consumer staple among most Iranian households in recent decades. However, the gradual reduction in the size of the college-aged cohort, as depicted in Figure 3.12, has led to a decrease in higher education enrollments.

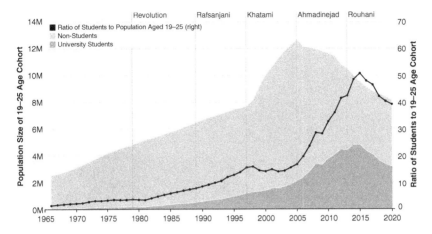

FIGURE 3.12. Changes in the nineteen to twenty-five age cohort and number of university students (left axis) and the ratio of university students to this cohort (right axis). Note that at any given time, part of the non-student population age nineteen to twenty-five may already have a university degree.

Sources: Statistical Yearbooks (1966–2019), Census Data (1956–2016), and Labor Statistics, Statistical Center of Iran; Institute for Research and Planning in Higher Education, Ministry of Science, Research, and Technology, irphe.ac.ir.

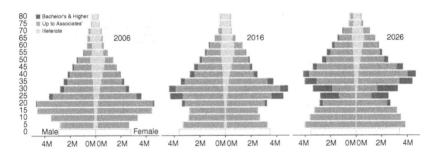

FIGURE 3.13. The educational attainments of Iranians by age and gender.
Sources: Statistical Yearbooks (1966–2019), and Census Data (1956–2016); Institute for Research and Planning in Higher Education, Ministry of Science, Research, and Technology, irphe.ac.ir.

Figure 3.13 illustrates the change in educational attainment among different genders and age groups in 2006, 2016, and the projections for 2026.[26] Between 2006 and 2016, the share of people aged 20 and higher with a higher education degree grew from 7% (2.9 million) to 11% (6.4 million). In this projection, over half the population aged 25–34, and 20% of the population aged 20 and higher (i.e., 12.5 million), will hold a higher education degree by the mid-2020s.

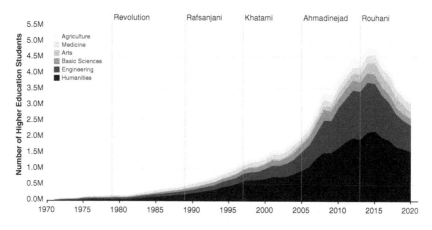

FIGURE 3.14. Number of university students by field of study.
Sources: Statistical Yearbooks (1966–2019), and Census Data (1956–2016); Institute for Research and Planning in Higher Education, Ministry of Science, Research, and Technology, irphe.ac.ir.

The trend in the number of higher education students broken down by their field of study is presented in Figure 3.14. The number of students pursuing postsecondary degrees rose approximately tenfold starting in 1995 to reach about 4.4 million in 2016, but has declined since then.[27] Among these students, a quarter are enrolled in an associate's degree program, about half are enrolled in a baccalaureate program, and the remaining are enrolled in a graduate program. By reducing the opportunity cost of education, the unwelcoming labor market of recent decades has had a decisive impact on boosting demand for continuation of education at the graduate level. The share of master's degree students rose from 4% to 22% between 1997 and 2016.[28] Based on the statistics from recent years, roughly two out of five students who earn a bachelor's degree will end up pursuing a master's program. Humanities and engineering are the largest fields of study in higher education, accounting for 46% and 30% of enrollment, respectively. Iran ranks fifth worldwide in terms of the number of recent graduates in STEM (science, technology, engineering, and mathematics) subjects in 2016,[29] after China, India, the United States, and Russia, all countries with larger populations than Iran.

Women currently make up 46% of all higher education students.[30] While engineering is dominated by male students, women make up the majority of students in all other fields of study, particularly in medicine and basic sciences where they have accounted for 65% of students for almost two decades. As discussed earlier, despite the closure of the gender gap in education, female labor force participation has remained fairly low. This implies that, contrary to its fundamental undercurrents, Iran has stayed near the bottom of the U-shaped trend that typically exists between women's participation in the economy and their average educational attainment.

Despite this considerable increase in the number of university "seats," the quality of higher education has not increased proportionately. One indicator showing this disproportionate expansion very clearly is the number of faculty per student. New faculty recruitment has failed to keep up with the growth in the number of students, resulting in a significant drop in the faculty-to-student ratio from 18% in 2005 to less than 8% in 2018 (Figure 3.15).[31] This reduction to less than half indicates that, although the universities have expanded their "seats" to accommodate more students, they lack the proper educational capacity to instruct them. The lack of sufficient investments in infrastructure and human resources in tandem with unmeritocratic recruitment and promotion of the faculty, academic repression and purge (which started with the cultural revolution in early 1980s), a corrupt admissions system that allows the regime's elite to enter university without having the merit or requirements (*sahmiye-ha*), brain

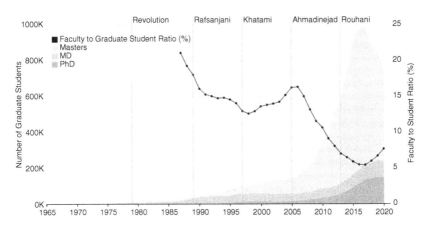

FIGURE 3.15. Number of students in medical and graduate schools (left axis) and the ratio of faculty members to these groups of university students (right axis).

Sources: Statistical Yearbooks (1966–2019), and Census Data (1956–2016); Institute for Research and Planning in Higher Education, Ministry of Science, Research, and Technology, irphe.ac.ir.

drain (see chapter 8), and a productionist approach to research which focuses solely on numbers and indicators with no regard for the actual outcome (see chapter 9) are among the main reasons the expansion of higher education has failed to help with the development of Iran in spite of its tremendous potential.

Besides its traditional and universal benefits, the educational system during the Islamic Republic era has served a strategic purpose as schools and universities provide a countrywide platform for shaping the thoughts and ideology of future generations, thus allowing the regime to access the deepest roots of society. In fact, all Iranian citizens who are below the age of about 50 at the time of this writing have gone through a long, systematic educational agenda the chief aim of which was to turn them into committed citizens who support the revolution's ideology and beliefs. In fact, education, in conjunction with the monopoly on media, was perceived by the Islamic Republic as the main pillar of its efforts to legitimize its rule and suppress cultural and political diversities.

SUMMARY

Iran's working-age population and its labor force have expanded by nearly fivefold between 1960 and 2020. A low economic participation rate (hovering around 40%) together with high unemployment (typically 12–15%) have been the defining features of Iran's labor market since the inception of the Islamic Republic. In fact, the labor participation of Iran is comparable only to that of countries such as Syria and Yemen which are experiencing civil wars. Even more shocking are the trends in the minimum wage which, in real terms, is at the same level in 2020 that it was in the 1960s. Lack of sufficient job opportunities is mainly attributed to demographic pressures, a hostile business environment for small private enterprises, which could have been the main drivers for job creation, a large public sector which inflates wage expectations, large foreign exchange revenue from natural resources which inhibits growth of labor-intensive manufacturing, and skill mismatches. We will return to this issue in chapter 4 to provide an analysis of the trends in national investments and capital formation which are the drivers of economic growth and job creation. Parallel to the drastic changes of population and labor force is an equally large change in the stock and rate of human capital formation in Iran. The literacy rate increased from about 10% in the middle of the twentieth century to nearly 90% in 2020, and educational attainments, measured in terms of mean years of schooling, increased at an extremely rapid rate from a mere four years in 1990 to ten years in 2018.

In contrast to positive developments in quantitative aspects of education, the quality and effectiveness of education have been poor. For example, the performance of Iranian students in major international student achievement tests has consistently been at the bottom third of participating countries. As a result, despite remarkable improvements in numerical indicators of human capital formation, as well as increasing access to technology such as computers and means of communication, the labor productivity in Iran (expressed as non-oil GDP per employed worker) has not increased over the past several decades. Besides shortcomings in the quality of education and poor links between educational materials and the needs of the country, the inability of the Iranian higher education system to contribute to economic growth is in part due to the purge of many competent professors during the academic cleansing efforts in the early 1980s, which has been followed by extensive patronage and unmeritocratic appointments in universities, and in part due to the shallow and populist policies of the regime for promotion of research in universities. These issues will be discussed in chapters 8 and 9, respectvely.

4

THE ECONOMY

THIS CHAPTER DISCUSSES historical trends in Iran's path of economic development and its future trajectory. In the first part of this
chapter, we provide an overview of historical patterns in the Iranian
economy by focusing on macroeconomic indicators such as economic
growth, share of economic sectors, employment, inflation, inequality, capital formation, and international trade. In the second part, we
will shed light on some of Iran's most pressing economic challenges by
quantifying their magnitude and future trajectories. The broad discussion of economic development in this chapter will be supplemented in
the next three chapters with more detailed information on the performance and challenges of the financial, energy, and agricultural sectors.

ECONOMIC GROWTH

Since the start of the twentieth century, the economy of Iran has undergone three periods of sustained growth (1925–1941, 1953–1976, and 1989–
2011) and numerous slumps (1941–1945, 1951–1953, 1978–1988, 2012–2021).
Most of the above important economic turning points were induced by
critical political events: the rise of Reza Shah to the throne and end of the
Qajar dynasty (1925), the Anglo-Soviet invasion of Iran and abdication of
Reza Shah (1941), the oil nationalization movement and the coup d'état
(1951 and 1953), mass demonstrations and the revolution (1978 and 1979), the
end of the Iran-Iraq War (1988), and oil sanctions (2011). As we explained

in chapter 1, the end of the last period of growth was a gradual process caused by the Islamic Republic's dysfunctional institutions and political decay as well as oil sanctions (2011–2015 and 2018–present time in 2021).

In more recent decades, the trends in economic growth of Iran have had a significantly greater variance compared to that of many developing countries. This is largely due to the state's poor macroeconomic management (e.g., failure to mitigate the effects of oil shocks) and lack of a political mechanism to discourage politicians from taking unsustainable populist policies by holding them accountable for the effects of their policies in the long run, which requires stable programmatic political parties as well as free and fair elections, both lacking in the Islamic Republic.

Although no official statistics of the aggregate level of economic activity exist prior to 1959, it has been estimated that at the beginning of the twentieth century, when Iran was under the rule of Mozaffar ad-Din Shah Qajar, the per capita GDP and share of agriculture in the economy were $370 (in 2020$) and 50%, respectively.[1] This level of per capita output had remained more or less unchanged by the time Reza Shah came to power in 1925. Less than two decades later and at the onset of the Anglo-Soviet invasion of Iran during World War II in 1941, which also led to the abdication of Reza Shah, the per capita GDP had already reached $730 (2020$)—double the level at the beginning of Reza Shah's reign.[2] Although about a third of the output was lost by the end of World War II in 1945,[3] the economy fully recovered prior to 1951 when Mosaddegh became the prime minister. Although Mosaddegh successfully nationalized the oil industry, the economy soon experienced another deep slump due primarily to the British embargo on Iranian oil, which brought Iran's crude production to almost a complete halt. Between the coup in 1953 and the end of the 1950s, the economy of Iran expanded at a respectable pace, raising the per capita GDP to $1,200 (in 2020$). In the meantime, the share of agriculture in the economy plunged to less than 30%.[4]

The rest of this chapter focuses on key developments in the economy of Iran after 1960 with more emphasis on the postrevolution epoch. Figure 4.1 shows the average values of some of the key economic variables (real GDP growth, inflation, employment, and oil revenue per capita) within the following periods: 1960–1969, 1970–1978, 1979–1988, 1989–2004, and 2005–2021. (We note that the last four periods are identical to the periods considered to evaluate the quality of governance in chapter 1.) The overall economic situation in each period can be summarized as follows.

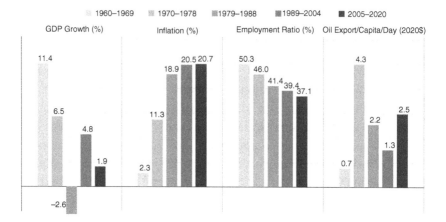

FIGURE 4.1. Average annual values of real GDP growth, inflation, employment ratio (share of working age population employed), and oil exports per capita per day (in 2020$) between 1960 and 2020.

Sources: Economic Time Series Database and Other Statistics, Central Bank of Iran (cbi.ir); Statistical Yearbooks (1966–2019), Census Data (1956–2016), and Other Economic Statistics, Statistical Center of Iran.

1960–1969

In the 1960s, for the first time, Iran had all major institutional prerequisites and foundations of growth (including a functional judiciary and the Central Bank which was established in 1960), political stability, access to capital thanks to rising oil revenues, and relationships with both the Western and Soviet blocs which helped Iran access new technologies. Early in this period, the Shah's White Revolution of 1963—which also benefited from the support of the Kennedy administration—allowed the state to strengthen its rule in the villages which at the time still accommodated nearly two-thirds of the population. This period also witnessed a stark improvement in technocratic capacity and entrepreneurial activities, particularly in the domain of industrial manufacturing. As discussed in previous chapters, the rapid economic development of this period catalyzed a substantial social mobilization which, together with the egalitarian, democratic, and religious aspirations of the nation, ultimately led not only to the overthrow of the Shah but also to the end of the dynastic era as the nation's oldest political institution.

During this period, the real GDP expanded at an average annual rate of 11.4% (8.5% on a per capita basis) with the growth rate never falling below 6.7% (Figure 4.2). The per capita GDP increased from $1,200

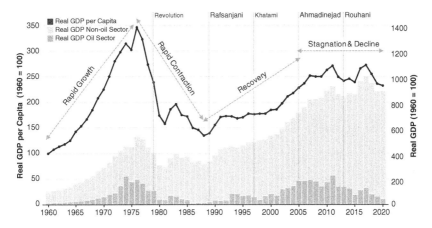

FIGURE 4.2. Real GDP per capita (left axis) and real GDP by oil and non-oil sectors (right axis) both relative to 1960.
Sources: Economic Time Series Database and Other Statistics, Central Bank of Iran (cbi.ir).

(2020$) in 1960 to $1,900 by the end of the 1960s due in part to the ramp up in oil production which increased from nearly one million barrels per day at the beginning of this period to four million barrels per day by 1970. However, on both an absolute and per capita basis, the oil revenue in this period was significantly lower than its levels in the next half century. The share of industry in the economy increased from about 14% in 1960 to 22% by 1970 (Figure 4.3)—a level which has not changed much thereafter. The 1960s was the last decade in which average inflation was single-digit, average economic growth was double-digit, and also the last period in which the number of employed people was still larger than the number of adults who were unemployed or economically inactive.

Gross and net capital formation rates in this period hovered around 32% and 20% of the GDP, respectively (Figure 4.4). Of the 1.3 million new jobs created in this decade, the shares in the agriculture, industry, and service sectors were 23%, 44%, and 33%, respectively. According to our estimate, on average, 200,000 people annually migrated from rural areas to cities during this time which would imply that nearly 20% of the urban population were rural residents a decade earlier.

1970–1978

While there is a reasonable degree of agreement across the political spectrum about the impressive economic developments of the 1960s,

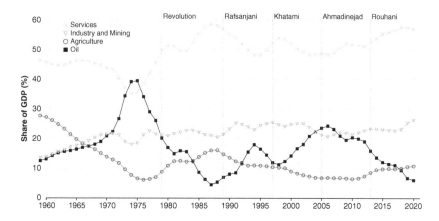

FIGURE 4.3. Shares of different sectors in the Iranian economy.
Sources: Economic Time Series Database and Other Statistics, Central Bank of Iran (cbi.ir); Statistical Yearbooks (1966–2019).

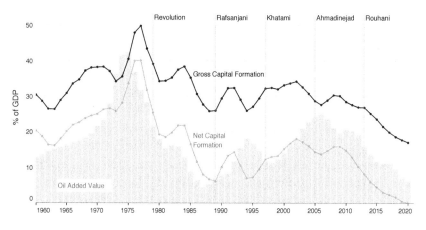

FIGURE 4.4. Gross and net capital formation and oil added value relative to GDP. A two-year moving average is applied.
Sources: Economic Time Series Database and Other Statistics, Central Bank of Iran (cbi.ir); Statistical Yearbooks (1966–2019).

the economic performance of Iran during the last decade of the Shah is still a highly controversial subject. On the one hand, contrary to the grim image publicized by the Islamic Republic regime for decades, the economic conditions leading to the 1979 revolution were far from sluggish. On the other hand, contrary to the Shah's exaggerated view of the state of the economic progress and the glorified picture that monarchists depict from that era, the growth during 1970s was of a lower quality compared to the previous period (i.e., it was dominated by natural resources revenue while corruption was on the rise and income distribution was hugely uneven). In this period, the real GDP increased at an average rate of 6.5% (5.9% for non-oil GDP), and the per capita GDP reached its historic record high of $6,500 (2020$) in 1976.[5] The average daily crude production of this period amounted to 5.3 million barrels of oil (MMbbl), which corresponds to a 160% increase compared to the 1960s. Such a large surge in oil production, which was partly necessitated and enabled by the 1973 Arab oil embargo, was technically feasible thanks to the presence of a relatively small quantity of easy-to-extract oil in Iran's supergiant fields, allowing for a sharp production rise over a short time (see chapter 6). Beside production volume, the average price of oil in this period was almost double that of the 1960s, increasing the per capita oil revenue from an average of $0.7 per day in the 1960s to $4.3 per day (2020$) during this period.[6] As a result of the oil windfall, the average gross and net capital formation rates in this period surged to 41% and 32% of GDP, respectively (Figure 4.4).

In this period, nearly 70% of the 2.1 million newly created jobs were in the industrial sector which at the time constituted about a fifth of the economy.[7] Also, the gap between the shares of the agriculture sector in the GDP and employment in this sector reached its highest level (9% and 44%, respectively). The rate of internal migration from villages to cities increased to an average of 260,000 per year, but the share of urban population who had migrated from rural areas over the decade before decreased to 16% compared to 20% in the previous period.[8] Iran's tourism industry also witnessed a significant growth in this period. The number of foreign tourists visiting Iran surged from 350,000 in 1970 to 700,000 in 1977, generating $500 million per year (2020$).[9]

The staggering oil revenue and the resulting surge in Iran's purchasing power in the international markets, along with the Shah's exaggerated perception about the role of his own political maneuvering in increasing global oil prices in 1973–1974, were among the chief reasons that he increasingly shifted his attention toward international affairs and away from the domestic socioeconomic challenges and their alarming signs. Due to an imprudent macroeconomic policy which allowed for the consumption of unprecedented sums of petrodollars in the domestic economy, the aggregate demand increased substantially and gave rise to a sharp increase in inflation through the Dutch disease phenomenon.[10] The inflationary pressure of the last few years of the Shah, which reached its climax in 1977 (1356 Persian calendar), played an important role in mobilizing broader groups in the lower and middle classes against the Pahlavi regime and adding an economic dimension to the movement, which until that point mostly revolved around demands for political freedom (by students) and reactions to the Shah's top-down moderniza-tion agenda (by the clergy and *bazaar*). The economic grievances of the less privileged classes due to rising inequality and dissatisfactions among *bazaaris,* whose institution had come under attack by not only an anti-profiteering campaign to control prices but also by modern methods of manufacturing, distribution, and retail, played a key role in the fall of the Pahlavi regime.[11]

1979–1988

The first decade of the Islamic Republic rule was accompanied by an economic free fall such that the GDP per capita plunged at an aver-age rate of 6.1% per year, reaching a level in 1988 that was last observed more than two decades earlier in 1965. The combined effects of economic mismanagement of the new revolutionary government, the cost of war, lower oil exports, and the fast population growth of the time (about 4% per year) resulted in a drastic decline in the per capita income. The po-litical turmoil of the time is reflected in the frequent changes of govern-ments within the first two years of the revolution: Bazargan (February to November 1979), Banisdar/Rajaei (February 1980 to June 1981), Rajaei/Bahonar (August 1981), which was then followed by the first stable gov-ernment of the Islamic Republic, the Khamenei/Mousavi administration (October 1981 to August 1989). In this period, the average rates of gross and net capital formation in the economy decreased to 33% and 16% of the GDP, respectively. Job creation in this period, which according to official statistics amounted to 2.2 million,[12] was dominated by the public sector which had appended the then newly confiscated enterprises. This in turn inflated the government wage bill and reduced real wages and public investment. Despite the dedication of the newly established regime to ending, if not reversing, the rural to urban migration by promoting agriculture and life in villages, nearly 400,000 people migrated from the countryside to urban areas on an annual basis in this period. The migration to cities in this period was also accompanied by a reduction in the number of farmers from 3.5 million at the onset of the revolution to 3.3 million by 1988.

In spite of using economic grievances for mobilizing lower classes against the Pahlavi regime, particularly in the two years leading up to the revolution, the faction of the revolutionaries that ultimately became dominant had never clearly explained their economic plans beyond rhetoric. Needless to say, Khomeini did not have the slightest clue about economic principles. Beyond his infamous quote that "Economics is for donkeys," his views on proper economic management can be summarized as the provision of free housing, water, electricity, and transportation; opposition to usury; praise for the social and economic role of the *bazaar*; and a shallow and outdated understanding of the concept of independence—which was naively interpreted as self-sufficiency in production of everything, a view which served as the basis for decades of ill-fated draconian import-substitution dogma.

In an essay published a few months prior to the revolution,[13] Mehdi Bazargan—a prominent figure among Khomeini's close circle who went on to become the first prime minister after the revolution—summarizes the economic difficulties of the Shah's time as inflation; scarcity of basic goods; general shortcomings related to housing, school, health, water, electricity, marriage, etc.; and most importantly, traffic jams and air pollution. Neither he nor any other of Khomeini's aides offered a clear economic plan to address what they depicted as excruciating economic conditions. However, Bazargan made it clear that the *bazaar* and industries should be kept in the private sector, but if and when the Shah's regime was replaced with a benevolent government, industries should be nationalized while the *bazaar* should remain private so that it could retain its *free spirit*. However, it did not take long after the establishment of the Islamic Republic—which, rather than being the promised benevolent government, turned out to be more predatory compared to the Shah's regime—for the economic recession to begin and for welfare to deteriorate for broad classes of society.

Against the above backdrop, the constitution of the Islamic Republic views the role of the economy as a means to *help man move toward God*.[14] In the spirit of this ideology, the constitution gives control of all major segments of the economy to the benevolent theocratic government. More specifically, it declares "all large-scale and mother industries, foreign trade, major minerals, banking, insurance, power generation, dams, and large-scale irrigation networks, radio and television, post, telegraph and telephone services, aviation, shipping, roads, railroads and the like" should be owned by the government. To fulfill this provision, the first major economic action taken by the new regime was the confiscation of private industries and banks which led to a significant expansion in the role of government in the economy at the expense of losing much of the country's entrepreneurial capacity and, more importantly, setting a bad precedent regarding enforcement of property rights, a legacy that continues to impede development even today. Another major event of the early days of the revolution that has had a detrimental impact on economic performance to this day was the hostage crisis, which made it clear that the new regime did not feel obliged to follow international laws.

Other provisions in the constitution of the Islamic Republic with far-reaching impact on Iran's path of development are the calls for national self-sufficiency in food and science. We will provide a detailed explanation of the adverse effects of these two dogmatic provisions in chapters 7 and 9, respectively.

It took about a decade for the Islamic Republic regime to take the deteriorating economic condition of the nation into account when deciding about an important political and ideological matter, namely the war with Iraq. In 1988, after selfishly declining previous international offers to end the Iran-Iraq War on much better terms and with hundreds of thousands less casualties, Khomeini ultimately accepted the United Nations proposal (UNSC Resolution 598) to end the war. This was only after incurring major military losses and significantly reduced support from the people for the cause of war, as well as dire economic conditions reflected by the massive budget deficit (about 50%, see Figure 1.5 in chapter 1), which was in part due to vanishing oil revenues in the last years of war (see chapter 6). Thanks to the infrastructure inherited from the hefty investments of the Pahlavi era along with continuation of oil exports, albeit in modest amounts, and draconian market control measures and rationing, the government managed to prevent the worst forms of economic hardship such as famine. Similarly, large investments in military equipment that were made during the last decade of the Pahlavi era played an important role in enabling the revolutionary state, with its inexperienced leadership, to defend the country against the Iraqi invasion.

1989–2004

This period starts with selection of Khamenei as the second supreme leader of the Islamic Republic regime and encompasses the presidency of Rafsanjani (1989–1997) and Khatami (1997–2005), which are commonly known as eras of reconstruction and reforms, respectively. At the time of this writing, this is also the only period during which the economy registered a modest level of sustained growth under the rule of the Islamic Republic. In this period, real GDP increased at a rate of 4.8% per year on average which, together with reduced population growth rates (1.7% per year), resulted in a modest annual per capita output growth of about 3.1%. By the end of this period, the GDP per capita reached $3,800 (2020$). Due to lower prices, the annual oil revenue in this period registered an average of $29 billion (2020$), which is lower compared to an average of $34 billion in the 1979–1989 period and $70 billion in the 2005–2021 period.

In early 1990s, having no other alternative to stimulate growth, Rafsanjani implemented a series of reforms aimed at partial liberalization of the economy in line with the policy package commonly known as the Washington Consensus which was advocated at the time by the International Monetary Fund and the World Bank. Although some observers refer to these reforms as Rafsanjani's Perestroika,[15] it seems that he was more influenced by the Chinese version of reforms toward economic liberalization implemented by Deng Xiaoping which successfully protected the Communist Party from social pressures demanding political freedom. Among the set of reforms implemented initially were various degrees of deregulation, reduced rationing and price control, exchange rate unification, creation of free-trade zones, issuance of public bonds (*Oragh-e-Mosharekat*), and the relaunch of the stock exchange market. The compounding effects of these reforms allowed for larger public investments which, along with a better utilization of the existing production capacity, helped end the economy's downward trend after about a decade. However, despite initial success, the conflicts between the state's economic goals and lack of prudent policies which led to accumulation of large foreign debt whose maturity coincided with falling oil prices, gave rise to a deep economic stagflation in 1994. Ultimately, in 1995 when inflation soared to 50%,[16] causing significant grievances and at least one major protest, many of the reforms (e.g., the unified exchange rate regime) were reverted to avoid further political instability.

The beginning of Khatami's presidency coincided with the Asian Contagion of 1997 which caused a stark decline in oil prices. At its lowest point in 1998, the Brent crude price fell to about $10 per barrel (i.e., $15 in 2020$).[17] From 1999 to the end of Khatami's second term in 2005, oil prices increased by approximately fourfold which, along with reduction of tensions with the West, helped the economy expand at a respectable rate while inflation eased to 10–15%.[18] Some of the important institutional developments of Khatami's presidency include the creation of the Oil Stabilization Fund (*Hesab-e-Zakhire-Arzi*), licensing private banks and credit institutions (some of which later became Ponzi schemes), and a second attempt to unify different exchange rates in 2002.

Between 1989 and 2005, gross and net capital formation somewhat recovered, registering average values of 31% and 13%, respectively (Figure 4.4). The economy added 8.6 million new jobs in this period, corresponding to an average of 530,000 jobs per year which is significantly higher than the averages for the previous period of 1979–1989 and the next period of 2005–2021, when the average annual number of jobs created were 270,000 and 330,000, respectively.[19] A sizable portion of the new jobs came from agriculture as the number of farmers increased from 3.3 million at the beginning of this period to 4.6 million in 2005.[20] Despite a modestly better economic performance, unemployment never fell below 10% in this period, and the employment ratio continued its secular decline.[21] The growth of agriculture in this period was achieved by nearly a 50% increase in the country's water consumption. As will be discussed in chapter 7, unsustainable water consumption over prolonged periods of time has created a full-fledged water crisis with far-reaching ramifications for current and future generations.

2005–2021

This period encompasses the presidency of Ahmadinejad (2005–2013) and Rouhani (2013–2021). With $1.1 trillion (2020$) in oil export proceeds[22] and a favorable demographic structure conducive to rapid economic growth, this period was Iran's singular opportunity to improve the economy and lift millions of people out of poverty. However, the per capita GDP at the end of this period in 2021 stayed at the same level that it was in 2005, while the currency devalued by ~3,000%, and average inflation soared to over 20% with a more recent peak of 45% in 2020.[23] (While the official statistics claim that inflation hovers around 45% at the time of this writing in 2021, there is every reason to believe that this claim is false and the true figure is much higher.) Imports continued their increasing trend from the previous period to reach a peak of $112 billion in 2011 before declining by roughly 20–30% in the next decade.[24] Capital formation plunged continuously in this period to the extent that net capital formation has entered negative territory since 2020. Trading partners in the developed world (e.g., Japan, Germany, Italy, and France) were replaced with China, Iraq, Turkey, and Afghanistan.[25] The economy created about four million new jobs, of which an unprecedented share of 80% were in the service sector.[26]

As will be discussed in chapter 5, one of the main challenges during this period was related to the financial system. The Central Bank's overly relaxed supervision led to mushrooming of banks and nonbank financial institutions (credit institutions and *Qarz-al-Hasaneh*) that essentially ran a Ponzi scheme. By increasing the liquidity demand, these institutions pushed deposit interest rates to unprecedented levels even when inflation was not too high (e.g., 2016–2017) and the real economy was in recession. Moreover, mandating banks to lend to the government and semiprivate corporations—which is routinely done by the state to fill the budget deficits—further exacerbated the situation by increasing frozen assets in the banks' balance sheets, ultimately forcing them to borrow heavily from the Central Bank.

An important policy change during this period was the energy subsidies reform of 2010 which was meant to free up resources for a direct cash transfer scheme. While the program arguably had a short-term positive impact on the poor, it rather quickly lost its effect as the government chose not to increase the payments to keep up with inflation. The monthly cash transfer at the time of this writing in 2021 is about $1.5 per person (5¢ per day). Ahmadinejad also implemented a few other large-scale economic projects, including a partial transfer of some of the state-owned enterprises to low-income households (*Saham-e-Edalat*) as a pro-poor method of privatization. These shares remained nontransferable for about a decade until, in an effort to alleviate the pressure of the deep economic crisis on the poor, the government of Rouhani finally made these shares sellable on the Tehran Stock Market in 2020 (their value at the highest point was no more than $500 per person). Construction of millions of affordable houses (*Maskan-e-Mehr*) was another ill-designed and poorly executed megaproject of this period which led to a huge spike in government debt and inflation. Furthermore, over $100 billion worth of state-owned enterprises were privatized in this period,[27] of which an overwhelming share were sold to nongovernmental public organizations, often at hugely discounted prices. By the time Ahmadinejad left office in 2013, the per capita GDP and number of employed people were the same as eight years earlier.[28]

When Rouhani took office in 2013, oil exports were cut in half due to international sanctions, and the economy was in another episode of stagflation. The main mechanisms by which sanctions affected Iran's economy include reducing oil revenue, increasing fiscal deficit and inflation expectations, increasing international transaction costs, disrupting industries by interrupting the supply of imported intermediate goods, and lowering expenditures and investments by households and firms. The fall of oil prices in late 2014 and early 2015 further reduced Iran's oil export revenue to about a quarter of its presanctions level. The government overlooked the economic demands of the nation to push Khamenei's disastrous nuclear ambitions for many years until the economic pressures reached a point in 2015 that could no longer be neglected. Then, similar to the dire economic landscape around 1988 that was instrumental in forcing Khomeini to accept the ceasefire, a deep economic crisis played a major, although belated, role in persuading the supreme leader, this time Khamenei, to agree to the Joint Comprehensive Plan of Action (JCPOA) in July 2015. After the implementation of the JCPOA in January 2016, recovery of the oil sector helped the economic growth rate rise from deep negative values. However, before long, the next administration in the United States abandoned the nuclear deal and unilaterally reimposed oil sanctions. By the time the new sanctions were imposed in August 2018, the one-off effects of the oil export recovery had been fully realized and the economy was already back on its long-term, low-growth paradigm; inflation was on the rise; capital flight near its highest record; and capital formation at its lowest record, while the state was more than ever paralyzed with internal conflicts, corruption, and lacked the legitimacy needed to push painful economic reforms forward. Between the beginning of 2018 and end of 2020, the per capita income contracted by 15%, currency was devalued by about tenfold, and tens of millions of people in the working and middle classes fell into poverty. In fact, as discussed in chapter 3, the minimum wage of Iranian workers in 2020 plunged to less than $2.00 per day, implying that the per capita income in the families of most low-skilled workers was less than a dollar per day—lower than the $2.00 per day threshold commonly used to define abject poverty. As a result of the nuclear program—which never had economic justification, particularly in recent decades given Iran's enormous natural gas discoveries and production—the country lost more than $200 billion directly from the shrinkage of its oil revenues until 2020. Needless to say, this staggering amount of money went into the pockets of other major producers such as Saudi Arabia, Russia, Iraq, and the United States.

While the real GDP per capita can be used to understand the overall trends in the economy and the average standard of living, the distribution of income should also be considered when evaluating the economic conditions of different classes. Despite forty years of egalitarian rhetoric, Iran's income inequality is rather high. A recent study estimated that the top 10% of the population in Iran earns about half of the total income, while the share of income going to the next 40% of the population (the economic middle class) and the bottom 50% are about 35% and 15%, respectively.[29] Ironically, the Islamic Republic regime—after four decades of claiming to be for the oppressed (*mostazaf*) and demonizing capitalism—has managed to create an economy in which income inequality is almost exactly similar to that of the United States, which has always served as a symbol for the viciousness of the oppressors in the regime's propaganda.[30] Finally, although data for measuring wealth inequality in Iran are not available, it is almost certain that wealth is significantly more concentrated than income, particularly given that taxes on capital gains, inheritance, and property in Iran have been virtually zero. Through a comparison of Iran with other countries with similar levels of income inequality, it seems plausible that the top 10% of the population in Iran is likely to own upward of 60% or potentially even 70% of private capital.[31]

Decomposition of Iran's economic growth over the past half century reveals that, among the three sources of output growth (capital, labor, and productivity), a rise in capital inputs has had the highest contribution to growth by a large margin.[32] In addition to insufficient levels of investments during the Islamic Republic compared to the 1960–1979 period, a significant decline in the growth of total factor productivity[33] (TFP) has also contributed to the poor economic performance in this period.[34] The lack of productivity gain in the economy over such a prolonged period of time could be attributed to large misallocations of credit and other resources by the state (which, as explained in chapter 1, has a low capacity and wide scope) as well as the entrenchment of various forms of corruption in the political system.

Enacting an effective monetary policy is a vital requisite for long-term economic planning, hence among a government's most important tasks. However, as will be discussed in detail in the next chapter, high inflation has been a defining feature of the Islamic Republic's economy to such an extent that, since the 1990s, Iran has been consistently among the worst in the world in terms of inflation. The chronic high inflation in Iran is attributable to the poor governance of the regime in a number of different ways: a low tax base, irresponsible and unnecessary public expenditures, dysfunctional central banking, and favoring political stability over reforms. As discussed in chapter 1, due primarily to tax exemptions on the commercial activities of nongovernmental public organizations such as bonyads, *Oqaf* (public and quasi-private charitable endowments), and IRGC-affiliated corporations which control large parts of the economy, as well as small or zero tax on inheritance, capital gains, and property, Iran has one the smallest tax-to-GDP ratios in the world. Corruption in tax and customs offices of the government has also contributed to the low levels of taxes extracted from the *bazaar* and major importers, who are often among the regime's elite, and their patronage networks. A large government wage bill due to the operation of the regime's extensive propaganda machine (including numerous religious organizations), financing of proxy military forces in other countries, corruption in granting government contracts, and heavy subsidies on food and energy inflate government expenditure and contribute to the fiscal deficit. Furthermore, due to the regime's diminishing legitimacy and loss of social capital, many obvious economic reforms are deemed too politically risky (e.g., true privatization of loss-making state-owned corporations, and reduction of subsidies). These reforms are always associated with short-term pain and hence may prove destabilizing, as for example evidenced by the uprisings in 2019 in response to the gasoline price increase. Finally, the low technocratic capacity of the Central Bank and its insufficient autonomy in setting goals and implementing them (see chapter 5) also have contributed to the Islamic Republic's disastrous performance in ensuring price stability.

One of the common mistakes made by some observers when arguing the root causes of Iran's poor economic performance is the exaggerated emphasis on the detrimental outcomes of class struggle for growth. Such claims have at least two fundamental flaws. First, there has been no viable mechanism in modern Iran for members of a socioeconomic class to act collectively to bring about major policy changes with implications for growth that are exclusively beneficial to them (and neutral or undesirable to other classes). This is in large part due to the crackdown on civil society by the Islamic Republic and lack of programmatic parties that can be held accountable for their economic policies beyond political cycles. For example, some argue that a large retail sector, the *bazaar*, or speculators in the market are what suppress manufacturing and other productive economic activities in Iran. While there is no doubt that the economic policies of the state create winners and losers, phenomena such as large store-to-population ratios are themselves a consequence, and not the cause, of a poor economic environment. Had the interests of the so-called nonproductive classes been influential in terms of steering the economic policies, they would have first prevented the explosive growth of their own sectors through regulation in order to protect their profit margins. By and large, the expansion of petty bourgeoisie in the service sector has been a product of high population growth of the past decades and lack of job opportunities elsewhere in the economy. Some aspects of income distribution, such as low labor wages, have important structural explanations such as the presence of what is known as the dual economy, where the supply of labor is virtually unlimited during early stages of development. This issue is intensified in contemporary Iran by an explosive population growth and labor productivity stagnation which, as explained previously, is due to the Islamic Republic's poor quality of governance. Second, any definition of class, particularly if based on a relationship with the means of production, inevitably places people with vastly different or opposing ideological views and even different economic interests into the same group. Therefore, focusing too much on the issue of class struggle (or even large income disparities) as a cause for the poor overall economic performance of the past decades in Iran is fundamentally problematic, or is at best not seeing the forest for the trees. There also seems to be no emerging mechanism through which class conflicts per se will become a determinant to growth in Iran's foreseeable future unless they cause social instability, which in turn hinders growth.

Another common misinterpretation of the underlying causes for Iran's disappointing economic performance is related to the role of geography. While geography and climate played an important role in shaping civilizations and the dynamics of state building in the premodern era, their relevance to different levels of economic prosperity of nations has consistently diminished since the Industrial Revolution. For example, Iran's lack of a powerful naval force in the previous centuries could have been partly attributed to lack of forests to supply timber in the Persian Gulf,[35] but such random geographical factors have little impact on a country's military power today. Similarly, land characteristics had profound impacts on many aspects of life in the premodern and early modern eras. Suitability for agriculture and other characteristics of land were the main determinants of the population size, population distribution, and prosperity of countries. They were also among the main causes of war between tribes or countries, which in turn helped establish centralized state power. Today, due to the ever-increasing role of technology and human capital as determinants of growth, rich and poor countries can be found in almost every corner of the world, every climate, and with any level of natural resources. Therefore, any apparent outsize influence of geography and climate on the poor economic condition of a country should now be seen as a symptom of the lack of development rather than a cause for it.

Today, after decades of insufficient and noninclusive economic growth, the signs of stress in the Iranian economy are intensifying rapidly. The employment ratio is among the lowest in the world. Severe water scarcity has become the new norm, threatening future output from the agriculture sector, which can lead to disastrous food insecurity and hunger (see chapter 7). Even in the absence of sanctions, the revenue from oil exports will be woefully insufficient to drive growth in the future. In the absence of large investments and use of advanced extraction technologies, significant oil production growth in the mid-term seems unlikely (see chapter 6). Despite implementation of an import substitution agenda for decades, the industrial sector has failed to incentivize innovation and attract private investments and has no significant comparative advantage to compete in the international arena due to low productivity.

The experiences of many rapidly developing nations suggest that foreign direct investments (FDI) could have played an important role in advancing Iran's economy, particularly given its chronic struggle with shortage of capital and lack of access to advanced technology. Over the past quarter century, however, Iran has only attracted an average FDI of

$2 billion per year with its maximum never even reaching $5 billion. Lack of foreign investments and technology transfer are among the chief reasons why Iran fails to take advantage of its highly educated population, low-cost labor, and reasonably functional transportation infrastructure.

EXTERNAL SECTOR

Oil revenue has historically been the primary source of foreign currency for Iran and, in turn, the main determinant of the aggregate level of imports. Figure 4.5 illustrates Iran's exports of oil and non-oil goods and services, along with the aggregate level of imports since 1960. Iran's oil export proceeds have undergone numerous episodes of drastic rise and decline due in part to political shocks such as the 1951 oil nationalization movement and the subsequent coup in 1953, the 1973–1974 Arab oil embargo, the 1979 revolution, the 1980–1988 war with Iraq, and oil sanctions (2012–2015 and 2018–present time in 2021). The largest oil export revenues, particularly when assessed in comparison to the size of the whole economy, were earned in the periods of 1974–1980 and 2007–2011. A more detailed account of the domestic and international developments affecting Iran's oil sector will be provided in chapter 6.

Compared to oil exports, Iran's non-oil exports have undergone fewer erratic changes. In the early 1960s, Iran's annual export of non-oil goods and services amounted to less than $1 billion (2020$). This value increased at a modest rate to nearly $15 billion in 1978. Shortly after the revolution and in spite of the lower real exchange rates (see chapter 5), which could have been conducive to the growth of tourism and export of manufactured and agricultural products, the non-oil exports underwent a stark decline due to irresponsible actions of the revolutionary state such as taking American diplomats hostage and being hostile toward rich countries from which Iran received most of its tourism revenue. Taking foreigners and Iranians with dual citizenship hostage is still conducted today by the Islamic Republic as a routine method for generating financial and diplomatic ransom. In the postwar epoch, non-oil exports once again started to expand, albeit at a slower pace, until about 2000. Since then, stemming from the explosive growth of natural gas production (from the South Pars field), which formed the underpinnings of growth for the petrochemical and energy-intensive industries, non-oil exports have expanded at a respectable pace to the extent that in 2019, their aggregate value ($55 billion[36]) has become equivalent to the export of three million

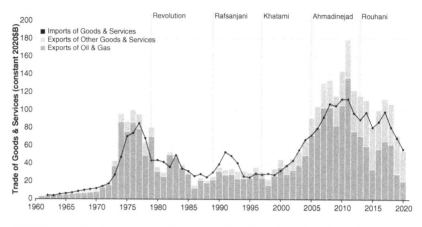

FIGURE 4.5. Iran's exports and imports of goods and services (2020$).
Sources: Economic Time Series Database and Other Statistics, Central Bank of Iran (cbi.ir); Statistical Yearbooks (1966–2019).

barrels of crude oil per day at $50 per barrel. (It should be noted that Iran reports the exports of all petroleum-derived fuels, natural gas liquids [NGLs], lease condensate, and petrochemicals under non-oil exports.)

While the total value of Iran's imported goods has changed drastically over time (often in a pattern that ensures a slight current account surplus to compensate for capital flight), the composition of imported goods has not varied significantly when considering the breakdowns by main groups. As shown in Figure 4.6, between the early 1960s and 2018, the share of machinery and electrical goods in the import mix has hovered around 25%, the share of foodstuffs and animals increased from less than 5% to about 25% of the imports, the share of chemicals increased from about 10% to 17%, and the share of vehicles and other means of transportation has consistently hovered around 5%. Given Iran's active pursuit of an import substitution policy since the early 1960s,[37] one would expect to see larger changes in the composition of imported goods across multiple decades compared to the observed pattern. While a more detailed examination of imported goods at a subgroup level would likely reveal more dynamism, it nevertheless can be concluded that the import substitution growth policies of the past decades have been either fairly static in terms of the overall structure (due, for example, to the presence of powerful interest groups) or have failed to bring about significant changes in Iran's industrial output, or a combination of both.

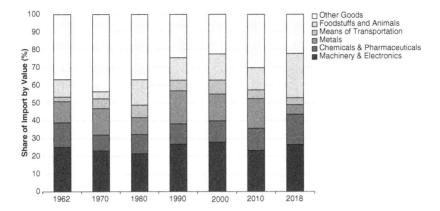

FIGURE 4.6. The shares of different broad groups of goods in Iran's import mix. *Sources:* Statistical Yearbooks (1966–2019).

Contrary to the composition of imported goods based on broad groups which has remained relatively unchanged over long periods, Iran's major trade partners have changed several times since 1960 (Figure 4.7). The top ten trade partners before the revolution were almost exclusively from the developed countries of the time. During the last four decades of the twentieth century, which spans equally across the Pahlavi and the Islamic Republic regimes, Germany had been consistently the first or second trading partner of Iran. The United States was one of Iran's main trade partners before the revolution, but trade came to an abrupt stop soon after the revolution and never recovered again (due primarily to sanctions). Trade with the United Kingdom, which had been, in relative terms, on a decline in the two decades leading to the revolution, somewhat recovered in the decade after the revolution, before starting to diminish rather quickly in the twenty-first century. Since around 2005, a major shift in Iran's trade has taken place where trade with developed countries has been substituted with developing countries including China, India, Turkey, Afghanistan, and Iraq. China, which was not even among the top ten trading partners until 1995, has become the biggest partner since 2013 amid international sanctions on Iran for its nuclear program. Part of these rearrangements, such as the rise of trade with Japan (1970–1990), South Korea (1980–2000), and China (2000–2020), reflected rapid economic growth of these countries and their higher shares in global trade. In the long run, the inclination of Iran toward developing and emerging markets will inevitably deprive the country

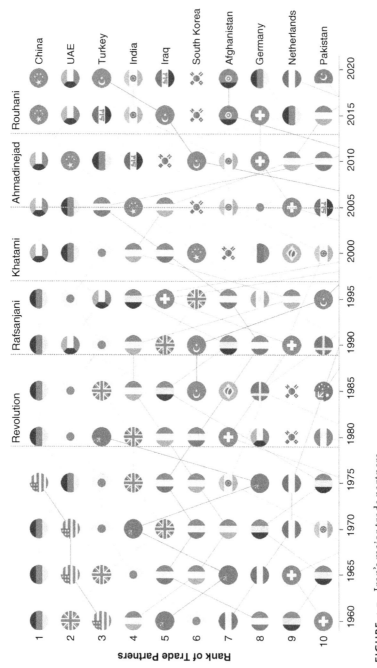

FIGURE 4.7. Iran's major trade partners.
Sources: Statistical Yearbooks (1966–2019).

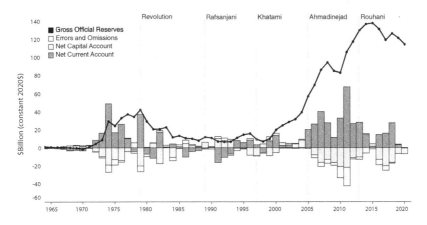

FIGURE 4.8. Balance of payments (net current account, net capital and financial account, and errors and omissions) and gross international reserves.

Sources: Economic Time Series Database and Other Statistics, Central Bank of Iran (cbi.ir); Statistical Yearbooks (1966–2019).

of new technologies developed in the West, hence adversely affecting productivity. Overall, the compounding effects of low capital formation and investment, which was discussed in the previous section, along with the shift in the origin of imported goods from industrial countries such as Germany and Japan to less developed countries will have far-reaching consequences on economic growth, particularly in the industrial sector.

Contrary to the current account which, except for a few years, always had a positive balance in recent decades, the balance on the capital account in Iran has usually been negative (Figure 4.8), particularly during the period of 2005–2020 in which a total of $170 billion was lost in capital flight. As a result of running a surplus in the net current and capital accounts, Iran accumulated a sizable stock of foreign currency during the 1970s, reaching a peak of $42 billion (2020$) at the onset of the revolution. This trend reversed during the first decade of the Islamic Republic where Iran lost much of its foreign reserves. However, due primarily to rising oil prices and an increase in the export of NGLs and petrochemicals, Iran accumulated a total of $130 billion in foreign currency between 2000 and 2015. Since 2015, a combination of lower oil prices, sanctions, mass capital flight, and nontransparent expenditures lumped into "errors and omissions" resulted in a loss of about a third of the reserves by 2020.

ECONOMIC IMBALANCES AND FUTURE TRAJECTORY

At the time of this writing in 2021, the Iranian economy is undergoing its deepest crisis since the inception of the Islamic Republic. After more than four decades of the regime's mismanagement, over half of the country's 85 million people live in poverty; net capital formation—which has undergone a secular decline for two decades—is now in negative territory; groundwater resources have been largely depleted (which in turn increases the risk of widespread hunger and internal conflicts among different regions); the massive wealth embedded in hydrocarbon and mineral resources has been exhausted without being replaced by enduring financial or physical assets; two-thirds of the working-age population are unemployed or are out of the workforce; about half of the demographic window of opportunity has passed with no savings made to support the largest cohorts of the population that will reach retirement in the coming decades; political and administrative corruption is among the highest in the world; and the flux of brain drain and capital flight is depriving the country of the essential elements for future growth. As discussed in chapter 1, at the roots of Iran's catastrophic economic performance is the Islamic Republic's poor system of governance.

As discussed earlier in this chapter, Iran's real GDP per capita in 2020 still hovers around the same level that it was at the turn of the century—a level which is significantly lower than its historical peak registered half a century ago just before the revolution. Erosion of state legitimacy and social capital along with entrenchment of corruption, particularly in the form of powerful interest groups within the state, have gradually hampered the state capacity for embarking on economic reforms, even in the most obvious cases such as fuel subsidies. Natural resource reserves—which directly constitute about a quarter of the value added in the economy—were unsustainably extracted for decades without being replaced with durable assets to ensure income generation in the future. Moreover, the country's catastrophic privatization process is coming to an end while it neither boosted productivity and innovation nor reduced the financial burden of many loss-making state-owned enterprises on the government. Instead of financing its expenditure by expanding the tax base, the government has covered the budget deficit with seigniorage,[38] withdrawals from the National Development Fund, and directed lending from banks, which has undermined the proper function of the financial system. We note that Iran's fiscal deficit of

8–10% of GDP in recent years is on par with that of the Soviet Union in its last years during 1985–1991.

Even though the vast majority of public debt in Iran is denominated in local currency (thus constantly reduced by the country's high inflation), the stock of public debt (including nonsecuritized debt) in Iran has reached about 50% of the GDP.[39] Historical trends in Iran's primary deficit and effective interest payments on public debt are shown in Figure 4.9. This figure also shows Iran's other major deviations from the conditions associated with normal sustainable growth: the financial health of banks (which need to increase their capital adequacy ratio to 8% and reduce nonperforming loans to 5% of gross loans), gross capital investments (which need to increase to ~30% of GDP), and the country's water use (which will be discussed at length in chapter 7). Using this simple framework, we estimate that the size of Iran's annual economic shortfalls (relative to its GDP) has increased from less than 15% in 2011 to over 35% in 2020 and will likely reach 40% in the next few years. The results imply that Iran's primary deficit, effective interest payments, and other major economic deviations in the coming years will hover around $130 billion per year, of which about $35 billion is needed to improve banks' financial health as a one-off payment and will not be carried over to next year once paid.

As the result of sanctions, Iran's annual oil exports—which amounted to $50–60 billion prior to sanctions—have slumped to approximately $5–15 billion in 2019–2021. This development is not only causing intolerable fiscal pressure but also pushing the balance of payments into deeper negative values. By 2021, the foreign reserves of the country, which had already been in decline even before the US withdrawal from JCPOA (Figure 4.8), have shrunk by over 10% compared to their peak in 2015 (Table 4.1). As will be explained in chapter 6, the recent paradigm shift in the global oil market from scarcity to abundance[40] has made the global economy less vulnerable to disruptions from a medium-sized producer such as Iran.

The past two decades in Iran have been a period of economic stagnation, environmental degradation, and political decay. Without decisive policy response, these crises will accelerate and bring the economy to a state of total collapse. For decades, Khamenei and the regime's elites have opposed even the slightest demands for a change in the way the country is ruled. Iran's prolonged period of economic stagnation and

TABLE 4.1. Selected economic indicators of Iran.

Indicator	Unit	2011	2012	2013	2014	2015	2016	2017	2018	2019	2020[a]
Real GDP Growth	%	3.1	-7.7	-0.3	3.2	-1.6	12.5	3.7	-5.4	-6.5	0–0.7
Market Exchange Rate	T/$	1890	3570	3020	3390	3400	3700	4600	13200	15200	24600
Inflation	%	21	30	35	16	12	9	10	31	41	36[b]
Gross Foreign Reserves[c]	$B	92	104	118	126	128	123	114	124	121	114
External Debt	$B	19	8	7	7	9	10	10	11	9	9
Balance of Payments	$B	21	12	13	9	2	-5	-8	10	-3[a]	-7
Current Account	$B	59	23	25	14	1	13	15	27	3	-1
Goods	$B	68	29	29	18	5	19	22	33	7	3
Exports	$B	146	97	93	89	63	82	96	93	59	50
Oil & Gas	$B	119	68	65	55	32	53	63	61	29	21
Non-oil	$B	27	29	28	34	31	29	33	33	30	29
Imports	$B	78	69	64	71	58	63	74	61	52	47
Services, Income, Transfers	$B	-10	-6	-5	-5	-6	-8	-7	-7	-4	-4
Capital Account	$B	-19	-10	-9	1	2	-12	-19	-16	-7	-6
Errors and Omissions	$B	-18	-1	-3	-6	-1	-6	-5	-1	0[a]	0
Nominal Gross Public Debt	% GDP	35	43	41	42	42	49	49	47	48	47
Change in Gross Public Debt	% GDP	-3.0	8.0	-1.7	0.5	0.7	6.8	0.0	-1.7	0.6	-0.6
Interest Payments	% GDP	3.0	3.0	2.9	2.9	3.2	3.1	3.8	4.0	4.5	5.1
Banks Recap. & NPL Reduction[f]	% GDP	7.2	8.2	8.5	7.6	7.8	8.3	8.5	8.8	8.7	8.2
Capital Investment Shortfall[g]	% GDP	1.0	6.1	8.4	7.4	10.5	12.0	12.3	14.6	15.9	15.9
Adaptation to Water Scarcity[h]	% GDP	1.8	1.8	2.4	2.7	3.0	2.9	3.1	2.9	3.3	3.8

(a) estimated by authors based on partial data availability, (b) potentially underreported, (c) sum of gross foreign reserves of the Central Bank, NDFI, and commercial banks, (d) method adapted from IMF Public Debt Sustainability Analysis framework ("Productivity in the Iranian Economy (1375–1395), The Central Bank of Iran," in Farsi, 2018), (e) residual values (2011–2016) were calculated by considering primary deficit and automatic debt dynamics obtained in this work and changes in gross public debt as reported in references (Iran 2018 Article IV Consultation, International Monetary Fund, 2018; "Evaluation of Public Debt Sustainability of Iran in the Medium-Term," Majlis Research Center, 2016), (f) capital needed to raise banks' capital adequacy ratio to 8% and reduce NPLs to 5% of gross loans, (g) calculated as the gap between the actual gross capital formation and a desirable level equal to 30% of GDP (as observed a decade earlier), (h) see **Chapter 7**.

Sources: Economic Time Series Database and Other Statistics, Central Bank of Iran (cbi.ir); Statistical Yearbooks (1966–2019), Census Data (1956–2016), and

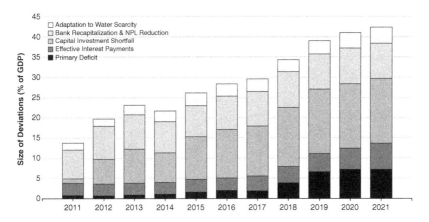

FIGURE 4.9. Deficits and deviations from normal conditions for sustainable growth (see Table 4.1 for detailed information).

political decay resembles the Brezhnev era in the Soviet Union where reforms were blocked by a coalition of the state and powerful interest groups—the former motivated by favoring political stability and the latter for its entrenched interest in the status quo. Observing Khamenei's response to the current crisis in Iran, it is hard not to think of Nero who, according to the popular legend, sang a song and played the fiddle while Rome was burning.

SUMMARY

Since the beginning of the 1960s, when statistics on aggregate levels of output have become available, the economy of Iran has undergone four distinct phases of growth and contraction: (1) between 1960 and the revolution, real GDP per capita increased from $1,200 (2020$) to its historic record high of $6,500, (2) between the revolution and 1988, the real per-capita GDP shrank to less than half its prerevolution level, (3) between 1989 and 2005, the economy recovered and the real per capita GDP reached a level equal to that of early 1970s, and (4) between 2005 and the time of this writing in 2021, the per capita income has remained stagnant while inequality has risen. In 2021, at least half of Iran's 85 million population still live in poverty with millions under the abject poverty line (i.e., income less than $2 per day). Iran's catastrophic economic performance is directly rooted in the poor system of governance of the Islamic Republic regime. In addition to most of its past challenges, the Iranian economy will face a number of new or intensified challenges in the coming decades which can hinder its future growth. First, a looming paradigm shift in the global energy markets from scarcity to abundance will significantly reduce the amount of national wealth Iran could otherwise generate from its vast remaining hydrocarbon reserves. Second, as the demographic window of opportunity inevitably comes to a close during the 2040s, the population support ratio will decline and further reduce national savings and investment. Third, the high and increasing level of corruption, particularly in the form of grand or political corruption, not only will continue to distort resource allocation but also will make major economic reforms even more difficult, if not impossible. Forth, depletion of natural resources in general and groundwater in particular will likely cause major socioeconomic dislocations with dire consequences for growth and development. Finally, new global trends in automation and use of artificial intelligence will deeply impact developing countries such as Iran with a competitive advantage in labor-intensive manufacturing due to their low-cost labor.

5

THE FINANCIAL SECTOR

A HIGHLY DEVELOPED FINANCIAL sector is a result of, and a contributor to, economic development. Developing the financial sector leads to higher rates of savings and capital accumulation and better investments. One of the main mechanisms by which a developed financial sector improves economic conditions, particularly in developing countries, is its vital role in the growth of small and medium-sized enterprises, which are far more labor intensive than large firms. This chapter explains the evolution of Iran's financial sector with a focus on the banking system. We begin by discussing the institutional background and the performance of the Central Bank of Iran (CBI) and evaluate its success in controlling inflation and the exchange rate. We then describe major developments in Iran's banks, with a focus on measures of financial depth and credit allocations, and compare them with those of other countries to put the discussion in a broader context. Finally, we discuss Iran's looming financial crisis, its root causes, and potential future impact on the economy.

Based on Razieh Zahedi and Pooya Azadi, "Central Banking in Iran," Working Paper 5, Stanford Iran 2040 Project, 2018.

CENTRAL BANKING

In this section, we first discuss the existing structure and institutional set-up of the CBI and subsequently evaluate its performance over the past few decades. The Central Bank of Iran (*Bank-e-Markazi*) is a government organization that conducts the nation's monetary policy. The CBI was originally established in 1960 by Iran's first Monetary and Banking Act[1] to issue currency and serve as the government's banker. The Second Monetary and Banking Act of 1972[2] expanded the CBI's responsibilities to include the issuance of currency, implementation of monetary policy, and supervision of banks. According to this act, the CBI's objectives were defined as follows:

- Maintaining the value of the currency
- Maintaining equilibrium in the balance of payments
- Facilitating trade transactions
- Assisting in the economic growth of the country

According to decades-long international consensus, a central bank's primary goal is to ensure price and financial stability, to which other goals should be subordinate. In fact, price and financial stability constitute the only promises that central banks can deliver in the long run.[3] As such, we only assess the performance of the CBI with regard to achieving these goals while acknowledging that the CBI was also assigned other goals that under specific conditions might have been inconsistent with its primary goal of ensuring price stability.

Interactions between fiscal and monetary policy, the Islamic finance framework, and institutional governance are the key factors affecting the performance of Iran's Central Bank. As discussed earlier, the government of Iran has chronically run significant fiscal deficits over the past four decades. With limited access to international financial markets and an underdeveloped capital market, the government has always tapped into the domestic banking system and the National Development Fund of Iran (NDFI) for financing the budget deficit. Fiscal dominance has resulted in the loss of the Central Bank's control over its balance sheet and impaired its ability to carry out an effective monetary policy. In an attempt to address this issue, legislation was passed in the early 2000s to ban the government from financing the deficit through seigniorage (issuing more money by the Central Bank). However, before long, the reform proved ineffective as the government was (and still is) permitted to borrow from the state-owned banks—an act with an indirect but equally harmful impact on the CBI's balance sheet. The composition of the CBI's balance sheet is also affected through the purchase of government-held foreign currency from oil exports. To avoid an expansion of the monetary base (high-powered money or *payeh-e-pooli*), the CBI has to go through a full sterilization process by which oil dollars are exchanged for rials in the foreign exchange market.

Another pivotal feature pertinent to CBI performance is the role that Islamic finance principles play where they have created a strong linkage between the real and financial sectors—causing risk spillovers between the two sectors and adding to the vulnerability of the economy as a whole. Over decades, the Islamic finance framework has created a complex and burdensome environment for the government to issue public debt, which in turn has suppressed the development of financial markets. For example, the CBI has not been able to use open market operations, discount windows, repurchase agreements, reverse repos, and interest rates on excess reserves, as they are not seen as compliant with Sharia law (we note that, in recent years, some of these restrictions were relaxed to help the CBI control the soaring inflation). As such, the CBI ought to utilize more direct instruments (e.g., statutory determination of the profit rate and credit rationing), which are known to be ineffective for controlling inflation and are prone to misallocation of resources. Furthermore, the contractual nature of Islamic banking undermines the Central Bank's potential for supervision of commercial banks and credit institutions, giving rise to higher risks in the financial sector.

Another consequential factor in central bank performance is the quality of its governance. Independence, transparency, and accountability are considered the three pillars of good governance for modern central banking. Many central banks around the world—from both economically advanced and developing countries—have already been granted more independence and autonomy to protect the long-term interests of their nations against the demands of short-sighted and populist politicians which cause future inflation to rise. However, no changes in this regard have been implemented in Iran, and the CBI still has little goal and operational independence. In practice, the appointment and removal of CBI's governors have been based solely on the discretion of the president. In this arrangement, the degree to which a candidate for CBI's governor is deemed obedient to the president becomes a more important selection factor than the candidate's actual merits for the job. In fact, the Central Bank in Iran has always served as a quasi-fiscal arm to finance the state's deficit while simply overlooking its primary task of ensuring price stability when in conflict with the demands of the government, and in some cases, powerful interest groups such as those of the IRGC's banks and financial institutions. In addition, the members of the Money and Credit Council (MCC, *Shoraye-Pool-va-E'tebar*), the highest authority for setting monetary policy, are appointed based on their official positions in other government organizations (not as individuals for their professional expertise and merits). While certain benefits can be obtained from some level of coordination between the Central Bank and the government, the heavy presence of government officials among the MCC members not only undermines the independence of the CBI but also routinely creates a conflict of interest for those MCC members with responsibilities in other organizations.

Today, communication with the public and transparency in design and implementation of monetary policy play a key role in the basket of tools that central banks use to influence expectations. However, the CBI has failed to effectively and honestly communicate with stakeholders and has persistently surprised the public, resulting in public mistrust of the Central Bank, which in turn deteriorates its ability to shape market expectations when needed.

In addition to securing price stability, the CBI is responsible for the overall stability of the banking system. To this end, the CBI is expected to set and enforce prudent bank regulations and routinely update them in accordance with the best international standards. In the last part of this chapter, we will provide an assessment of the CBI's performance in its role in safeguarding the stability of the banking system.

Inflation

Despite the substantial progress that central banks around the world have made to keep inflation in a desirable range (typically 2–4%), Iran has persistently experienced high (average 20%) and volatile (standard deviation of 9%) inflation over the past half century (Figure 5.1).[4] High inflation is known to discourage investment, stimulate capital flight, intensify income inequality, create anxiety in society, and make long-term decision-making by economic agents challenging. In the late 1970s and 1980s, high inflation was a matter of daily life in many countries, including the United States and many other developed economies of the time.

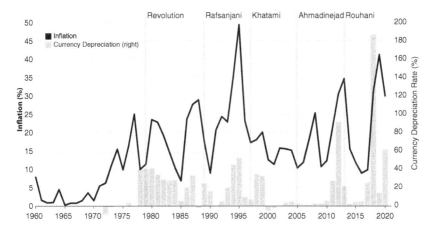

FIGURE 5.1. Trends in inflation and currency depreciation rate between 1960 and 2020.

Sources: Economic Time Series Database, Central Bank of Iran (cbi.ir); International Monetary Fund, DataMapper (imf.org/external/datamapper/datasets); Statistical Yearbooks (1966–2019), Statistics, Statistical Center of Iran.

However, in the late 1980s and early 1990s, switching from quantitative measures and currency pegging to directly targeting inflation through interest rates allowed many countries to overcome their persistently high inflation. At the time of this writing in 2021 and according to the official statistics, inflation in Iran hovers around a staggering rate of 45%, while there is a significant amount of anecdotal evidence that the true rate could be even much higher. To put this figure into a broader context, we note that at the time of this writing, only about twenty countries around the world have double-digit inflation rates, with only half a dozen of them dealing with inflation of 20% or higher.[5]

The quantitative theory of money asserts that in the absence of permanent nonmonetary shocks, inflation is correlated with money growth, particularly in the long run. Figure 5.2 shows the growth rates of the monetary base (or high-powered money, which is the total amount of currency in circulation and bank reserves held with the Central Bank) and broad money (or M2, which includes currency in circulation as well as demand and time deposits). In the decade leading to the 1979 revolution, the monetary base and broad money supply, on average, increased at staggering rates of 37% and 33% per year, respectively, giving rise to a persistent double-digit inflation for the first time after World War II.

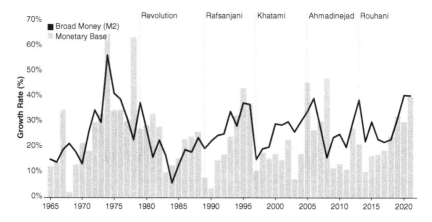

FIGURE 5.2. Annual growth rates of the monetary base and broad money (M2) in Iran.

Sources: Economic Time Series Database, Central Bank of Iran (cbi.ir); Statistical Yearbooks (1966–2019), Statistics, Statistical Center of Iran.

TABLE 5.1. Selected financial and economic indicators of Iran.

Parameter	1970–78	1979–88	1989–2004	2005–20
Monetary Base Growth	37%	23%	19%	25%
Broad Money Growth (M2)	33%	20%	27%	28%
Inflation	11%	19%	21%	21%
Private Credit to GDP Ratio	28%	31%	27%	48%
Banks Reserves Ratio	17%	17%	23%	12%
Real GDP Growth	6.5%	−2.6%	4.8%	1.9%

Sources: Economic Time Series Database, Central Bank of Iran (cbi.ir); International Monetary Fund, DataMapper (imf.org/external/datamapper/datasets); Statistical Yearbooks (1966–2019), Statistics, Statistical Center of Iran.

During the period of 1979 to 1988, the money supply growth somewhat decelerated but rose again to high levels in the years following the Iran-Iraq War. Table 5.1 summarizes trends in the growth rates of the monetary base, broad money, and inflation for the periods considered in the previous chapters.

The structure of the CBI's assets and liabilities provides important insights into the dynamics of money growth and monetary policy in Iran. The expansion of the CBI's balance sheet can be primarily attributed to the budget deficit and, to a lesser degree, to the partial sterilization of oil revenue (Figure 5.3). More specifically, the main drivers of this expansion

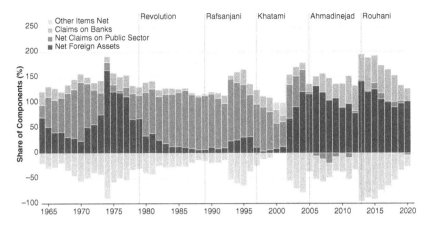

FIGURE 5.3. Shares of different components of the monetary base.
Sources: Economic Time Series Database, Central Bank of Iran (cbi.ir); Statistical Yearbooks (1966–2019), Statistics, Statistical Center of Iran.

were to direct financing of the government deficit during Rafsanjani's two terms and Khatami's first term, an increase in oil revenues during Khatami's second term and Ahmadinejad's first term, and financing of the government deficit indirectly through state-owned commercial banks during Ahmadinejad's second term and both of Rouhani's terms. As discussed in the previous section, since the early 2000s, there has been a shift in the source of government budget financing from the Central Bank to commercial banks, which consequently reduced the CBI's claims on government and expanded its claims on banks (Figure 5.3). In other words, the mere shift in the source of financing for the persistent and massive fiscal deficit of the country has not mitigated its inflationary pressure.

Figure 5.4 shows the ratio of broad money to the monetary base (a.k.a. M2 multiplier) and the share of time deposits (i.e., interest-bearing bank accounts) in the broad money. During the last few years of the Pahlavi regime, the M2 multiplier and share of time deposits in broad money were hovering around 3 and 60%, respectively. With real interest rates in deep negative territory and people's savings in decline due to economic recession, both the multiplier and the share of time deposits decreased during most of the 1980s. Since the end of the Iran-Iraq War, the multiplier and share of time deposits have been on the rise: between 1990 and 2020, the M2 multiplier increased from about 2 to 7, and the share of

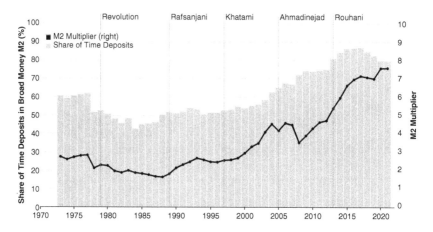

FIGURE 5.4. Trends in share of time deposits in broad money (M2) and M2 multiplier defined as the ratio of broad money (M2) to the monetary base.
Sources: Economic Time Series Database, Central Bank of Iran (cbi.ir); Statistical Yearbooks (1966–2019), Statistics, Statistical Center of Iran.

time deposits increased from 50% to more than 80%. The rise of the M2 multiplier between 1996 and 2009 was somewhat due to the reduction of the banks' reserve ratio (ratio of banks' reserves held by the Central Bank to deposits) which decreased from 30% to 10%, respectively. The faster growth of broad money compared to the monetary base during the 2010s (which led to a corresponding increase in the M2 multiplier from near 4 to 7) has occurred in the absence of any boost from a reduction of reserves requirements.

Exchange Rate

Like the central banks of several other large commodity exporters (e.g., OPEC members),[6] the Central Bank of Iran has historically used the exchange rate as a nominal anchor to control inflation. As shown in Figure 5.5, Iran had a fairly stable exchange rate prior to the revolution, but from the inception of the Islamic Republic in 1979 until 2020, rial has depreciated at an average annual rate of 24%. The depreciation has occurred in forms of crawling (e.g., 2002–2010) and bouts (e.g., 2012, 2018, and 2020). As a general rule, fundamental negative market pressure on a currency would reduce private wealth (depreciation of local currency) or public wealth (reduction of a central bank's foreign reserves), or a mix of both.

An important characteristic of Iran's currency exchange policy has been its multiple currency practices (MCP) (Figure 5.5) and various regulations to control the composition of imports. Different exchange rates were used to prioritize the import of essential goods (e.g., staple foods) and to push the government's import substitution agenda that was seen as a critical component of Iran's industrialization process. For example, the official exchange rate (*Nerkh-e-rasmi*) was designated for the import of essential goods, a competitive (*reghabati*) and preferential (*tarjihi*) rate for the import of specific goods, and a floating (*azad*) rate for other goods.[7] The first plan to unify multiple exchange rates in Iran after the revolution materialized in 1993 but was abandoned in the same year in the midst of the foreign debt crisis and high inflation (Figure 5.1). The second attempt to phase out MCP took place in 2002 amid more favorable economic conditions. However, on the first decennial anniversary of the reform, the Central Bank once again returned to the multiple exchange rate practice and has stayed with it to the time of this writing in 2021. The CBI has used various measures to stabilize the exchange rate in the market including attempts to reduce capital flight and force exporters to sell their foreign currencies at a rate determined by the CBI. However, these measures have not been successful, and the exchange rate market has experienced numerous episodes of sharp devaluations. The multiple exchange rate regime of the past few decades has not only resulted in suboptimal allocation of Iran's scarce resources but has also allowed for the growth of powerful import rent-seeking groups and entrenched corruption.

The relative movements in the exchange rate and domestic prices, which are routinely measured by the real exchange rate (RER), can provide important insights into the extent of disequilibrium in the foreign exchange market and cost competitiveness of an economy in international markets. The higher the value of RER, the more expensive the exports and the cheaper the imports. Figure 5.5 shows changes in Iran's RER over time using 1960 as the base year. As this figure shows, Iran experienced a large decline in its RER in the years after the revolution, reaching a new bottom in 1993 when the country underwent an external debt crisis. The next downward correction of RER occurred with the implementation of the exchange rate unification plan in 2002. After that, with a fixed exchange rate, the RER almost monotonically increased until 2012 when sanctions triggered a bout of currency depreciation. A more

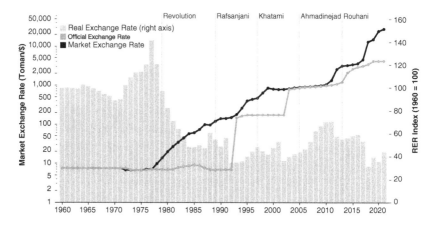

FIGURE 5.5. Trends in rial's official and market exchange rates (left axis) and real exchange rate (RER) in Iran indices (1960 = 100) calculated based on rial and US dollar consumer price indices and average of the official and market exchange rates (right axis).

Source: Economic Time Series Database, Central Bank of Iran (cbi.ir).

severe bout of currency devaluation occurred in 2018 when the United States withdrew from the nuclear deal and reimposed oil sanctions on Iran. At the time of this writing in 2021, the RER in Iran is at the bottom of its range since 1960.

Due to crude oil production shocks of the past decades along with large fluctuations in the global oil market, the contribution of oil and gas exports to the Iranian economy varied over a large range. Over the past half century, the share of oil in the GDP varied between 2% and 40%, and its share in the central government budget varied between 10% and 80%.[8] In 2000, to cope with the macroeconomic challenges of such large fluctuations in oil revenues, like many other large commodity-exporting countries, Iran created a countercyclical fund, the Oil Stabilization Fund (OSF), to help smooth its budget expenditures. After about a decade, Iran established its second natural resource fund, the National Development Fund of Iran (NDFI), to facilitate public investment and to serve as inter-generational savings. However, neither of these two funds—the OSF with a countercyclical objective or the NDFI with an intergenerational savings objective—has delivered the expected results. The former has become obsolete due to persistent budget deficits while the latter has turned into a mere quasi-fiscal arm of the government. Between its inception in 2011 and 2020, the NDFI has received some $100 billion—equivalent to 20%

of oil export proceeds. However, as yet another example of institutional weakness and lack of fiscal discipline, the NDFI was mandated to give considerable amounts of banking facilities and make large deposits with the commercial banks (in domestic currency). As a result, the NDFI, parallel to the Central Bank, has made large injections of petrodollars into the foreign exchange market.

Reforms

Major structural and operational reforms are needed in order to restore the ability of the CBI to conduct effective monetary policy. First and foremost, the issues of chronic fiscal dominance and large public debt need to be addressed, as sound public finance is a prerequisite for effective monetary policy. To this end, current government debt should be securitized to generate cash flow for the banks to mitigate their liquidity problems and provide opportunities for investment. This will provide banks with collateral in the interbank market and enable the CBI to effectively conduct open market operations.

One can infer from the historical monetary data presented earlier that high inflation—as long as it did not provoke social unrest—has persistently been of little concern to the government. In fact, a prolonged period of fiscal dominance has inverted the traditional roles of the fiscal and monetary policies: inflation has been predominantly determined by decisions made in the fiscal domain while economic growth and government solvency have been among the top priorities of monetary policy. In fact, by reducing the debt in real terms, high inflation has consistently benefited the country's major debtors to the banking system (the government itself and a small group of the regime's political elite and their patronage networks). Given the sizable portion of nonproductive expenditures (e.g., on ideological causes) and implicit energy subsidies in the budget, as well as the potential for higher public revenue by taxing *bonyads,* which have been tax-exempt since their inception, even a substantial cut in fiscal expenditures could be planned in such way that it would be benign to the provision of public goods and services. However, it is clear that any meaningful change in this realm will require a wide consensus among various political players whose short-term interests are in fact the reason such reforms have been politically infeasible thus far.

In addition to much-needed fiscal reforms, Iran should embark on a number of fundamental reforms in the structure, governance, and operation of the Central Bank to avoid a similar catastrophic outcome from monetary policy in the future. The CBI should make price stability the primary objective of the country's monetary policy, to which all other objectives would be subordinate. The CBI operation should also ensure financial stability as long as it does not contradict its primary objective of price stability in the long term. In this paradigm, instead of surprising the public with its decisions, the CBI should publicly announce and justify its target inflation for the mid-run and make institutional commitments to achieve that. The CBI should also make it clear to the public that it will allow the exchange rate to align with levels warranted by the fundamentals, although it may continue to smooth out fluctuations in the short run. Also, politicians, once and for all, must understand that by not allowing the CBI to focus on controlling inflation, the goals of unemployment reduction and economic growth will not be achieved in the long run. After all, the success of this reform will require the CBI to be given more autonomy, while having the backing of the political authorities, and to develop a greater degree of technocratic capacity.

The second group of reforms should aim to improve the quality of the CBI's governance with the overarching goal of making it independent, transparent, and accountable. Although some degree of institutional coordination between the Central Bank and the government is needed, the independence of the Central Bank should shield it from discretionary decisions of the political authorities who tend to prioritize short-term gains over long-term economic benefits. Theory and empirical data suggest that in developing countries like Iran, political independence—that is, the absence of political influence on Central Bank goals or personnel—is an indispensable ingredient for the success of the monetary policy.[9]

Contrary to the strategy of the Central Bank of Iran of systematically refraining from revealing its intention for future moves, the prevailing strategy among modern central banks is to be highly predictable to economic agents. Economic decisions are shaped by expectations; transparency is a modern institutional solution to influence these expectations. The CBI can improve the outcome of monetary policy if it becomes more transparent about its objectives, its strategy for reaching them, and the rationale for its key decisions. It is important that communications to the public be clear and easy to interpret. Transparency will help the CBI regain its currently eroded public confidence and therefore be able to effectively anchor inflationary expectations. Otherwise, in case of a financial crisis, lack of public confidence in the CBI will amplify the economic damage and make the recovery period longer. To hold the CBI accountable for its performance and decisions, a clear metric, such as deviation from the target inflation rate over a period of time, should be used to evaluate its performance.

COMMERCIAL BANKS

The expansion of Iran's economic activities in the 1960s and 1970s was accompanied by a rapid growth of the banking sector; by 1978, there were three dozen commercial and specialized banks, of which twenty-eight were private.[10] However, soon after the revolution, banks and other industries were nationalized (details can be found in the Banks National-ization Act[11] and the Law for Administration of the Banks[12]). This trans-formation—along with a general contraction in the level of economic activities—warranted an extensive bank consolidation which ultimately reduced the number of banks to about a dozen,[13] a development that substantially eliminated competition in the banking sector. It is gener-ally believed that the changes in the structure and governing rules of the central and commercial banks, along with the departure of many of their experts and managers, hurt the performance of the banking sector at that time[14]. In 1983, the banking rules were amended to comply with the principles of a usury-free Islamic finance framework, including the concept of a non-interest-bearing banking system.[15] A defining feature of Islamic banking is the prohibition on predetermined payments (i.e., interest or *riba*) in all forms of transactions, thus restricting the use of funds solely to a profit-and-loss-sharing basis.[16] Today, Iran is probably the only country in the world whose financial operation is fully compliant with Islamic finance principles (at least in de jure terms).[17] In addition to the rules and regulations above, the policies of the public banks are guided by five-year development plans and annual government budgets.

Due to the lack of access to international financial markets, Iran's economy almost solely relies on domestic banking for the provision of funds for the establishment of new firms, development of existing busi-nesses, maintenance, and working capital. Despite this heavy reliance on domestic banks, the financial sector in Iran is rather undeveloped even within the standards of developing countries. Figure 5.6 compares Iran's financial depth (defined as the ratio of private credit to GDP) with that of China, India, Turkey, and South Korea. After four decades of trial

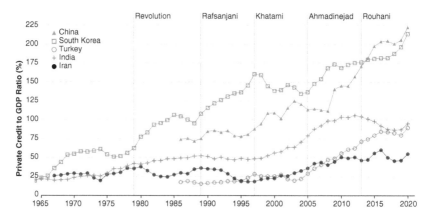

FIGURE 5.6. Financial depth (ratio of private credit to GDP) in Iran and selected countries.

Sources: Economic Time Series Database, Central Bank of Iran (cbi.ir); Total Credit to Private
Non-Financial Sector, Bank for International Settlements.

and error with financial policy, Iran's financial depth in 2020 stands
at the same level as it was at the onset of the 1979 revolution, while the
other countries mentioned have significantly increased the availability
of credit per unit output. As will be discussed shortly, due to their impaired balance sheets, the lending capacity of Iranian banks has dropped
significantly over the past few years, causing the credit-to-GDP ratio to
drop from its record high of 60% in 2016 to 40% in 2019.

Figure 5.7 shows how shares of different sectors from total bank credits
have changed during the same periods considered in earlier chapters.
In the last decade of the Pahlavi regime, bank loans, on average, were
allocated to different sectors as follows: 42% services and trade, 22%
manufacturing, 17% construction, and 9% agriculture (with the remaining allocated to other uses). After the revolution, the share of services
and trade sector from bank credits dropped to about half, before rising
again in the last period (2005–2020) to the same level observed before the
revolution. On the contrary, the shares of manufacturing and agriculture
increased until the end of 1989–2005 period but underwent a significant
decline thereafter. The share of construction spiked soon after the revolution but has been on a declining trend since the end of the 1979–1988
period. Moreover, in recent years, more than 60% of the allocated credit
was for the provision of working capital, while only less than 10% was
dedicated to the establishment of new businesses.[18]

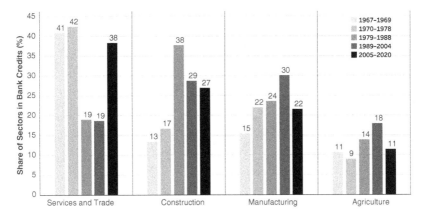

FIGURE 5.7. Share of different sectors in outstanding bank loans between in different time periods.
Sources: Economic Time Series Database, Central Bank of Iran (cbi.ir); Statistical Yearbooks (1966–2019), Statistics, Statistical Center of Iran.

FINANCIAL STABILITY

The banking system in Iran is faced with multiple intertwined crises that have brought the country's financial sector to the verge of a major collapse. In fact, it is now plausible that the consequences of previous irresponsible actions and economic misconduct, which have thus far been limited to low output growth and high inflation, will morph into a full-fledged financial crisis that would, in turn, result in a significant loss of output and employment. The problems in the banking system in Iran are rooted in fiscal dominance, institutional weakness of the CBI, endemic corruption, and general misconduct in the banking system itself.

Figure 5.8 delineates the extent to which some of the key financial soundness indicators (FSI) of Iranian banks have changed between 2005 and 2019. These indicators include capital adequacy ratio (CAR), return on assets (ROA), ratios of nonperforming loans (NPLs), banks' claims on government, and banks' debts to the CBI to the total loans. The figure depicts a marked deterioration of the banking sector's health in terms of accumulation of non-income-generating assets (NPLs and claims on government), buildup of debt to the Central Bank, decline in banks' ability to absorb losses (CAR), and lower profitability (ROA).

Cash flow problems and inadequate capital constitute two of the most pressing issues facing Iran's banking system. The cash flow problem is a

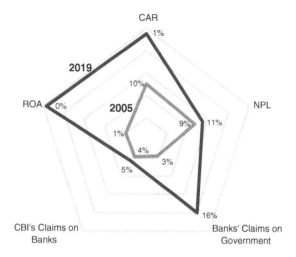

FIGURE 5.8. Comparison of selected financial soundness indicators of Iranian banks in 2005 and 2019. For all variables, the center represents the desirable side of the range and the outmost layer represents the undesirable side.

Sources: Economic Time Series Database, Central Bank of Iran (cbi.ir); Statistical Yearbooks (1966–2019), Statistics, Statistical Center of Iran; International Monetary Fund, Article IV Consultation, Country Report No. 18/93, 2018; International Monetary Fund, Article IV Consultation, Country Report No. 07/100, 2007.

consequence of high interest rates and the accumulation of non-income-generating assets, which itself is caused by massive government debts (directed lending), overvalued and illiquid fixed assets due to speculative investments in real estate, and large amounts of nonperforming loans. The underlying reason for the latter issue is the lack of enforcement of banking regulations by the Central Bank and the judiciary, allowing distressed banks to continue operation without recapitalization.[19] In addition to all these, high interest rates and sluggish economic conditions exacerbated the problems and made the repayment of debt more difficult. Based on conservative official estimates, the total amount of banks' NPLs hovers around 10% of the loans. It is important to note that these estimates of NPLs exclude the rolled over loans which comprise a significant portion of the fresh loans. In the absence of effective supervision by the Central Bank, these problems, although somewhat masked by inflation and liquidity growth, were hidden for a long time. In fact, by using complex and convoluted accounting tricks, the banks were able to roll over toxic assets and register them as fresh loans, allowing them to book interest income, pay dividends to shareholders, and give lucrative bonuses to managers.

Since around 2005, to avoid liquidity risk, the banks have had to offer high interest rates on deposits to attract more resources. While a sizable portion of banks' assets were unable to generate revenue, paying high interest rates on the liability side amplified their cash flow problems which gradually impaired their balance sheets and reduced their capacity to grant new loans. In addition, with the increasing penetration of unregulated credit institutions (*Moasesat-e-E'tebari*) free to offer higher interest rates, competition to attract new deposits led to a price war and a Ponzi scheme. Meanwhile, with higher interest rates, the cost of borrowing in the real sector increased and, through the adverse selection effect, put more pressure on the banks' balance sheets. This situation resulted in a downward spiral of higher interest rates and a further rise of NPLs. Increasing the relative size of banks and credit institutions served as a protection against bankruptcy (by becoming too big to fail). Indeed, in recent years, many of these financial institutions have received uncollateralized support from the Central Bank.

At the same time, an explosive growth rate of liquidity (M2) led to an expansion of banks' size without a corresponding increase in their capital, causing the capital adequacy ratio in the banking system to reach an unprecedented low level of about 1%, which is far below the Basel II and Basel III international standards that recommend minimum CAR levels of 8% and 10.5%, respectively. The accumulation of NPLs, along with insufficient capital, is a precursor for bank failure and trigger for a deep financial crisis.[20] Since 2019, the actual net capital position of the banks in Iran, on average, is effectively negative.

Further, corruption and an outdated accounting system, far from the rules of the International Financial Reporting System (IFRS), have exacerbated the challenges in banks' balance sheets and masked the very issues that need to be addressed by the CBI. Reporting and monitoring of financial soundness indicators have been limited, and the CBI has failed to report problems and alert banks and other stakeholders that they need to manage the issues in a timely manner.

Impairments in the banks' balance sheets affect not only the banks' risk management performance and their operating profitability but also their connections with the international banking system. Avoidance of IFRS standards came at the expense of the banks' disconnecting with their international counterparts. However, due to the overwhelming role of banks in Iran's financial market, it is the real sector that ultimately shoulders the burden, as it is highly dependent on bank credit. As mentioned above, despite a rapid growth in broad money supply, the real sector has consistently faced liquidity and cash flow problems. In fact, without decisive and immediate reforms, a banking crisis in Iran is very likely. If this happens, such a crisis will likely have far-reaching effects on the economy, such as low credit and GDP growth for a prolonged period of time.[21] Historical data indicate that the GDPs of countries that experience a major banking crisis collapse significantly, and it often takes a long time for the output to recover to its pre-crisis levels. Further, banking crises have relatively larger real effects in developing countries due to less developed bond and equity markets and difficulty in providing support for troubled banks.[22]

SUMMARY

In this chapter, we evaluated the performance of the financial system in Iran with a focus on the Central Bank and commercial banks. We also outlined a number of fundamental reforms without which the objectives of monetary policy in general, and the objective of price stability in particular, will remain unattainable.

Iran's average inflation rate of more than 20% over the past decades demonstrates that high inflation—as long as it doesn't provoke social unrest—has persistently been of little concern to the government. Besides fiscal dominance, lack of proper monetary instruments at the CBI's disposal is responsible for the poor outcome of Iran's monetary policy. Although the Central Bank is eventually responsible for preserving the value of money, its performance should be judged with consideration for the degree of difficulty imposed by exogenous uncontrollable factors. Both of the aforementioned causes for high inflation in Iran—fiscal dominance and the lack of proper monetary instruments at the CBI's disposal—are to some extent the consequences of the larger issue of poor governance in the country. Iran would have had a significantly smaller fiscal deficit, hence lower inflation, had the state been more responsible with respect to its expenditures and more willing to tax some of the large, quasi-private conglomerates (such as *bonyads*) that have been tax-exempt since their inception. Some other obvious reforms that could have helped control the fiscal deficit, such as a reduction in energy subsidies, were also omitted as the power structure in Iran leaves hardly any incentives for politicians to justify taking such socially expensive moves. Failure to control inflation, however, has benefited the country's major debtors besides the government itself: the Islamic Republic's elite and their patronage networks. The benefit to these groups has come at the expense of putting a hidden regressive tax on all citizens with consequences that are in sharp contrast with the state's own pro-poor rhetoric and stated values. The second most important cause of high inflation—lack of proper monetary instruments—is a result of decades of reluctance to use market-based tools because they were not perceived as compliant with the usury-free principles of Islamic finance. In fact, the CBI has suffered from a legacy of inefficient laws and regulations that are attributed to the ideology of the Islamic Republic. It is important to note that Iran is probably the only country in the world where all dimensions of the financial sector are restricted by these rules.

Despite the heavy reliance of the Iranian economy on the banking system, its financial depth has remained almost unchanged for decades. This is partly due to the accumulation of toxic assets in banks' balance sheets which significantly reduced capacity for granting loans. We also argued that the CBI has failed to monitor and supervise the banking system which, in turn, has pushed the economy to the verge of a major financial crisis. The chapter provided a set of institutional reforms along with best international practices to address the aforementioned challenges. First and foremost, the current government debt should be securitized to generate cash flow for the banks to mitigate their liquidity problems. This will provide banks with collateral in the interbank market and enable the CBI to effectively conduct open market operations. The law governing the CBI should be revised to provide operational autonomy and limit the way in which the government has been able to dominate the Central Bank's policies. We also discussed the exchange rate policy and argued that it should be part of a coherent macroeconomic policy.

6

THE ENERGY SECTOR

SINCE THE BEGINNING OF OIL production in Iran over a century ago, the petroleum sector has played a central role in shaping the country's path of economic and political development in multiple ways. In this chapter, we provide an overview of historical trends in Iran's energy landscape and discuss their future trajectories. The first part of the chapter is concerned with rates of production, consumption, and export of crude oil and natural gas. We then focus on the role of oil revenue in financing the government budget and the future impediments for continuation of the past trends due to depletion of Iran's oil reserves and the looming paradigm shift in the global oil markets from scarcity to abundance. We also estimate economic losses associated with the misallocations of natural gas to its various end uses by the government. Finally, we will describe supply and demand for electricity and discuss the economic feasibility of nuclear energy given Iran's vast natural gas and renewable resources.

Iran currently holds the fourth and second largest proven reserves of crude oil and natural gas in the world, respectively.[1] An overwhelming majority of Iran's gas reserves are found in deposits that are not associated with significant quantities of crude oil, and until the end of the twentieth century, the gas sector had been fairly underdeveloped. Natural gas and oil constitute the primary sources of energy for Iran's domestic consumption with marginal contributions from coal, nuclear,

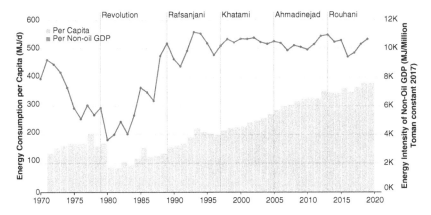

FIGURE 6.1. Trends in the energy consumption per capita (left axis) and per non-oil GDP (right axis) in Iran (calculated based on the lower heating values of oil products and natural gas).

Sources: Statistical Yearbooks (1966–2019), Statistics, Statistical Center of Iran; Review of 26 Years of Iran's Energy Statistics, Ministry of Energy, Tehran 2015 (in Farsi); Iran's Energy Balance 1393, Ministry of Energy, Tehran, 2014 (in Farsi).

and renewables including hydropower, solar, and wind. While crude oil has historically been Iran's primary source of external revenue, the use of natural gas has almost exclusively been limited to the domestic market where it provides an increasingly larger share of the country's primary energy mix (from about a quarter in the 1970s to three-quarter in 2020).[2]

Since 1970, due to the combined effects of rapid population growth and higher per capita energy consumption, Iran's primary energy demand has expanded by over tenfold.[3] Figure 6.1 shows trends in Iran's energy consumption per capita and per unit of economic output (non-oil GDP). The per capita energy use of Iran has quadrupled over the past half century—a rate which has been significantly higher than the global average increase of roughly 50%.[4] Since 1990, Iran's energy consumption per unit of output has stayed flat—a trend which diverges from the declining global trends stemming from energy efficiency improvements.

This increasing per capita energy consumption has been partly due to low energy prices. Figure 6.2 illustrates how the prices of gasoline and electricity in real terms have changed over the past half century in Iran. As illustrated, the real gasoline prices in Iran have undergone five distinct phases: a 40% decline between 1970 and the onset of the revolution, a

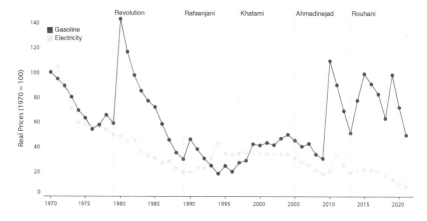

FIGURE 6.2. Trends in real domestic prices of gasoline and electricity between 1970 and 2021 (1970 = 100).
Sources: Statistical Yearbooks (1966–2019), Statistics, Statistical Center of Iran; Iran's Energy Balance 1393, Ministry of Energy, Tehran, 2014 (in Farsi), and news archives.

more than twofold increase in the months after the revolution, a long and drastic decline through the mid-1990s, a partial recovery through 2010, and finally a period of multiple spikes each followed by a few years of cooling off due to inflation. It should be noted that throughout all these decades, the price of gasoline has been centrally set by taking into account only domestic calculations such as budgetary constraints and risk of social unrest with no regard for gasoline's opportunity cost which is determined by international prices. The price of electricity in real terms saw an initial 80% decline between 1970 and 1990, followed by a slight increase through the mid-2000s, and a further decline since then. The regime's eroded legitimacy and fear of widespread unrests are the underlying reasons why the state has refrained from the implementation of an energy subsidies reform, although such reform seems to be obvious from an economic standpoint.

CRUDE OIL

Iran's rate of crude production over the past half century has undergone multiple changes due to disruptions caused by the political turmoil of the revolution, the war with Iraq, patterns of investment, and geologically driven factors (Figure 6.3). Under the 1954 consortium agreement between Iran and a half dozen Western oil companies, the production of crude oil in Iran increased rapidly from about a million barrels per day (MMbbl/d) in early 1960s to nearly five MMbbl/d by the end of 1972. The new consortium agreement between Iran and foreign companies which took effect in 1973 soon boosted the production to about six MMbbl/d (which is still the record high after half a century) but failed to deliver the eight MMbbl/d which was originally envisioned. However, beginning in 1978, first due to the political instability around the time of the revolution, including the famous strikes in the National Iranian Oil Company (NIOC), and then due to the revolution and termination of the consortium contracts, outbreak of war with Iraq which caused physical damage to Iran's oil production facilities, lack of new investments, and natural decline of existing fields, Iran's production was cut significantly and hovered around half of the previous peak level between the 1979 revolution and the end of war in 1988. In the postwar period, the production capacity of Iran gradually increased and stabilized in the range of 3.5 to 4.0 MMbbl/d until the oil sanctions of 2012–2015 which reduced Iran's crude export and production by about one million barrels per day. Between 2018 and the time of this writing in 2021, due to the new round of sanctions imposed unilaterally by the United States, Iran's oil export plunged to a range of about 0.2–0.5 MMbbl/d according to the data published by OPEC and other international agencies (Iran never reports its actual export volume during sanctions).[5] As a result of these drastic changes in Iran's crude production, the share and importance

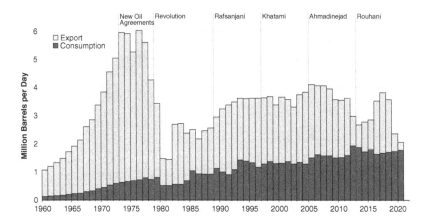

FIGURE 6.3. Iran's crude oil production between 1960 and 2020.

Sources: Statistical Yearbooks (1966–2019), Statistics, Statistical Center of Iran; Economic Time Series Database and Other Statistics, Central Bank of Iran (cbi.ir); Monthly Oil Market Report, 2018–2021, OPEC.

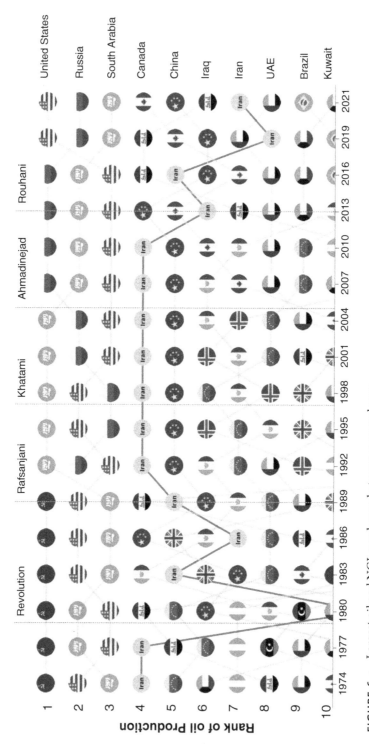

FIGURE 6.4. Largest oil and NGL producers between 1974 and 2021.

Source: US Energy Information Administration, eia.gov.

of Iran in the global oil market has also varied significantly over time (Figure 6.4): from the fourth global producer prior to the revolution, to anywhere between the fifth and tenth during the first decade after the revolution, back to the fourth position after the war until 2010, then between fifth and eighth until the present time in 2021.

The domestic consumption of crude oil has steadily increased from about 0.1 to 1.8 MMbbl/d between 1960 and 2020. Since 2000, the per capita consumption of petroleum-derived products in Iran has increased from 6.3 to 6.8 barrels per year while the real GDP per barrel of fuel consumed has increased by one-third.[6]

Oil export proceeds have played a decisive role in Iran's state-building process over the past century and have shaped the elites' attitude toward entrepreneurship and rent-seeking activities. Prior to nationalization of oil in 1951 under Prime Minister Mosaddegh, Iran was receiving only a small fraction of the profits from the Anglo-Persian Oil Company which was operating the country's oil fields. For example, Iran received a mere 18% of the oil profits in 1948. In a major shift after nationalization and in line with the then new terms of oil agreements between Middle Eastern countries and Westerns oil companies, Iran managed to secure half of the oil profits when the 1954 agreement was negotiated with the consortium companies (in which US oil companies gained a 40% share).[7] Parallel to this agreement, which granted the consortium companies the drilling and production rights only in the southwestern region, the Iranian government partnered with other foreign oil companies to discover and produce oil in the remaining parts of the country. In these joint ventures, Iran's share varied between 75% and 90%.[8] Overall, Iran's crude production increased from near zero in 1954 to nearly five million barrels per day in 1972.[9] In 1973, several years prior to the end of the first consortium agreement, Iran successfully renegotiated with the consortium companies a renewed twenty-year agreement with more favorable terms. In the ensuing years of this new agreement, Iran not only benefited from the then soaring oil prices but also from higher production and a larger share of profits, leading to a large rise in the country's oil revenue (Figure 6.5). However, before long, due to a combination of lower prices, natural decline of the fields, and political turmoil, oil revenues started to decline by 1977.

In 1979, which marked the first year of the Islamic Republic regime, the doubling of crude prices counterbalanced the large drop in Iran's export volume, helping the country's oil revenue to remain almost intact. However, in 1980–1981, the termination of the consortium agreement and US sanctions imposed on Iran due to the hostage crisis resulted in a further drop in oil exports and a significant blow to oil revenues. Despite a partial production recovery in 1982 (to 2.5 MMbbl/d), plunging oil prices gradually reduced Iran's crude revenue to levels not seen since the 1950s—eventually persuading Iran to accept the cease-fire in 1988. In the postwar period through the end of Rafsanjani's first term, when oil prices were relatively stable, a further rise in production capacity resulted in a modest increase in the country's oil revenues. However, during the period of 1993 to 1998, while production was held constant at 3.6 MMbbl/d, oil prices dropped significantly, due in part to weak demand caused by the Asian financial crisis. From that point to the financial crisis of 2008, oil prices and Iran's oil revenue increased almost steadily. When the global demand was restored by 2011, Iran earned its highest per capita oil revenue since 1979.

Around that time, the regime, and for that matter, many global energy experts, had concluded that the oil market had already reached an inelastic phase where demand could no longer be met by smooth responses from producers. The natural decline in production of conventional oil fields along with insignificant amounts of new oil discovery were believed to bring global oil production to a peak in the medium term and an inevitable decline thereafter.[10] The popular peak oil theory of the time predicted that, like the United States where oil production has been on a constant decline since 1970, other major oil producing countries would soon reach their production peak, thereby causing global supply to decline. In Iran's math, given the slow rate of recovery of the Western powers from the financial crisis and their heavy dependence on imported crude oil, these economies were unable to bear the burden of another price shock on top of crude's price tag of $100 per barrel at the time. What the regime catastrophically failed to see, however, was the rapid development and implementation of new technologies in the oil industry, particularly in the United States, which allowed for commercial extraction of oil from tight resources. In addition, global efforts to decarbonize economies due to growing concerns about climate change and higher oil prices, which by that time had lasted for a decade, were finally resulting in improvements in fuel efficiency in the transportation sector and a larger market share for alternative fuels, hence smaller

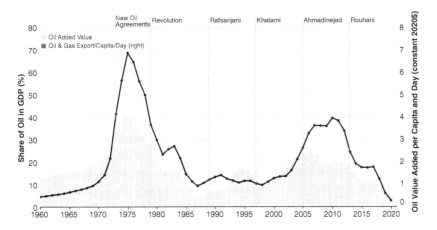

FIGURE 6.5. Share of oil in Iran's GDP (left axis) and oil export per capita and day (right axis).
Source: Economic Time Series Database and Other Statistics, Central Bank of Iran (cbi.ir).

demand for petroleum fuels compared to previous projections. All in all, in 2012 and contrary to Iran's calculus, the United States and its allies managed to cut Iran's oil exports by half without pushing oil prices to higher levels. Under these sanctions, Iran's oil revenue in 2012–2014 was reduced to half. Later, as the price of oil started to fall in late 2014, Iran's crude revenue further decreased to a third of its pre-sanction value. It was under these conditions that Iran struck a nuclear deal with the global powers. After the implementation of this deal, Iran produced oil at its full capacity of about 3.7 MMbbl/d for three consecutive years before being subjected to new sanctions in the second half of 2018. Along with lower prices, this new round of sanctions brought Iran's oil revenue to low levels that the country had not seen for seven decades.

According to Iran's official statistics, the country holds 155 billion barrels of proven liquid hydrocarbon reserves in 2020, of which two-thirds is crude oil and the remainder is natural gas liquids (NGLs).[11] At current production capacity, these reserves would correspond to a reserve-to-production ratio of nearly 70 years for crude oil (assuming production at full capacity of 3.8 MMbbl/d) and over 150 years for condensates. However, due to reasons outlined below, the amount of wealth embedded in oil reserves is unlikely to yield comparable financial wealth for current and future generations.

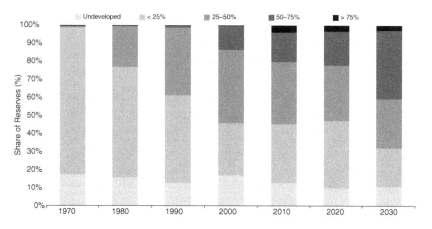

FIGURE 6.6. Depletion levels of Iran's oil fields based on reserves that were already discovered (authors' estimates based on data compiled from various sources).

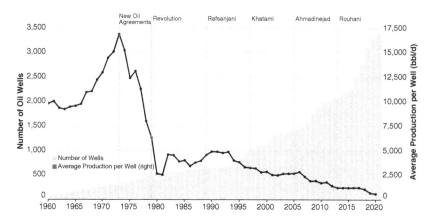

FIGURE 6.7. Number of Iran's oil wells and their average production between 1960 and 2020.

First, having produced some seventy-five billion barrels of oil thus far,[12] a significant portion of Iran's production will come from mature fields with depletion levels upwards of 50% (Figure 6.6). For comparison, at the time of Iran's peak production in the mid-1970s, oil was almost entirely produced from oil fields with depletion levels less than 25%. Since that time, the average productivity of Iran's oil wells has decreased to less than 10% of its peak level (Figure 6.7). Keeping all maintenance and gas injection activities at the current level, every year Iran would have to bring a minimum of 250,000 bbl/d in new capacity online to compensate for the decline in productivity of its existing wells which hovers around 6% per annum according to our estimate.

Thus far, with an average production cost of around, or even less than, $10 per barrel, most of Iranian crude oil lies near the bottom of the global oil cost curve. By 2030, about 40% of Iran's oil reserves, and at least a similar share of the production capacity, will be associated with fields that have already produced more than half of their ultimate recoverable crude. This would mean Iran can no longer entirely compensate for the natural decline of its oil fields, especially the supergiants, through infill drilling—a relatively inexpensive solution that could be implemented with domestically available technology—and instead would be in need of significant investments in secondary and tertiary production technologies which are more complex and have higher production costs.

Given current uncertainties in the global oil markets, US sanctions, and looming political instability inside the country, it would be improbable, if not unthinkable, for Iran to be able to absorb meaningful amounts of foreign investments in its oil sector in the medium term. Since the implementation of the nuclear deal in early 2016 through mid-2018, when new sanctions were imposed, only two international companies made agreements with NIOC despite the significant efforts of Iran and the more favorable conditions of new contracts offered (i.e., Iran Petroleum Contracts, IPC). In any case, the production cost of Iran's future oil will be higher compared to the country's current average of about $10 per barrel.

In addition to sanctions, Iran's oil revenue has also been affected by the paradigm shift in the global oil market of the past decade which has fundamentally, and perhaps permanently, changed the global oil landscape from scarcity to abundance.[13] This paradigm shift, which stemmed from twin changes on the supply and demand sides of the market, has already manifested itself in lower oil prices since 2015 as well as in large downward revisions to forecasted oil prices of the next decades (e.g., 50% reduction in the US Energy Information Administration [EIA] long-term forecast between 2012 and 2019).[14] On the demand side of the market, due to stricter climate policies to reduce carbon emissions, besides the economic motivations of the oil-importing countries to improve their energy security, major innovations and investments have been made in technologies related to electric vehicles, fuel efficiency, and renewable energy, thereby exerting a significant downward pressure on oil demand. On the supply side of the market, recent technological advances in hydrofracking, horizontal drilling, and big data and analytics have lowered the production cost of oil from tight resources to a range of $30–60 per barrel,[15] resulting in an increase of US total oil supply from nearly 8 MMbbl/d in 2010 to 18 MMbbl/d in 2020.

As a result of the above developments on both sides of the market, the timing of "peak oil" has not only been postponed well into the future but also its underlying cause will no longer be a geology-driven decline of supply, but a peak of demand caused by a combination of climate policies and technological advancements. More importantly, in the long run, the relative price of oil is unlikely to be significantly higher than the marginal cost of production for those producers who can move into and out of the market more quickly than other players (e.g., US tight oil producers).

The future oil production of Iran will depend primarily on when the sanctions end, how the political landscape of the country looks at that time, and the outlook of the oil market—all of which are extremely uncertain factors at the time of this writing. Anecdotal evidence suggests that, through the use of domestic capabilities for gas reinjection, maintenance activities, well workover, and infill drilling, Iran may retain its production capacity for a few years into the sanctions. However, the current sanctions are much stricter compared to the previous ones and were imposed at a time when the economy was more fragile, which makes it even harder to divert domestic resources for expenses such as oil production capacity maintenance that are not of vital immediate concern. In any case, it seems unlikely that Iran's crude production and export by 2025 will exceed 4 and 2 MMbbl/d, respectively. Together with low prices, which are expected to last at least in the medium term, the added value of the oil sector in Iran is likely to remain around one dollar per capita per day if sanctions are lifted.

Although the Islamic Republic almost never allocated a significant share of oil revenue for intergenerational savings purposes, Iran's low crude production (relative to its reserves) was not necessarily perceived negatively until recently, as it would have left more reserves for the future when the value of oil in real terms was forecasted to be significantly higher. However, given the paradigm shift in the global oil market from scarcity to abundance, it is likely that Iran will ultimately hold significant amounts of stranded oil reserves. The extent of the impact of this some-what depends on the rate at which Iran can convert its underground oil resources to durable financial and physical assets in the coming decade or two. Nevertheless, the regime's irresponsible foreign policy, which is the sole cause of the current and previous oil sanctions, and insufficient investments in the oil sector will ultimately have substantial adverse impact on the wealth of the nation. For example, in a hypothetical sce-nario where Iran's crude production since the 1979 revolution was higher by only one MMbbl/d—a figure which could have been easily achieved given Iran's large reserves and low production costs relative to competi-tors—and assuming a conservative rate of return of only 3% on the extra proceeds, the nation's total wealth (i.e., net stock of capital) would have been double what it was in 2020. All in all, Iran's national wealth loss due to oil reserves that could become stranded in the future is estimated to be between five to fifteen times its current GDP.

NATURAL GAS

With the establishment of the National Iranian Gas Company in 1965, development of Iran's natural gas industry started almost half a century later than its oil sector. Until then, Iran's gas fields were mostly undis-covered (or undeveloped), and natural gas was almost entirely produced as an unwanted by-product of crude oil which had to be flared at the production facilities.[16] In the mid-1960s, Iran signed a contract to export gas to the Soviet Union which in turn resulted in the development of the first major gas infrastructure in the country including a large pipeline from the southwestern oil fields to Astara near the Caspian Sea. In ad-dition to the trans-Iranian pipeline and gas transport infrastructures, which were to be used for domestic purposes as well, the export of natural gas to the Soviet Union provided financing for some of the major state-owned projects such as the Isfahan Steel Company and the Arak Heavy Machinery Plant which were important elements of the state's industrial policy. In the meantime, the consortium companies also increased the utilization of associated gas in their own operations in addition to mak-ing a sizable amount of gas available for other uses. Since then, with the discovery and development of several gas fields, including the supergiant South Pars, an overwhelming majority of Iran's gas reserves and current production are from deposits without significant quantities of crude oil (nonassociated fields). The South Pars/North Dome field is by far the

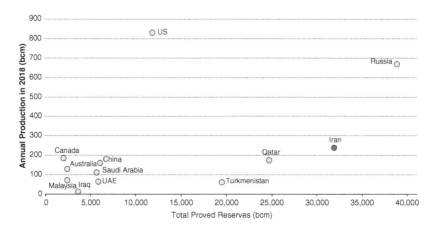

FIGURE 6.8. Total proved reserves of natural gas and annual production of select countries.

Source: BP Statistical Review of World Energy, London, June 2020.

largest discovered gas reserves in the world, and its development, now in its third decade with total investment reaching $100 billion, has been the largest project implemented by the Islamic Republic thus far. In 2021, with 32 trillion cubic meters of proved reserves and an annual production rate of 240 billion cubic meters, Iran holds the second largest recoverable gas resource in the world and is the third largest producer after the United States and Russia (Figure 6.8).[17] To put Iran's current gas production into context, the economic value of Iran's produced gas at international prices (~$150,000/million cubic meters [mcm] in 2019) was worth $40 billion, which would be equal to 10–20% of its economy. Despite the rise in the amount of produced gas over past decades, the demand for gas has seen an equal or even larger growth. The main factors contributing to soaring demand for natural gas include expansion of the national gas grid to most households, population growth, displacement of liquid fuels by natural gas in the power sector, as well as construction of petrochemical plants and other energy-intensive industries, many of which are economically viable only when gas is priced below its opportunity cost for the country (e.g., gas export price). In the remainder of this section, we first provide an overview of natural gas production and its outlook in Iran. We then explain how the amount of produced gas is currently allotted to different uses and discuss the pivotal role it plays in shaping the regime's development policy and as a source of rent and corruption.

Compared to crude oil, the production of natural gas in Iran has undergone far less erratic changes throughout its history. This is due to a more stable aggregate production capacity, lack of direct vulnerability to sanctions (Iran's gas exports have been insignificant until recently), and lack of production quotas imposed externally by intergovernmental organizations (e.g., OPEC). Over the past half century, the annual production of natural gas in Iran has steadily increased at the rate of 15 mcm/d to reach 750 mcm/d in 2019 (Figure 6.9). The production rise since early 2000 is almost entirely attributable to the completion of different phases of the South Pars field (twenty-four phases in total, of which only one remains to come online in 2021). Although discovery of new natural gas resources has never been a top priority for Iran, it already has half a dozen undeveloped fields, mostly offshore, to tap into after the development of the South Pars is completed. However, these undeveloped fields are substantially smaller than the South Pars and by no means can benefit from the same economy of scale and manufacturing-like development approach which were instrumental in the development of the South Pars field. It is also expected that current producing fields, including the South Pars, will start to decline in the near future. As a result, despite the sizable potential of Iran's natural gas green fields, it seems improbable that the country's total gas production can be boosted significantly.

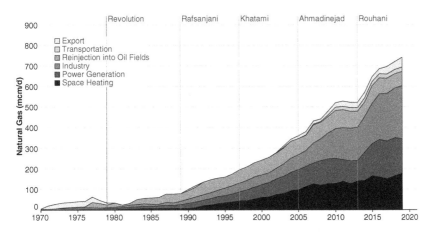

FIGURE 6.9. The supply and uses of natural gas in Iran between 1970 and 2019. *Sources:* Statistical Yearbooks (1966–2019), Statistical Center of Iran; "Review of 26 Years of Iran's Energy Statistics," Ministry of Energy, Tehran 2015 (in Farsi); Iran's Energy Balance 1393, Ministry of Energy, Tehran, 2014 (in Farsi).

A defining feature in the history of the natural gas sector in Iran is that both the price and the allocation priority of gas have been centrally determined by the government in the absence of any form of free market mechanism. Over the past decade, the price of gas in Iran for end users has typically hovered around 50% of the Henry Hub and 10% of residential gas prices in the United States, respectively. As a result of such cheap prices and despite the continuous expansion of the supply side, there has never been sufficient gas to fully meet the demand. Space heating (25%), power generation (22%), industry (34%), reinjection into mature oil fields (9%), transportation (3%), and exports (7%) have constituted the main uses of natural gas in recent years. Since more than 90% of Iranian households are already connected to the national distribution pipeline, a rise in demand for space heating—which has historically been given the highest allocation priority among all uses—will likely slowdown in the future. Similarly, over the past decades, natural gas has, to a large extent, replaced liquid fuels in power plants, implying that the future demand in this sector will primarily depend on economic and population growth and hence will be much slower compared to its past trend.

Another large consumer of natural gas in Iran is its large and growing petrochemical industry. Started in the mid-1960s with a fertilizer production plant in Shiraz, the capacity of the petrochemical industry in Iran grew at a modest rate before the revolution to reach nearly 3 million metric tons by 1979. However, since the early 1990s, the petrochemical industry, in tandem with Iran's gas extraction capacity, has gone through a hockey-stick growth where its production weight and value in 2019 has reached 30 million metric tons and $15 billion, respectively. It is also likely that in the coming decade, the largest demand growth for gas will come from the petrochemical industry. Despite relatively large investments and decades of central planning, the output of Iran's petrochemical plants is dominated by basic products (e.g., ethylene, methanol, ammonia, urea) due to lack of vertical integration. As a result, the added value of the industry as a whole is fairly low, and its profitability relies primarily on heavily subsidized gas (which has historically been about a quarter of the industrial gas prices in the United States).

Given that Iran was a major importer of gasoline for a few decades, significant efforts were made to replace part of domestic transportation fuels with compressed natural gas (CNG). To this end, Iran offers cheap CNG beside the relatively large investments made in refueling infrastructure and vehicle fuel tank manufacturing. Despite some initial success in expanding the country's CNG fleet, the growth has almost completely diminished in recent years.

For almost two decades between the mid-1990s and mid-2010s, Iran was a net importer of natural gas despite the country's large and growing supply. However, this situation has changed, and Iran has become a net exporter of gas yet again, although its export amount is only a fraction of Qatar's, with whom Iran shares the South Pars/North Dome field. Another strategic use of natural gas with very high economic return is immiscible reinjection of gas into mature oil fields to mitigate the natural decline of these fields. Recently, it has been estimated that roughly four thousand barrels of oil has been produced per million cubic meters of gas injected. At an oil price of $50 per barrel, this would mean a $200,000 revenue per million cubic meters of injected gas, which is greater than the average added value for the use of gas by the petrochemical industry. Despite favorable economics, there has never been enough gas to meet the plans for enhanced oil recovery.

Figure 6.10 shows sector-specific natural gas consumption and the order in which the government allocates gas to various sectors, according to anecdotal evidence. Due to a lack of a readily available alternative, the provision of natural gas for households and commercial buildings has always had the highest allocation priority as evidenced by the government's decision to redirect more gas from other sectors or even import gas from Turkmenistan to satisfy the peak demand in the cold days of winter. Similarly, the government also ensures an undisrupted supply of gas for the country's large CNG transportation fleet due to its critical role in passenger transport. The second group of natural gas uses, which includes power generation, industry, and exports, receive gas below their full capacity or contract, particularly in peak seasons. In fact, the power sector still consumes a sizable amount of liquid fuels (diesel and fuel oil) which are not only significantly more expensive than natural gas per unit of embedded energy but result in much higher local air pollution. Despite its comparatively high economic return, gas injection into declining oil fields always receives the lowest priority when allocating gas (especially for dry gas) because it is perceived as postponable.

In addition to the marketed gas, Iran still produces a substantial amount of associated gas that is wastefully flared at the oil wells due to lack of infrastructure to compress and treat it.[18] In fact, Iran has

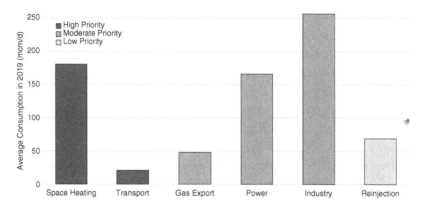

FIGURE 6.10. Natural gas allocation priority and consumption by end use in 2019.

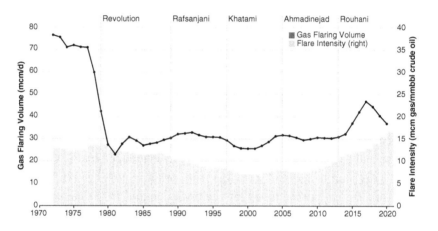

FIGURE 6.11. Amount of flared gas (left axis) and flare intensity (right axis), defined as the ratio of the flared gas to total crude oil recovered.

Sources: Statistical Yearbooks (1966–2019), Statistics, Statistical Center of Iran; Iran's Energy Balance 1393, Ministry of Energy, Tehran, 2014 (in Farsi); J.P.C. Carey, "Iran and Control of Its Oil Resources," *Academy of Political Science* 89 (1974); Global Gas Flaring Reduction Partnership (GGFR), World Bank.

consistently been among the top gas-flaring countries, both in absolute terms and per amount of oil produced (known as flare intensity). Figure 6.11 illustrates trends in Iran's total flared gas volume and flare intensity since 1970. The initial decline in the amount of flared gas in the ensuing years of the revolution is attributable to a large decline in the country's oil production. Between the end of the war to about 2010, the volume of flared gas remained constant, and flare intensity was slightly reduced. However, as more gas became available from the gas fields, Iran once again started to ignore investments in this area and flared an increasing amount of associated gas over the past decade.

ELECTRICITY

In general, changes in electricity consumption of countries are strongly correlated with their economic growth. In the case of Iran, however, this relationship is somewhat masked by other factors such as fast rates of population growth and urbanization, availability of gas from the South Pars field, heavy subsidies on electricity prices, and large variations in economic output itself due to the volatile nature of oil revenues.

Between 1960 and 1979, Iran's gross annual power generation increased from 0.6 to 20 terawatt hours (TWh), corresponding to an average annual growth of nearly 1 TWh.[19] After the revolution, electricity generation continued to grow at an average rate of 7 TWh per year to reach 310 TWh in 2019. On average, about 17% of Iran's gross electricity generation is lost in transmission and distribution.[20] For comparison, the average electricity transmission and distribution losses of the Organisation for Economic Co-operation and Development (OECD) countries is currently about 6%.[21] Figure 6.12 shows trends in Iran's net electricity production and consumption since 1970. In rough terms, the residential and industrial sectors each consume one-third of the generated electricity,

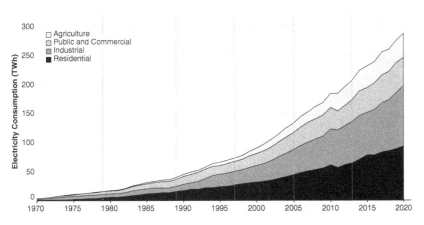

FIGURE 6.12. Trends in electricity consumption of Iran between 1970 and 2020 by major sectors.

Sources: Statistical Yearbooks (1966–2019), Statistics, Statistical Center of Iran; Review of 26 Years of Iran's Energy Statistics, Ministry of Energy, Tehran 2015 (in Farsi); "53 Years of Iran's Electricity Statistics 1346–1398," Ministry of Energy (in Farsi).

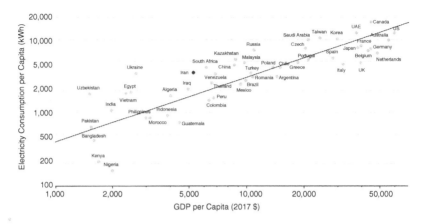

FIGURE 6.13. Per capita GDP and electricity consumption of selected countries in 2017.

Sources: Statistical Yearbooks (1966–2019), Statistics, Statistical Center of Iran; "Review of 26 Years of Iran's Energy Statistics," Ministry of Energy, Tehran 2015 (in Farsi); US Energy Information Administration, eia.gov; "53 Years of Iran's Electricity Statistics 1346–1398," Ministry of Energy (in Farsi).

with the remainder used equally in the public and agriculture sectors. The annual demand of the residential sector has increased from 1 TWh in 1970 to 93 TWh in 2020 due to a combination of population growth, improved access, and higher consumption per customer. The growth of power consumption by the industrial sector, which has been similar to that of residential use, has far exceeded the growth in the sector's added value. This disproportionate rise in the electricity demand of the industrial sector is due to the combined effects of electrification (fuel substitution); a shift toward more energy-intensive industries such as refining, iron and steel, food and beverages, and cement; and lack of investment in energy efficiency. Among these sectors, the electricity consumption for agriculture, which primarily uses electricity for operating water wells and irrigation pumps, has increased at the fastest rate. Of nearly 500,000 water wells in the country, about half have already switched from diesel to electric pumps.[22] Overall, Iran's electricity demand is higher than the expected value based on its level of economic output (Figure 6.13).

Since the early 1970s, as a result of parallel developments in domestic production of natural gas and advancements in gas to power technology in the world, electricity generation in Iran has increasingly relied on natural gas (Figure 6.14) to the extent that in recent years, the share of natural gas in Iran's power generation mix has reached almost 90%, while liquid fuels, hydropower, nuclear, and other renewables collectively constituted the remaining 10%. The average amount of hydroelectric power generated by Iran's growing number of dams has stayed virtually flat for more than a decade, suggesting that the natural capacity for expansion of hydroelectric power generation has largely diminished. Because of the higher efficiency of the newly installed combined-cycle power plants, the mean efficiency of Iran's thermal power plants improved from 31% in 1990 to 38% in 2018.[23] For the sake of comparison, the average efficiency of gas-fired power plants in the United States is currently around 44%.[24]

Despite the massive direct and implied costs Iran has paid for its only nuclear power plant in Bushehr (which is estimated at tens and hundreds of billion dollars, respectively), nuclear power accounts for a mere 1.2% of the country's power generation capacity. While detailed analysis of Iran's motives for the pursuit of its controversial and consequential nuclear program falls beyond the scope of this chapter, here we only emphasize that, with the discovery of the South Pars gas field in the early 1990s and from a purely techno-economic perspective, it was certain that gas-fired power plants would by far be Iran's most financially viable choice for power generation in the foreseeable future. Also, as far as energy security is concerned, gas power plants are a much safer alternative to atomic energy given the availability of domestic fuel and conversion

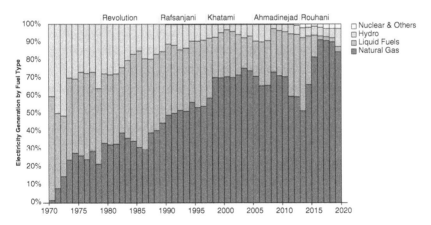

FIGURE 6.14. Share of power generation by type of fuel between 1970 and 2019.
Sources: Statistical Yearbooks (1966–2019), Statistics, Statistical Center of Iran; "Review of 26 Years of Iran's Energy Statistics," Ministry of Energy, Tehran 2015 (in Farsi); "53 Years of Iran's Electricity Statistics 1346–1398," Ministry of Energy (in Farsi).

technologies. The capital investment of new nuclear power on a per kilo-watt basis has been about ten times higher than a gas-combined cycle.[25] With recent advances in solar and wind technologies, similar to the case of gas-combined cycles, a tenfold gap has been created between the capital required for nuclear power and renewables for a similar output.[26]

Based on sector-specific projections, it is estimated that Iran will need to add about 150 TWh to its gross electricity to meet its domestic demands by 2040.[27] In addition, it has to compensate for the retirement of some of the older power plants. In principle, there are four alternatives for future expansion of the country's power generation capacity:(1) upgrading and retrofitting existing plants, (2) construction of new gas-fired combined-cycle plants, (3) construction of new nuclear reactors, and (4) development of large-scale wind and solar farms.

Upgrading and modernization of low-efficiency power plants, which are old or consist of single-cycle power stations, has the potential to fulfill about a fifth of the future demand growth (30 TWh) at a fairly low marginal cost. The construction of new gas-fired combined-cycle plants, as in past decades, will likely make up bulk of Iran's future capacity additions. Depending on the (shadow) price considered for natural gas, which itself depends on the opportunity cost for marginal consumption, the cost of electricity generation by new combined-cycle plants will be in the range of 1–7¢ per kilowatt hour (in 2021). Despite unfavorable economics, the Islamic Republic still insists on expanding nuclear power by commissioning the second phase of the Bushehr power plant which can generate about 8 TWh when fully operational and is also planning the construction of a few other reactors of varying sizes. However, with the expected downward trends in relative price of oil and gas in the long run, caused by a permanent paradigm shift from scarcity to abundance, the regime will likely have less political will and hard currency in the coming decades for such financially unjustifiable and politically expensive projects. As a result, a significant expansion of nuclear energy in Iran seems improbable at the time of this writing.

In addition to enormous reserves of natural gas which, if needed, can be used for power generation for several centuries, Iran has great potential for non-hydro renewable electricity. Notably, 30 million hectares of land in Iran receive solar irradiance of greater than 250 watts per square meter, and over 2 million hectares have a mean wind speed of 8 meters per second or higher which makes them ideal places for

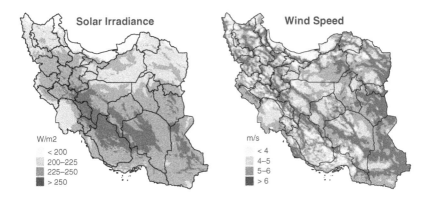

FIGURE 6.15. Annual average global horizontal irradiance (GHI) and wind speed.
Source: Vaisala 3TIER Services Global Solar Dataset; Vaisala 3TIER Services Global Wind Dataset, www.vaisala.com.

harnessing renewable energy. The distribution of this land across the country is shown in Figure 6.15. The ultimate viability of renewables in Iran depends not only on the costs of solar panels and wind turbines and the associated cost of capital but also on the added value for the marginal consumption of natural gas which will be freed up. In other words, as long as decisions with respect to distribution of natural gas are centrally made by the government in the absence of any form of market mechanism, the question of economic viability of renewables will be inseparable from where the displaced gas will be allocated.

SUMMARY

By the time of this writing in 2021, Iran has earned a total of $1.9 trillion (in constant 2020$) from crude oil exports, of which $1.5 trillion was obtained since the 1979 revolution. Over the past half century, on average, oil revenue has accounted for about 20% of the GDP and 45% of government revenue. With nearly 150 billion barrels of liquid hydrocarbon reserves, Iran can potentially continue to produce crude oil and gas condensates for several decades into the future. However, given the structural challenges of the global oil market, Iran's underinvested industry, and rising domestic demand for petroleum-derived fuels, it is unlikely that oil export revenue can resume and sustain its historical role as the driver of economic growth even in the absence of any oil sanctions. Thus far, with an average production cost of less than $10 per barrel, Iran has been able to compensate for the natural decline of its oil fields (i.e., estimated at about 6% per year) through a combination of domestic and international finance and technology. However, as the share of mature fields in Iran's crude production increases over time, it becomes increasingly more difficult, and expensive, for Iran to maintain its production capacity or augment it further.

A permanent reduction in the contribution of oil in financing public expenditures would have a number of important implications. In the short to medium term, it exacerbates the country's fiscal deficit and forces the government to cut subsidies and social safety nets, and even some of its economically unproductive but politically important expenditures on causes related to the ideology of the Islamic Republic. In the long term, the state must extract more taxes from citizens and quasi-public organizations, which will likely improve the institutions of democratic accountability. The reduction of petrodollars will cause depreciation of the currency, which, on the one hand, reduces the purchasing power of the people and, on the other hand, can boost the export of labor-intensive and agricultural goods and foster tourism depending on the country's political and business environments.

Iran is ranked second and third, respectively, in terms of reserves and production of natural gas in the world. Contrary to large swings in the crude production rate, the natural gas sector has undergone a relatively monotonic expansion over the past half century, during which the total amount of produced gas increased by more than tenfold. At the production rate of 750 million cubic meters per day (mcm) in 2020, natural gas provides three-quarters of Iran's primary energy demand. In the most plausible scenario, natural gas production in Iran will continue to grow over the next decade but at a much slower rate compared to the 2010s due primarily to smaller size of undeveloped fields and the natural decline of the South Pars field. Future exports, which will produce much larger revenues for the state than proceeds from domestic sales, will have to compete with the fast-growing petrochemical industry whose profitability is primarily dependent on cheap natural gas. At an average international price of $150,000/mcm, the value of Iran's natural gas production exceeds $40 billion per year (i.e., 10–20% of GDP). Given that this resource is allocated to different uses in the absence of a market mechanism, natural gas has become one the major sources of rent and patronage in the Islamic Republic regime.

Electricity demand has also seen a sharp upward trend where it mono-tonically increased from less than 1 TWh in 1960 to 310 TWh in 2019. The residential and industrial sectors each consume a third of the generated electricity, and the remainder is used by the public and agriculture sectors. Iran's electricity demand is much higher than the expected value based on its GDP. The electricity loss in Iran is estimated at 17% which is nearly three times higher than that of the OECD countries. Thanks to parallel developments in domestic production of natural gas and advancements of gas to power technology in the world, natural gas has consistently increased its share in Iran's electricity generation mix to the extent that it now accounts for almost 90% of the power generation while all other sources combined provide the remaining 10%. Importantly, despite the massive direct and indirect costs that the country has paid for its nuclear program—which are estimated to be in the range of tens and several hundreds of billion dollars, respectively—nuclear power constitutes no more than 1% of the mix and has production costs that are much higher than combined-cycle power plants and even renewables.

7

THE AGRICULTURE SECTOR

DUE TO THE LARGE AMOUNT of water used for farming, water consumption in Iran has consistently exceeded the level that is defined as the initial water stress threshold (i.e., a quarter of total renewable water) by approximately fourfold. As a result of this gap between the demand for water and the sustainable supply, Iran is heading for a full-fledged socio-environmental crisis with a decisive impact on the well-being of current and future generations. Besides the visible signs of Iran's water crisis in its shrinking lakes, drying rivers, and overdrafted aquifers, the downward trends in the country's water availability are evident in escalation of interregional and intersectoral conflicts over water. The longer the current situation persists, the more damage will be done to the environment and the less likely it will be that the environment can be restored to its normal state.

The underlying solution to address Iran's water problem is obvious: consumption should be regulated and reduced, water productivity should be improved, and wastewater should be treated and reused in the system. However, managing the economic and social costs associated with these potential remedies is not a trivial undertaking. In each hydrological year, the available water is distributed among four major sectors: municipal, industry, agriculture, and the environment. The demands for water differ significantly among these sectors in terms of quantity, quality, and shadow prices (i.e., willingness to pay for a marginal unit of water input).

Considering the vital role of water in people's daily lives and health, it is generally accepted that the priority for direct human use, municipal water, is the highest among these sectors. Also, given the substantially higher marginal benefits of water for industrial applications compared to the agriculture sector, industry would typically gain allocation priority should there be a local competition between the two sectors for water. Despite their relatively higher allocation priorities, municipal and industrial water consumption in Iran constitutes just about one-tenth of the total water use and thus inherently lacks the capacity to affect the water crisis in the grand scheme of things. Therefore, reducing the water used by agriculture remains the only viable option to address Iran's ongoing water crisis. This goal may be achieved through a combination of the strategies outlined above: regulating and selectively reducing irrigated farming, enhancing productivity (e.g., expansion of high-tech irrigation and greenhouses, and optimization of crop patterns), and reusing treated wastewater. However, a reduction in agricultural activities will have important consequences for the provision of food for the nation and employment for some four million farmers (see chapter 3)—the majority of whom are over the age of fifty and lack other professional skills and, as such, are unemployable in other sectors.

Thus far, the solutions implemented by the government to balance the supply and demand of water have almost entirely avoided any form of direct intervention leading to a reduction in the existing quotas. Instead, attempts have been focused on closing the gap by increasing the supply (construction of more dams, exploitation of more groundwater) and, to a lesser extent, incentivizing modern irrigation techniques to improve water use efficiency. However, the construction of more dams to capture surface water and the development of water wells for exploitation of groundwater that were once considered to be part of the solution are now perceived to be part of the problem. The trends in Iran's water withdrawal and dams in service over the past three decades are depicted in Figure 7.1.

Besides the provision of food and employment by the agriculture sector, strategic policies rooted in the ideologies of past decades have consistently advocated and incentivized farming to reach a state of food self-sufficiency. Food self-sufficiency, defined as the ratio of domestic production to total agricultural requirements, has long been a major goal for the agriculture sector in Iran. Historically, about 85% of the food consumed in Iran has been produced domestically. But food self-sufficiency

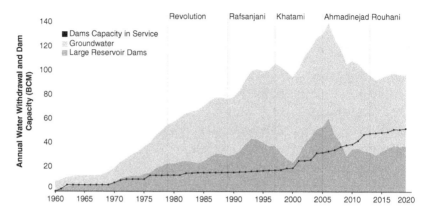

FIGURE 7.1. Iran's water withdrawal (surface water and groundwater) and the total capacity of dams in service. Sources of groundwater withdrawal include wells, qanats, and springs.

Sources: Statistical Yearbooks (1966–2019), Statistical Center of Iran; Iran's Water Resource Management Company, Iran's Dams Statistics (daminfo.wrm.ir).

does not necessarily translate into food security. The Food and Agriculture Organization of the United Nations (FAO) defines food security as "a situation that exists when all people, at all times, have physical, social and economic access to sufficient, safe and nutritious food that meets their dietary needs and food preferences for an active and healthy life." Food security therefore makes no a priori assumptions as to where the food originates but rather focuses on equitable and stable availability of food to people. By focusing on the origin of food or the capacity to produce it internally, a productionist approach addresses only the availability (supply) component of food security. As a result, a self-sufficient or even food-exporting country may still contain a large number of undernourished people whose low incomes are not sufficient to purchase food (e.g., Pakistan).[1] Meanwhile, some non-self-sufficient countries such as the United Kingdom and Japan, which produce less than 80% of their food,[2] are highly food-secure as they not only can afford to import food but also have no concerns about being the target of an international embargo. In any case, all countries engage in international food trade because not all crops constituting the food basket of a country can be grown within the political borders of that country due to limitations imposed by the climate. A country may therefore overproduce a specific crop based on its comparative advantage but be an importer of another crop.

The implications of Iran's water crisis will likely go beyond the mere issue of food security. Severe water scarcity can potentially be a cause of civil unrest in Iran, especially when combined with other factors such as high rates of unemployment and (the perception of) inequality. It can also trigger regional violence between upstream and downstream users over water resources.

In this chapter, we provide an overview of trends in the supply and demand for food in Iran and evaluate the country's sustainable capacity in terms of land and water endowments, considering potential future gains from investments in irrigation systems and infrastructure. Subsequently, we identify irrigated farmlands located in areas under extreme water stress or in areas inherently unsuitable for agriculture due to their land characteristics. We then introduce our proposed countrywide water scarcity adaptation plan to address Iran's water crisis. Finally, we estimate the ultimate changes in Iran's agricultural output and the economic consequences of the implementation of the proposed plan.

FOOD SUPPLY

Between 1960 and 2019, Iran's total agricultural production increased from less than 10 million metric tons to over 100 million metric tons (Figure 7.2).[3] An analysis of production at the crop level shows an

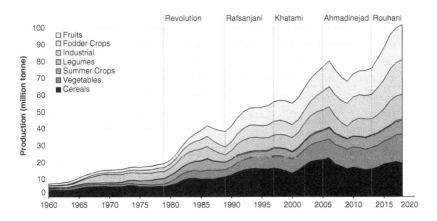

FIGURE 7.2. Trends in Iran's agricultural production by type of crop.
Sources: Statistical Yearbooks (1966–2019), Statistical Center of Iran; Annual Agriculture Statistics, Vols. 1–3, Iranian Ministry of Agriculture (in Farsi); "A Statistical Overview of Field Crops Harvested Area and Production in the Past 36 Years," Iranian Ministry of Agriculture, 2015 (in Farsi).

increasing trend for almost all major field crops grown in Iran. The rate of increase in production, however, shows marked disparities among crops due, in part, to shifts in crop patterns. The two crop groups with the highest rate of increase in production are fodders and vegetables. Despite decades of advocacy and support for wheat self-sufficiency, the rate of increase in wheat production lagged behind that of fodders and vegetables: average wheat production in Iran in the early 1990s was about 8 million metric tons, compared to an average of 13 million metric tons produced three decades later. Over the same period, the production of silage corn and vegetable crops has increased by eightfold and threefold, respectively. This increasing trend in the production of fodder and vegetables has dire consequences for water resources in Iran as the production of these summer-grown crops relies almost entirely on irrigation.

As shown in Figure 7.3, the official harvest areas of both field crops and orchards increased in the first decade after the revolution but have remained constant since the beginning of the 1990s.[4] The occasional downward strides observed in the total harvest area are mainly due to severe drought events, predominantly reducing the harvest area of rainfed wheat, which accounts for almost a quarter of the total area under cropping. Although the share of irrigated area in the total cropland increased soon after the 1979 revolution, no major changes in the relative distribution of farmlands with respect to irrigation have been observed thereafter (Figure 7.3). Despite the almost equal areas of rainfed and irrigated lands, about 90% of Iran's agricultural production is obtained from irrigated farming.

With over three million farm holdings, the average size of farms in Iran is fairly small (Figure 7.4). In 1960 and 2014, 91% and 87% of the farms were smaller than 100 hectares (ha), respectively.[5] On average, the size of irrigated farms (2.9 ha) is smaller than that of rainfed farms (6.9 ha).[6] (For comparison, the average size of farms in the United States is 175 ha.[7]) The size of individual farms has various implications related to the productivity, sustainability, and socioeconomics of agriculture. While smallholder farming is gaining popularity for its ecological (e.g., higher diversity and lower chemical inputs) and societal aspects (e.g., local markets), small farms are deemed to be less efficient, more expensive per unit of output (the economies of scale principle), and associated with agrarian poverty. Furthermore, small and fragmented farms with

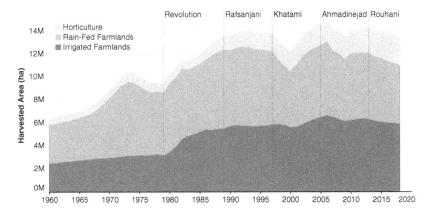

FIGURE 7.3. Changes in harvested area by type of farm.

Sources: Statistical Yearbooks (1966–2019), Statistical Center of Iran; Annual Agriculture Statistics, Vols. 1–3, Iranian Ministry of Agriculture (in Farsi); "A Statistical Overview of Field Crops Harvested Area and Production in the Past 36 Years," Iranian Ministry of Agriculture, 2015 (in Farsi).

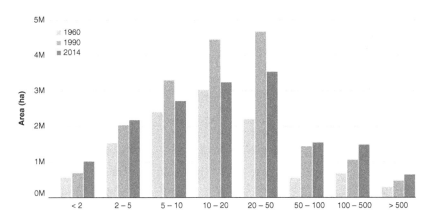

FIGURE 7.4. Distribution of Iran's farmland by size in 1960, 1990, and 2014.
Sources: Statistical Yearbooks (1966–2019), Statistical Center of Iran.

irregular geometry—typical of most farms in Iran—are less amenable to the use of machinery and implementation of modern irrigation and drainage systems.

Evaluation of Iran's land for agricultural suitability shows that on top of the well-known water limitations, land resources also pose significant barriers to sustainable food production for Iran's growing population.[8] A multitude of factors pertinent to the soil and terrain conditions—such as low organic matter, high salinity, and a mountainous topography—render

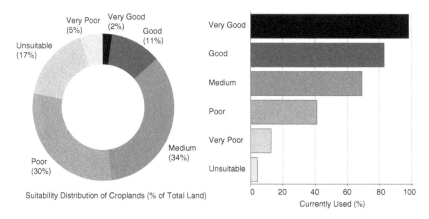

FIGURE 7.5. Agricultural suitability of existing cropland in Iran (left) and share of cropland from all land within each suitability class (right).

Sources: Mohsen B. Mesgaran and Pooya Azadi, "A National Adaptation Plan for Water Scarcity in Iran," Working Paper 6, Stanford Iran 2040 Project, Stanford University, August 2018.

the vast majority of Iran's land unsuitable for agriculture.[9] Only about 4% of the country's landmass can be considered as prime land with no limitation for cropping, all of which is already in use for agriculture (Figure 7.5). About 50% of the current farming acreage is poor quality land: a farming practice that is unsustainable and environmentally consequential. The data presented in Figure 7.5 strongly suggest that agriculture has exploited all the suitable land resources in Iran and has no room for further expansion. Furthermore, the land available to agriculture is likely to decrease in the future for various reasons such as land use change (e.g., urbanization) and land degradation (such as soil erosion, desertification, and salinization).

Although not very efficient, thus far, the agriculture sector in Iran has responded to the immediate food demand of the nation and contributed to Iran's economic growth. However, as discussed earlier, this development has occurred at the huge cost of deteriorating the land and depleting water resources. In fact, even in the absence of intended reduction in farming, it is likely that a shortage of water and deterioration of the soil will lead to an inadvertent and uncontrolled reduction in the output from the agriculture sector in the long run. However, inadvertent or not, if a reduction in agricultural output is not accompanied by sustained economic growth in other sectors, Iran will face a higher level of undernourishment and hunger.

FOOD DEMAND

Population size, per capita income, and diet constitute the fundamental determinants of food demand in a country. In contrast to very low-income and very high-income countries, the middle-income countries, such as Iran, are likely to experience food demand pressure from both the growth in their population size and people's income level. Therefore, in addition to the natural resource endowments of Iran that determine the country's inherent potential for domestic food supply, the current and future stages of the country's development should be taken into account when designing food security and environmental policies. In this section, we evaluate the historical impact of population and income growth rates on food demand in Iran and project future trends. To this end, we assume that the relationship between the changes in food demand with the growth rates of population and the real per capita income can be expressed by $d = p + n \cdot pci$, where d is the growth rate of demand for food, p is the population growth rate, n is the average income elasticity of demand for food, and pci is the real per capita income growth rate.[10]

Over the past three decades, despite a tremendous decline in the country's total fertility rate, Iran's population has increased by almost one million people per year (chapter 2) to reach 85 million in 2021. However, the population growth rate (p) declined from 2.5% in 1989 to 1.0% in 2020, and it is likely to decline further in the future as the largest cohort of the population, born in the years following the revolution, exits their fertility window. Assuming that Iran's future total fertility rate (TFR) will continue to stay at its current level of 1.9 (which is close to the replacement level of 2.1 births per woman), the population of Iran is projected to reach 90 million by 2030. This would mean that the annual population growth rate (p) will decline from 1.0% in 2020 to 0.7% by 2025.

The second term in the food demand equation ($n \cdot pci$) accounts for the dynamics of food demand as a country proceeds through different stages of development and per capita income (pci). The income elasticity of demand for food (n) is a measure that quantifies the percentage of change in demand for food (specific product or food as a whole) if the income level in a country changes by one percentage point. The income elasticity of demand for food varies substantially with both the type of commodity and the income level itself. Income elasticities for foods that are considered luxuries (e.g., some animal products) are greater than those for staple crops (e.g., wheat). Food comprises one of the largest

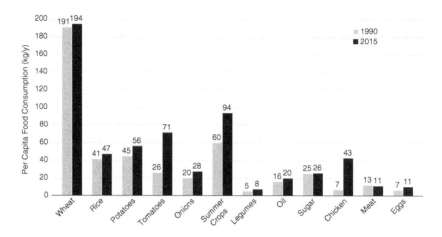

FIGURE 7.6. Trends in the per capita demand for select food (direct and indirect) in Iran.

Sources: Statistical Yearbooks (1966–2019), Statistical Center of Iran; Annual Agriculture Statistics, Vol. 1–3, Iranian Ministry of Agriculture (in Farsi); "A Statistical Overview of Field Crops Harvested Area and Production in the Past 36 Years," Iranian Ministry of Agriculture, 2015 (in Farsi).

shares in poor people's expenditures, but as their incomes grow, people often spend a smaller proportion of their total income on food—giving rise to a smaller income elasticity of demand for food. The average income elasticity of demand for food for very low-income and very high-income countries is typically around 0.8 and 0.1, respectively.[11] This would imply that the changes in food demand are much more sensitive to income growth when a country is at its earlier stages of development. Besides changes in the amount of food, per capita income also affects the country's food basket composition, which, in turn, affects the water demand by the agricultural sector. With rising incomes, people tend to buy more expensive foods such as fruits, vegetables, and animal products (meat, dairy, and fish) that are often associated with a higher water footprint. Typically, as per capita consumption of animal products rises, the direct consumption of cereals shrinks while the indirect demand for animal feed increases which, in turn, increases the total demand for cereals.

Figure 7.6 depicts changes in the select food basket of Iranians in 1990 and 2015. Based on long-term averages, wheat (200 kg per capita) has persistently dominated the food basket of Iranians while potatoes (50 kg per capita) and rice (45 kg per capita) constitute the other two major sources of carbohydrates.[12] With a per capita need of 71 kg, tomatoes

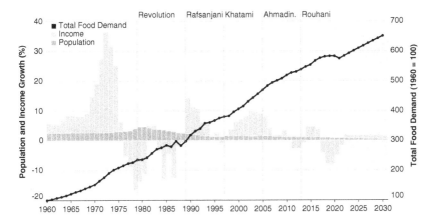

FIGURE 7.7. Estimation of the effects of population and real per capita income growth rates on the aggregate demand for food in Iran. A simple moving average was used to smooth out the real per capita income data. The average income elasticity of demand for food was assumed to vary in the range of 0.7 and 0.4 and scaled inversely with the real per capita income.

Sources: Statistical Yearbooks (1966–2019), Statistical Center of Iran; Economic Time Series Database, Central Bank of Iran (cbi.ir).

have acquired the highest share in the food basket among vegetables. An Iranian individual, on average, uses 20 kg of oil and 26 kg of sugar per year. Among crops that are mainly used for oil extraction and as feed for livestock and poultry, grain maize and soybeans have shown substantial increases in demand since 2000. The aggregate weight and value of the food consumed by Iranians in 2016 were 116 million metric tons and $37 billion, respectively. Based on the expected growth of population and per capita income (Figure 7.7), and future food prices,[13] we project that the total food demand of Iran will reach $46 billion by 2025.

WATER SCARCITY AND FOOD SECURITY

In this section, using recent estimates of total actual renewable water resources (TARWR), we first calculate Iran's water scarcity threshold, which defines the absolute maximum amount of water that can be used sustainably in the country. Subsequently, after accounting for future municipal and industrial water demands as well as potential water savings from investment in technology and infrastructure, we quantify the maximum amount of water left for the agriculture sector. We then introduce our proposed countrywide water scarcity adaptation plan that will bring the

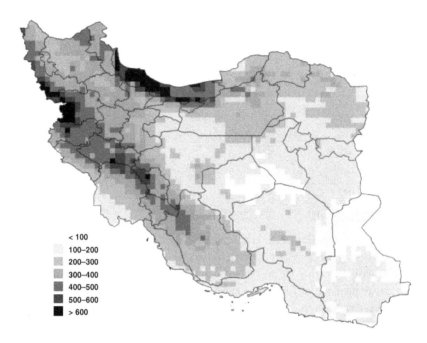

FIGURE 7.8. Long-term average annual precipitation in Iran between 1980 and 2010.

Sources: A. C. Ruane, R. Goldberg, and J. Chryssanthacopoulos, "AgMIP Climate Forcing Datasets for Agricultural Modeling: Merged Products for Gap-Filling and Historical Climate Series Estimation," *Agricultural and Forest Meteorology* 200 (2015).

total water use in Iran to an environmentally sustainable level. Finally, we calculate the amount of reduction in agricultural products as a result of the implementation of the proposed adaptation plan and estimate the associated economic costs both in absolute terms and relative to the future GDP.

Based on data presented in NASA's AgMERRA Climate Forcing Dataset for Agricultural Modeling (as shown in Figure 7.8),[14] the long-term (1980–2010) mean annual precipitation in Iran is about 236 mm (382 billion cubic meters [BCM]), which is consistent with data from precipitation monitoring stations in the country (Figure 7.9).[15] Temporal analysis indicates that the average precipitation has declined by 1.5 mm per year between 1980 and 2010. However, not all regions have been affected to the same degree, with the west and northwest of Iran showing the largest drop in precipitation. In general, about a quarter of the country has experienced a significant decrease in precipitation. Besides this decrease in precipitation, the average annual temperature of Iran has increased

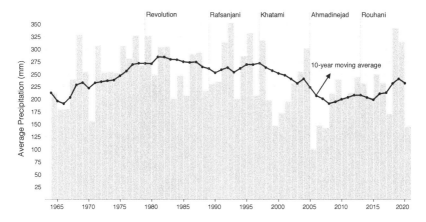

FIGURE 7.9. The average amount of precipitation in Iran between 1965 and 2020.

Sources: Statistical Yearbooks (1966–2019), Statistical Center of Iran; recent statistics published by the Ministry of Energy, Iran.

by 0.4°C per decade, which has given rise to higher water loss through evapotranspiration.[16] As a result of the combined effects of these two factors, the availability of TARWR in Iran, on average, has declined from 125 to 89 BCM[17] (TARWR is defined as the sum of the volumes of surface run-off, groundwater recharge, and the net cross-boundary water). A detailed account of Iran's water balance is provided in Appendix B.

A summary of the underlying assumptions used in this analysis is provided in Table 7.1. Currently, total water consumption in Iran is estimated at 96 BCM, exceeding TARWR by 8%, while to sufficiently mitigate the current water crisis, total freshwater consumption typically should not exceed 60% of TARWR.[18] That is, the total freshwater use should decrease to 53.4 BCM. Due to the higher priority of municipal and industrial water uses, we assumed that irrigated farming would be the only sector subject to reduction in water allocation. Hence, after subtracting future municipal and industrial water uses (12.1 BCM by 2025), 41.3 BCM freshwater will remain for irrigation. However, a proportion of the output loss caused by reduction in irrigation can be recovered by practicing rainfed farming on the affected irrigated lands. We have incorporated this factor in our analysis (see below). Under the proposed adaptation plan, the quantity of Iran's surface outflow will rise to 50 BCM (from primary and secondary sources), and the groundwater recharge and withdrawal will be fully balanced.[19]

TABLE 7.1. Assumptions used in the analysis for a five-year transition period to adapt to water scarcity. See Appendix B for more information on Iran's water balance.

Parameter	Beginning of Transition	End of Transition
Population growth		1% per year
Real per capita income growth		3% per year
Food intake basket		Same as 2015 (Figure 7.7)
Food price index growth		3% per year
TARWR	89 BCM	89 BCM
Total water consumption	96.4 BCM	53.4 BCM
Urban/rural and industrial water use	10.8 BCM	12.1 BCM
Agricultural freshwater use	85.6 BCM	41.7 BCM
Modernized irrigation area	1.6 million ha	3.0 million ha
Greenhouse area	24 k ha	38 k ha
Wastewater treatment and reuse	1.2 BCM	1.5 BCM
Additional water savings or supply		6.9 BCM
Expansion of modernized irrigation	–	4.2 BCM
Improvement of drainage and water transfer	–	1.8 BCM
Expansion of greenhouses	–	0.6 BCM
Additional reclaimed water	–	0.3 BCM
Compensation for set-aside land	–	30% of opportunity cost

In order to accurately evaluate the effects of reduction in agricultural water availability, the potential gains from technology in the future should be taken into account, including modernization of irrigation, expansion of greenhouses, and improvements in drainage systems and water distribution networks.

There is a common belief that adaptation of high-tech irrigation techniques (e.g., drip irrigation) brings about significant water savings by increasing irrigation efficiency, typically from below 50% to over 80%.[20] While such statements can be valid for savings at individual farms, they tend to overlook two unintended consequences that occur at the watershed scale when switching from traditional to modern irrigation. First, part of what is considered to be water loss in traditional irrigation is in fact recoverable and contributes to the environment water by returning to rivers and lakes or by percolating into the ground to recharge aquifers.[21] However, the quality of the return flow from farms is often lower than the primary water used for irrigation (e.g., contaminated with pesticides, fertilizers, and salts). Second, in the absence of physical control of water resources by the government, modernization of irrigation systems naturally leads to the expansion of croplands because, in a water-scarce country such as Iran, as long as water is available there is a tendency to use it. Owing to these commonly overlooked factors, the actual water savings by high-tech irrigation at a basin level is often less than that of individual farms.[22]

About 4 million hectares of irrigated farmlands (including both field crops and orchards) in Iran are deemed suitable for upgrading to modernized irrigation systems with current development occurring at nearly 100,000 hectares per year. The expected water savings from the implementation of modern irrigation systems for each hectare has been estimated at 4,000 cubic meters at the farm level. Based on data reported for the agricultural return flow in Iran (Appendix B), we assume that the basin-level water savings is 75% that of the farm-based estimates (3,000 cubic meters per hectare). Further, based on the recent data published by the Ministry of Agriculture in Iran,[23] we assume that the improvements in drainage (*zehkeshi*) and water transfer and distribution networks would result in an additional water savings of 0.2 BCM per annum.

Expansion of greenhouses could be another development that affects future agricultural water consumption in Iran. Since 2010, the total area of greenhouses in Iran has increased at an average annual rate of about 1,500 hectares to reach 24,000 hectares in 2021. In the analysis presented here, we assume that the rate of expansion of greenhouses will continue at the same rate by the end of the transition period.[24] Assuming 50% reduction in evapotranspiration (ET) and based on the latest data on Iran's crop mix produced in greenhouses (e.g., tomatoes, cucumbers, and peppers),[25] we estimate average water savings per hectare of greenhouse to be about 40,000 cubic meters. Given the above assumptions, we estimate the total additional water supply and savings from future expansions of high-tech irrigation, greenhouses, reclaimed water, and improvement in the drainage and water transfer infrastructure would add 7 BCM to agriculture's available water—implying a total annual allowable water use of 48.5 BCM for farming by the end of the transition period. Therefore, by the end of the transition period of the adaptation plan, the effective water availability for agriculture will be reduced by 43% relative to its current level. The subsequent part of this section explains how such a reduction in agricultural water allotment would affect the amounts, composition, and value of Iran's agricultural output.

It has been reported that 23% and 24% of Iran's total area is under critical and high groundwater stress, respectively.[26] Our analysis indicates that 34% of Iran's existing irrigated land (including both field crops and orchards) is located in areas classified as critical stress, 19% with high stress, and 47% with no or minimal groundwater stress, though these values vary significantly among different provinces (Figure 7.10, top panel). By assessing soil and terrain characteristics of Iran's land, as discussed earlier in this chapter, our analysis also reveals that 19% of Iran's existing irrigated land is located in areas classified as unsuitable, and 33% with very poor suitability (Figure 7.10, bottom panel). To meet the sustainability criteria for water use in our proposed adaptation plan, the exclusion of irrigated land under critical stress took precedence over that with low soil and topography suitability scores.

We followed the steps outlined below to estimate the impact of the adaptation plan on the output from the agriculture sector.

1. We first eliminated irrigated land located at the critical water stress zones (regardless of their land suitability score) to form an initial list of unsustainable irrigated land (UIL). About 34% of irrigated land were removed from production at this stage. However, this amount of reduction in irrigation farming was not sufficient to reduce the water consumption below the scarcity threshold.

2. From the remaining irrigated land, we eliminated land that had the least suitability scores and appended UIL accordingly.

3. For each province, knowing the cultivated area and crop production from irrigated land, we estimated the change in the production of each crop after elimination of the UILs. For example, if 10% of the irrigated land in a province fell within the UIL list, we reduced the irrigation production of each individual crop by 10% and estimated the corresponding reduction in water consumption. If the reduction in the total water use was still not enough, step 2 was repeated by adding more unsuitable land to the UIL list.

4. Finally, using crop simulation models,[27] we estimated the rainfed yields of wheat, barley, and chickpea as the potentially proper rainfed crops to be cultivated on the eliminated UILs (Figure 7.11). These crops constitute the vast majority of rainfed farming in Iran. Then, for each point, based on the relative producers' price,[28] we identified the best performing crop for rainfed farming in terms of economic return[29] and added the potential additional production of these crops to the existing rainfed production values.

The results obtained by pursuing the above procedure are listed in Table 7.2. Overall, once the adaptation plan is in full effect, we project

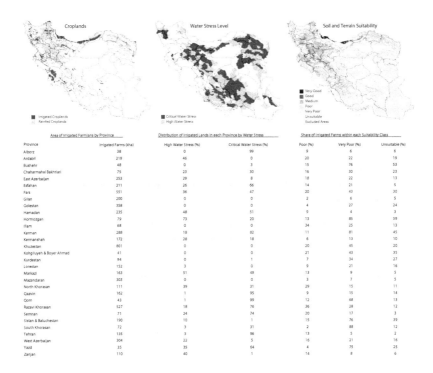

FIGURE 7.10. Maps of irrigated and rainfed cropland, water stress by study zone, and land suitability for agriculture. The table provides a breakdown of data by province.

Sources: Mohsen B. Mesgaran and Pooya Azadi, "A National Adaptation Plan for Water Scarcity in Iran," Working Paper 6, Stanford Iran 2040 Project, Stanford University, August 2018; Map of the Status of Iran's Underground Water at Sub-basin Level, Ministry of Energy, 2017; M. K. Gumma et al., "NASA Making Earth System Data Records for Use in Research Environments (MEaSUREs) Global Food Security-support Analysis Data (GFSAD) Cropland Extent 2015 South Asia, Afghanistan, Iran 30 m V001" [Data set]. NASA EOSDIS Land Processes DAAC, 2017.

Maps top: Croplands (Irrigated Croplands, Rainfed Croplands); Water Stress Level (Critical Water Stress, High Water Stress); Soil and Terrain Suitability (Very Good, Good, Medium, Poor, Very Poor, Unsuitable, Excluded Areas).

	Area of Irrigated Farmlands by Province	Distribution of Irrigated Lands in each Province by Water Stress		Share of Irrigated Farms within each Suitability Class		
Province	Irrigated Farms (kha)	High Water Stress (%)	Critical Water Stress (%)	Poor (%)	Very Poor (%)	Unsuitable (%)
Alborz	38	0	99	9	6	6
Ardabil	219	46	0	20	22	19
Bushehr	48	0	3	15	76	53
Chaharmahal Bakhtiari	75	23	30	16	30	23
East Azerbaijan	253	29	8	18	22	13
Esfahan	211	26	66	14	21	5
Fars	551	36	47	20	43	30
Gilan	200	0	0	2	6	5
Golestan	358	0	0	4	27	24
Hamadan	235	48	51	9	4	3
Hormozgan	79	73	20	13	85	59
Ilam	68	0	0	34	25	13
Kerman	288	18	82	11	81	45
Kermanshah	172	28	18	6	13	10
Khuzestan	801	0	0	20	45	20
Kohgiluyeh & Boyer Ahmad	41	0	0	21	43	35
Kurdestan	94	0	1	7	34	27
Lorestan	152	3	0	9	21	16
Markazi	163	51	49	13	9	5
Mazandaran	303	0	0	3	7	5
North Khorasan	111	39	31	29	15	11
Qazvin	162	1	95	9	15	14
Qom	43	1	99	12	68	13
Razavi Khorasan	527	18	76	36	28	12
Semnan	71	24	74	20	17	3
Sistan & Baluchestan	190	10	1	15	76	39
South Khorasan	72	3	31	2	88	12
Tehran	135	3	96	13	5	2
West Azerbaijan	304	22	5	16	21	16
Yazd	35	35	64	4	75	25
Zanjan	110	40	1	14	8	6

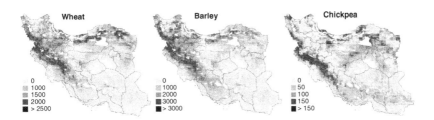

Wheat: 0, 1000, 1500, 2000, > 2500
Barley: 0, 1000, 2000, 3000, > 3000
Chickpea: 0, 50, 100, 150, > 150

FIGURE 7.11. Estimation of the average yields of rainfed wheat, barley, and chickpeas as three of the main rainfed agricultural products of Iran.

Sources: Mohsen B. Mesgaran and Pooya Azadi, "A National Adaptation Plan for Water Scarcity in Iran," Working Paper 6, Stanford Iran 2040 Project, Stanford University, August 2018.

TABLE 7.2. Changes in agricultural production after the implementation of the water scarcity adaptation plan.

Crop	Irrigated (kilo tonne) 2016	Irrigated (kilo tonne) Post-adaptation	Rainfed (kilo tonne) 2016	Rainfed (kilo tonne) Post-adaptation	Net Change (wt%)
Alfalfa	5894	3048	148	148	−47
Barley	2355	934	1369	2166	−17
Beans	229	148	1	1	−35
Chickpea	17	8	255	298	+12
Clover	270	193	230	230	−15
Cotton	159	67	2	2	−57
Cucumber	1672	805	9	9	−52
Fruits	19661	9190	1346	1346	−50
Grain corn	1171	669	0	0	−43
Lentil	9	5	74	74	−5
Melon	1477	522	13	13	−64
Onion	2395	1172	6	6	−51
Other crops	184	114	4	4	−37
Other fodders	2591	1397	255	255	−42
Other legumes	69	48	18	18	−24
Other oil crops	64	45	5	5	−27
Other summer crops	731	280	52	52	−58
Other vegetables	3667	1885	122	122	−47
Potato	4984	2817	11	11	−43
Rapeseed	55	34	13	13	−31
Rice	2921	2544	0	0	−13
Safflower	5	2	0	0	−64
Sesame	35	14	2	2	−58
Silage corn	11277	4462	39	39	−60
Soybean	124	97	16	16	−19
Sugar beet	5966	3413	0	0	−43
Sugarcane	7480	6014	0	0	−20
Sunflower	10	7	3	3	−24
Tobacco	21	11	0	0	−48
Tomato	5807	2551	21	21	−56
Watermelon	3905	1864	188	188	−50
Wheat	8843	5046	5749	6485	−21
Total	94049	49405	9950	11526	−41

that the weight and added value of Iran's agricultural production would shrink by 41% and 44%, respectively. However, not all crops will be affected equally. The production of wheat, barley, and rice will contract by only 21%, 17%, and 13%, respectively. In contrast to the staple crops, the production of less strategic products such as vegetables and summer crops will slump by some 50%.

In the rest of this chapter, we estimate the costs of our proposed adaptation plan as related to the development of modern irrigation systems and greenhouse structures. Typically, the capital costs of greenhouse construction is in the range of $100,000 to $500,000 per hectare depending on the type and available facilities. Considering an average cost of $300,000 per hectare and an average life expectancy of twenty years, the annual depreciation costs associated with the additional greenhouse farms to be built in the future are approximately $15,000 per hectare. Similarly, assuming a capital cost of construction of $1,800 per hectare and a life expectancy of fifteen years, the annual depreciation costs associated with high-tech irrigation are estimated at $120 per hectare. Therefore, an annual capital investment of $530 million is needed to maintain the additionally installed greenhouse capacity (24,000 ha) and high-tech irrigation (1.4 million ha) in the long run. Finally, there is no doubt that the losers of the proposed paradigm shift will need to be compensated as they will otherwise oppose any change. To this end, compensation equal to 30% of the opportunity cost of farming was assumed to be paid to the affected farmers for their set-aside land. The net additional expenditures on agricultural products are defined as the sum of Iran's net international trade of foodstuffs and the annual costs associated with maintenance of additional installed greenhouses and high-tech irrigation systems, plus the compensation paid to the farmers for the set-aside land. Iran's future GDP growth rate (including the impact of a reduction in agricultural activities) is assumed to be 3% per year. Since the consequences of reducing agricultural activities involve predominantly lower groundwater withdrawal and allocation of more surface water to the environment, the issues related to the quality of water were not considered in this study.[30]

The results of the analysis in terms of economic costs under the two scenarios of business as usual and the proposed adaptation plan are presented in Figure 7.12. We project that, while Iran's agricultural trade deficit under the business-as-usual scenario will remain in the range of $5–10 billion in the medium term, the annual costs associated with the

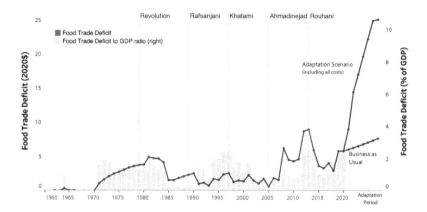

FIGURE 7.12. Historical trends and projections of future agricultural trade deficit (imports minus exports) under business as usual and adaptation scenario outlined in this chapter in constant 2020$ (left axis) and relative to GDP (right axis).

Sources: Mohsen B. Mesgaran and Pooya Azadi, "A National Adaptation Plan for Water Scarcity in Iran," Working Paper 6, Stanford Iran 2040 Project, Stanford University, August 2018.

adaptation plan, which include agricultural trade deficits and depreciation of additional equipment, will reach $25 billion by the end of its transition period. After the transition period, annual expenditures will rise at a smaller rate. Similarly, the ratio of adaptation costs to the GDP (Figure 7.12) will peak at 5.5% by the end of the transition period before it declines again with future economic growth. However, if the current trend in agricultural production continues, the ratio of food imports to GDP will likely decline in the long run because the growth rate of the economy will outstrip the rise in food demand. (Note that the income elasticity of demand for food (n) will decrease as the real per capita income (pci) rises.)

To put the implications of the proposed adaptation plan into context, we compare the ratio of food imports to GDP for a number of countries with different levels of income and water availability (Figure 7.13). Over the past decades, trade of foodstuff among countries has substantially expanded, and as a result, global food security has improved. In the meantime, the national agricultural policies aimed at maintaining a high degree of food self-sufficiency have been replaced by those that seek to maximize benefits from the country's comparative advantages. Although the share of agriculture in the economy decreases as a country becomes more developed, countries with higher income generally need to spend

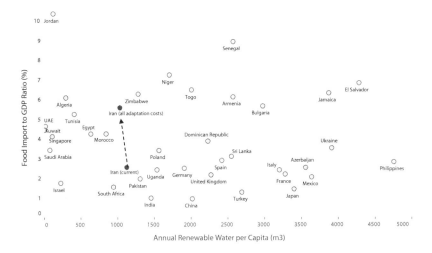

FIGURE 7.13. The ratio of food imports to GDP (2016) versus total annual renewable water per capita for selected countries with annual TARWR of less than 4,000 cubic meters per capita.

Sources: Aquastat Database, Food and Agriculture Organization of the United Nations; Countries GDP per Capita, World Bank Open Data, World Bank Group; Countries Trade of Food, World Integrated Trade Solutions (witz.worldbank.org).

smaller shares of their income on the import of foods from abroad.[31] It is expected that the adaptation plan outlined in this study will increase Iran's ratio of food import to GDP from its current level of 2.5% to 5.5%— which will still be well within a reasonable range considering Iran's per capita income level and water availability. Beyond the transition period, however, the ratio could decline if the economy grows at a reasonable rate.

Finally, we note that changes to the agriculture sector of Iran, whether part of an adaptation plan or simply an inadvertent consequence of lack of water for farming, could affect the well-being and distribution of millions of people living in rural areas. As discussed in chapter 2, about three-quarters of Iranians live in urban areas (roughly 430 cities or *shahrestans*), and one quarter live in rural areas (about 2,600 rural agglomerations or *dehestans*). Currently, about 6.4 million people, equivalent to 31% of Iran's rural population, live in areas known to have a critical condition with regard to groundwater stress, and another 4.0 million people live in rural areas experiencing high levels of groundwater stress (Figure 7.14). This means that Iran's water crisis could cause a massive redistribution of the population from the rural parts of the water-scarce regions toward the cities.

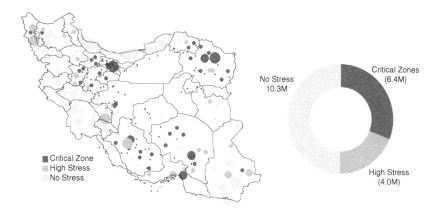

FIGURE 7.14. Distribution of Iran's rural population by groundwater stress level.

Sources: The 2016 Census Data, Statistical Center of Iran; Map of the Status of Iran's Underground Water at Sub-basin Level, Ministry of Energy, 2017.

SUMMARY

Over the past decade, Iran's water crisis has morphed into a new paradigm with its impacts now visible in the daily lives of millions of people. The underlying reasons that contributed to the genesis and exacerbation of this crisis are:

- The country's large and growing population
- Increased per capita food demand, especially for water-intensive crops, due to increase in per capita income
- Insufficient job creation in other sectors to absorb farmers, which has raised the social costs associated with potentially restrictive measures aimed at reducing farming activities
- Decades of irresponsible and ideologized policies that have advocated and incentivized food self-sufficiency as one of the main pillars for the country's independence
- Poor water resource management and governance with bias in favor of increasing water supply while making little effort to improve consumption efficiency. This is in part due to the presence of strong interest groups and corruption in the system that allowed for the construction of many unnecessary dams from the public budget while overlooking the development of several hundred thousand illegal water wells

- An increase in average temperature and decrease in average precipitation, both likely due to climate change

Today, the share of the environment from the total renewable water in the country has reached such low levels that diverting water from the environment has no additional capacity to alleviate water deficits in other sectors. Henceforth, the system represents a nearly zero-sum situation where a mere geographical or sectoral redistribution of the country's water endowment will only relocate the pain from one point to another within the system. The longer the situation persists, the interregional or intersectoral disputes over water rights that have occurred recently will become more frequent.

As long as water is available in Iran, there will be a tendency to use it. Therefore, restoring a sustainable balance in the supply and demand of water in Iran cannot be achieved without physical control of water resources by the government. Once the government is able to enforce a cap on the amount of water to be consumed, implementation of more efficient allocation rules and high-tech irrigation should be considered as supplementary steps. It is important to realize that without physical control of water by the government, the use of high-tech irrigation could in fact lead to an increase in water consumption, as the irrigated areas can expand when upgrading from traditional irrigation to high-tech irrigation. Further, the losers of the proposed paradigm shift will certainly need to be compensated from the public budget as they will otherwise oppose any reform.

Due to its high capital costs, enormous energy consumption, and massive environmental footprint, desalination (for purposes other than providing urban water) is ruled out as a potential solution to Iran's water crisis at large. Therefore, Iran's water scarcity problem should be addressed through a combination of water productivity gain (e.g., modernized irrigation), selective termination of some water-intensive activities, and an increased use of reclaimed water. The proposition presented in this chapter indicates that the potential gain from enhancement of agricultural water productivity (output per drop) in Iran, estimated at about 7 billion cubic meters (BCM), is not sufficient to fundamentally change the calculus given that about 44 BCM of water needs to be saved. Therefore, the ultimate resolution, to a large extent, should rely on reduced water allotments to agriculture. We estimate that an adaptation to water scarcity requires an additional annual spending of $300 per capita (2020$) on food imports and other costs. The total value of the imported foods (virtual water) will roughly equal a maximum of 5.5% of Iran's expected future GDP level in the next decade.

Given the realities of the water and soil landscape of Iran, we conclude that the hope for a high level of self-sufficiency in the long run is elusive. Instead of self-sufficiency, policymakers should make it their primary goal to ensure the nation's food security, which can be achieved by boosting other sectors of the economy to allow for the import of more food. Furthermore, the pronatalist agenda seeking to increase the total fertility rate above the current level, which is indeed close to the replacement level, should be abandoned as it will only exacerbate the ongoing water shortage and risk the food security of future generations. In order for policymakers to make informed decisions, experts and researchers should develop a modern water governance structure for Iran that encompasses a detailed spatial and temporal account of water availability at various scales, the maximum allowable use, and fair and economically viable water distribution among various stakeholders. Of particular importance is the determination of regional crop patterns optimized for water use, the suitability of climate, and economic profitability. Experts should therefore devote their efforts to research and outreach activities that produce tangible outcomes. They should also clearly and truthfully explain the realities of the matter to the policymakers and the public and avoid populist statements (e.g., "saving both agriculture and water is possible") to help develop a national plan to address the formidable water crisis facing Iran.

8

MIGRATION AND BRAIN DRAIN

IN THIS CHAPTER, we present trends in the international migration of Iranians and discuss their underlying causes and ramifications for the future of Iran. Our analysis is based on a dataset compiled from statistics published by national governments and international agencies. Additionally, we developed a classification algorithm to identify scholars of Iranian descent working in foreign countries through analyzing global publication records of the past decades.

While some of the underlying causes of Iran's brain drain are shared among most developing countries (e.g., lower wages compared to more developed economies), many of the main drivers of migration from Iran have roots in the unique sociopolitical landscape of the country. The regime's formal stance on the issue of elite migration has been in stark contrast with its de facto policies and actions. On the one hand, given the large number of dissidents among those who decide to leave the country, the regime considers migration as a blessing which purges problematic citizens and improves its political stability in the long run. On the other hand, in authoritarian regimes such as the Islamic Republic where elections and polls are devoid of true meaning, migration is commonly interpreted as an indicator of the level of dissatisfaction and hopelessness across different segments of society; therefore, while the regime does not consider brain drain as an important threat, it is nevertheless sensitive to public perception of the issue and, as such, downplays the magnitude and consequences of the ongoing brain drain crisis.

Herein, we seek to shed light on the extent, causes, and implications of migration and brain drain from Iran. To this end, we first present trends in the flow and stock of Iranian migrants with an emphasis on trends in the number of Iranian students and scholars abroad. We then explain the structural forces that collectively shape the decisions of Iranians to migrate. Finally, we discuss the extent to which the migration of highly educated people can affect the stock of human capital and the outlook of the country.

TRENDS IN MIGRATION FROM IRAN

The trend in the total stock of migrants and the migrant-to-population ratio of Iran over the past half-century are shown in Figure 8.1. According to the compiled data, the total number of Iranian migrants (including nonpermanent) increased from about 130,000 in 1970 to 480,000 in 1978, spiked to 830,000 in 1979, and then continuously increased to 3.1 million in 2019. In the meantime, the migrant-to-population ratio of Iran also steadily increased from approximately 0.5% in 1970, to 1.3% in 1978, to 2.2% in 1979, and finally to 3.8% in 2019. Since 1979, the annual flow of migrants from Iran has averaged about 63,000 people, with the largest spikes occurring in 1979, 2010, and 2016; see Appendix C for more detailed information about the annual number of migrants from Iran.

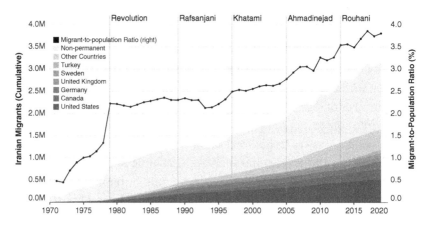

FIGURE 8.1. Trends in the stock of Iranian migrants (left axis) and the migrant-to-population ratio (right axis).

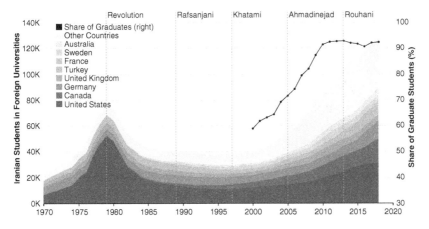

FIGURE 8.2. Number of Iranian-born students (excluding second-generation Iranians) in foreign countries (left axis) and share of graduate students among Iranian international students in the US (right axis).

The countries hosting the largest number of Iranian migrants in 2019 include the United States (32%), Canada (14%), Germany (11%), the United Kingdom (6%), Sweden (5%), and Turkey (5%). The data also reveals that, in rough terms, for every five Iranian migrants, three persons have migrated by obtaining permanent residency status or a work permit abroad, one person through university admission, and another person by being granted asylum. We also found that, since 1979, about 90% of Iranian migrants in the United States who meet eligibility requirements for naturalization have already become US citizens (see Appendix C for more detailed data on migration of Iranians to the United States).

Figure 8.2 depicts trends in the number of Iranian-born university students enrolled in foreign universities between 1970 and 2018. These values include both Iranian international students (who were on a student visa) and Iranian-born students who had already emigrated prior to enrollment at a university (hence were not considered as international students in their host countries). Assuming an average duration of study of four years to obtain a degree (see Appendix C), which in turn can be used to calculate the number of unique students from the enrollment data shown in Figure 8.2, we estimate that a total of about 700,000 Iranian-born individuals have attended foreign universities by 2019. The trend in the number of these students has shown three distinct phases: (1) the decade prior to the 1979 revolution, in which the number of enrolled students rose rapidly, reaching a peak of about 75,000; (2) the first two decades after the revolution, in which the number of enrolled students dropped sharply, ultimately stabilizing at around 40,000; and (3) the early 2000s to 2019, in which the number of students has increased steadily to reach an unprecedented level of about 130,000. Along with these variations in the number of students, some important characteristics have also significantly changed over time:

- During the 1970s, due to the rapid development and industrialization of Iran and the limited capacity of higher education in the country, graduates of foreign universities were in high demand and hence motivated to return home.[1] In contrast, an overwhelming majority of graduates from foreign universities remain abroad today. For example, among Iranian students in the United States, the tendency to return to Iran after graduation has declined from as much as 90% in 1979 to less than 10% in 2019,[2] which corresponds to the lowest rate of return among students of all nationalities in the United States.

- The share of students at the graduate level has dramatically surged over the past decades. For example, the share of graduate students among Iranian international students in the United States increased from 55% in 1979 to 92% in 2019.[3]

- As more Iranian families have migrated over time, the number of Iranian-born students who were residing abroad prior to university has increased accordingly. This group is typically more assimilated to their host countries compared to their parents or peers who migrated after admission to a foreign university at the postgraduate level.

Figure 8.3 illustrates trends in the number of Iranian diaspora scholars who published one or more papers in any given year between 1970 and 2019. As shown, in the decades leading to 2000, there was a steady but slow growth in the number of Iranian scholars abroad. However, since the early 2000s, this number has risen dramatically, corresponding with the substantial increase in the number of Iranian students in foreign countries as described above. A similar trend has been reported for the number of patents published by Iranian-Americans,[4] which reinforces the same conclusion regarding the rate of acceleration of brain drain from Iran that one can draw from the trends in the number of Iranian diaspora scholars.

To date, the cumulative number of Iranian scholars with an affiliation outside Iran exceeds 110,000. Based on the authors' latest affiliations,

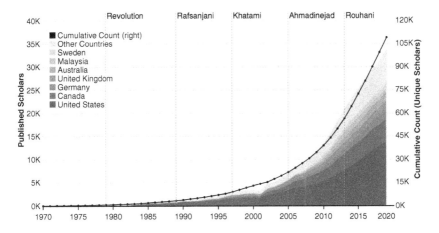

FIGURE 8.3. Number of Iranian diaspora scholars who published at least one article between 1970 and 2019. The total number of unique researchers is approximately 110,000. Based on data from Scopus.

Sources: Scopus Abstract and Citation Database, www.scopus.com, accessed January 2020.

we estimate that only about 2% of these researchers have returned to Iran, which is consistent with the official statistics of faculty recruitment in Iran[5] (see Appendix C for more information about the shares of foreign-educated individuals in academic and high-level government positions). In rough terms, this figure corresponds to one-third of Iran's total human resources in research based on head count and, arguably, a far greater share of that is based on productivity and influence. The countries that host the largest number of Iranian scholars are the United States, Canada, Germany, and the United Kingdom. Figure 8.4 illustrates the geographical distribution of all scholars of Iranian descent affiliated with universities and research institutions in foreign countries since 1980.

Since the 1979 revolution, nearly one million Iranians have fled the country and sought asylum elsewhere, with the largest number of claims filed in Germany, the United States, Turkey, and the United Kingdom (Figure 8.5). Iranian refugees are made up of a wide range of individuals, including political dissidents, social activists, artists, ethnic and religious minorities, and LGBTQ[6] individuals. Regrettably, many among the rejected and, to a lesser extent, recognized cases of asylum seekers are simply opportunists and pretenders whose real motivations are economic rather than fear of prosecution. What persuades these diverse groups of people to embark on uncertain and possibly irreversible and dangerous

FIGURE 8.4. The estimated number of scholars of Iranian descent affiliated with universities and research institutions in foreign countries between 1980 and 2019. Based on data from Scopus.
Sources: Scopus Abstract and Citation Database, www.scopus.com, accessed January 2020.

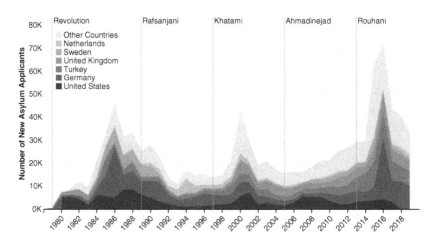

FIGURE 8.5. Number of new Iranian asylum applications filed between 1980 and 2019.

journeys to seek asylum elsewhere is primarily the Iranian government's violation of human rights and various forms of discrimination and repression which can be in the form of brutal or even life-threatening violence.

The trend in the number of Iranian asylum seekers after the revolution shows three distinct peaks. The first peak—occurring between 1984 and

1991, climaxing in 1986—was primarily due to the impact of the Iran-Iraq War and the consolidation of power in the Islamic Republic which was achieved with harsh crackdowns on political opposition. About a decade later, there was a second surge in the number of asylum seekers, which lasted for two years from 1999 to 2001. The surge in the number of Iranian asylum seekers during this period was partly due to ease of travel to Bosnia, which did not require a visa at the time.[7]

The student protests of 1999 (known as the *Kouye-e-Daneshgah* protests), which were the first widespread and violent uprisings in nearly two decades, could be one reason behind the increase in the number of asylum seekers in ensuing years. The third large wave of asylum seekers from Iran began in the aftermath of the 2009 presidential election which turned into an even bloodier protest than the student protests a decade earlier. The early 2010s also marked the beginning of a long period of economic stagnation which has lasted to date. The current wave culminated in 2016 when as many as 70,000 Iranians applied for asylum status. Of about a million Iranians who have applied for asylum since 1980, about one-third have been granted asylum while the remainder have been denied for failing to demonstrate that their fear of persecution is well founded.

DRIVERS OF MIGRATION

In this section, we provide an overview of the multitude of factors that collectively shape the environment in which Iranians make their migration decisions and discuss how these structural forces may evolve in the future. The push-pull theory of migration explains the start and continuation of migration flows over time based on the disparities between the place of origin and the destination, which could encompass a wide range of economic, environmental, demographic, social, and political factors. Depending on how they impact people's migration decisions, the drivers of migration can be categorized into four broad groups, namely predisposing, proximate, precipitating, and mediating.[8] As we will explain shortly, these drivers vary not only in terms of their ability to trigger and actualize migration—spanning from root causes to triggers to catalysts—but also in terms of how long their influence lasts.

Predisposing drivers, such as income disparities between developing and developed countries, are slow-moving factors which typically form the context for migration over multiple decades. Proximate drivers are those that, compared with predisposing factors, evolve over relatively

TABLE 8.1. Major drivers of migration from Iran.

Category	Drivers of Migration
Predisposing (evolve over very long term)	Lower per capita income compared to advanced economies
	Social and political repression, violation of human rights, and religious persecution
	Low quality of education compared to the developed countries
	Rise of labor mobility, urbanization, individualism, and secularism
Proximate (evolve over long term)	Economic stagnation, chronic unemployment, and bleak economic outlook
	Decay of government institutions (state, the rule of law, and accountability)
	Loss of social capital, prevalence of endemic corruption and crime
	Environmental challenges in large cities, particularly air pollution
Precipitating (events)	Iran-Iraq War, 1980–1988
	Academic cleansing program (officially cultural revolution) of 1980–1983
	Government crackdown on dissent and protests of 1999, 2009, 2017–2018, and 2019
	Major economic sanctions imposed in 2012 and 2018
	State's poor responses to natural disasters in recent years
	Monetary shocks (bouts of currency devaluation, very high inflation)
Mediating (catalysts)	Increase in internet penetration
	Increase in number of friends and family abroad

shorter periods and more directly affect migration decisions. Examples of proximate factors include periods of economic stagnation, chronic environmental issues such as water shortages and air pollution, and intensification of social and political repression over several years. Precipitating drivers are those that are linked to specific events that could trigger migration, such as natural disasters, war, financial crises, and government crackdowns. Finally, mediating factors are those that facilitate or restrict migration, such as means of transportation, consular services, and the availability of information about the benefits and drawbacks of migration from family or community networks. We note that these structural forces should not be viewed as deterministic factors that lead people to a certain decision about migration. Instead, they should be considered as an array of factors whose dynamic interplay increases the likelihood of a given decision over another. Table 8.1 provides a list of the drivers of migration in Iran for each of the four classes discussed above.

Predisposing Factors

The term *predisposing factors* is used to refer to the structural forces that affect migration decisions but are static or change very slowly

over time. The income disparity between Iran and destination countries is, arguably, the most important among these factors. Over the
past decades, the per capita income in advanced economies (e.g., the
United States and Canada) and popular destinations in the developing world for Iranian migrants (e.g., Turkey and Malaysia) have been
approximately ten times and three times larger than that of Iran, respectively. Similar gaps exist in the quality of education, particularly
at the postgraduate level.

The Iranian government's social and political repression and human
rights violations constitute other important predisposing factors that
motivate migration across different social classes. Lack of democratic
institutions (e.g., free and multiparty elections), crackdowns on civil
society, the mandatory hijab, pressure on religious minorities, draconian
interventions in relationships between men and women, and homophobia
are some embodiments of this issue.

Another important predisposing factor that has slowly, but fundamentally, changed the migration landscape in Iran is social mobilization, a term that refers to a cluster of changes in the society such as
the reproductive behavior, education, urbanization, exposure to mass
media, and mobility of labor which typically occur around the same
time for each nation.[9] A sharp decline in the fertility rate in Iran,
which started in the mid-1980s (see chapter 2), ushered in a new era
of parenting where the amount of time and money that parents could
spend per child increased significantly. Analogous to the concept of
capital investment, the increased level of per child expenditures on
education and training, as the most important investments in human
capital, has pushed the current generation of Iranian youth to higher
educational attainments compared to their previous counterparts,
and, the higher the educational attainments, the higher the international transferability. The increase in the effective costs of raising
a child (e.g., on education), in turn, further accelerated the fertility
decline in the country. Another predisposing factor which paved the
way for larger migration flows from (and within) Iran is related to the
country's move over the past century from a Malthusian equilibrium
and agrarian economy to an urbanized population where the majority
of the labor is in industry or service sectors and more mobile compared to the past, hence more susceptible to migration if warranted
by other factors.

Proximate Factors

Compared to the wage gap that exists between Iran and the developed world (which was discussed under predisposing factors), changes in individual income levels during cycles of economic expansion and contraction more directly affect migration decisions, and, hence, are classified as a proximate factor. Four distinct trends can be identified in historical per capita income in Iran (chapter 4): a sharp increase in the 1970s which was, to a large extent, due to oil windfalls; a sharp decline during the 1980s; a slow recovery through the mid-2000s; and stagnation since around 2005. As discussed earlier, major macroeconomic imbalances and deviations from normal conditions, such as the country's low investment, large public debt, and water scarcity, and a looming financial crisis, along with policy and political uncertainties, depict a bleak outlook for output growth in the foreseeable future. Today, an overwhelming majority of Iranians believe that their standard of living will not improve under the business-as-usual scenario in the Islamic Republic. Prolonged sluggish economic growth and poor economic prospects are among the most important drivers of migration in the past decade, especially for the highly educated elites who have a longer planning horizon and have more resources to cope with the uncertainties of migration.

In addition to economic factors, decay of the rule of law and democratic accountability (i.e., the political institutions that limit and check power) since the early 2000s has gradually led to a loss of state capacity and legitimacy, the spread of corruption, and the erosion of social capital, resulting in a state of hopelessness prevalent in Iranian society today.

Since they deteriorate the quality of life, critical and persistent environmental issues can be part of the calculus when people evaluate the potential risks and benefits of migration. Among the most significant of these issues for Iranians are the extreme air pollution in metropolitan areas and the water scarcity that is faced by most parts of the country. While the effect of air pollution in pushing people to migrate is not as significant as other economic and sociopolitical factors, it could be an impediment to the return of the migrants.[10] Iran's water scarcity, which is gradually becoming a full-fledged environmental crisis, has thus far only caused internal displacement of the population from water-stressed villages to nearby cities and other regions, but has not contributed significantly to international migration from the country. However, if the problem persists, the water crisis can potentially generate a flow of environmental refugees in the future.

Precipitating Factors

In contrast to predisposing and proximate factors that are embedded in the economic, social, and political landscapes, precipitating factors are linked to identifiable events that directly influence the migration decisions of individuals and households. Figure 8.6 displays a timeline of these events which begins with the volatile and hostile political atmosphere after the 1979 revolution and the eight-year war with Iraq. These events not only led to a flux of migrants and asylum seekers toward Europe and North America, but also caused massive internal displacement (from the western to central provinces in the case of the war).

Another important event which gave rise to the migration of university professors and their families from Iran was the regime's cultural revolution (1980–1983), which was an effort toward Islamification of universities through academic cleansing and modification of curricula.[11] In addition to the dire consequences of expelling some of the most qualified professors (which was followed by the recruitment of new faculty members based on commitment to the ideology of the revolution rather than merits), the ability of Iranian universities to contribute to the development of the country has been undermined by the short-sightedness of the state's research policies (see chapter 9), outdated and ineffective curricula, and a hostile environment for those who criticize the status quo. These issues play an important role in persuading many academics to pursue their career goals in a foreign country.

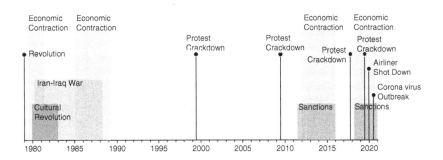

FIGURE 8.6. Major precipitating drivers of migration from Iran since 1979.

Other precipitating events that are among the causes of large flows of migrants from Iran were the government's crackdowns on major protests during the past two decades. These events include the crackdowns on the student protests in 1999 (*Kouy-e-Daneshgah*), the presidential election Green Movement protests in 2009, the protests in 2017–2018, and the protests in 2019 which were triggered by a spike in gasoline prices. The government's reactions to these four events became successively more violent, causing higher rates of posttraumatic stress in Iranian society.

The economic sanctions imposed on Iran in 2012 and 2018 in response to its nuclear program were among the most significant events of the past decade affecting the decision to migrate in a number of different ways. First, the sanctions exacerbated Iran's economic challenges by reducing government revenue, increasing international transaction costs, and, in some cases, disrupting industrial production by interrupting the supply of imported intermediate goods. Sanctions also intensify the sense of hopelessness, as no democratic path exists for the Iranian people to influence policies that led to the imposition of the sanctions in the first place, or to influence the regime's subsequent reaction to resolve the issue. Finally, by creating an uncertain atmosphere, the sanctions have changed people's financial behavior by disincentivizing investment in the real economy and incentivizing conversion of savings to foreign currencies or other liquid stores of value, which over time loosen the economic ties of people to the country and increase their international mobility.

Besides the impact of sanctions and the sluggishness of the real sector of the economy, sporadic financial shocks—manifesting in high inflation and periods of steep currency devaluation—can also be classified as precipitating events that trigger migration. These shocks primarily stem from the state's politically driven and dysfunctional monetary policy and cause widespread social frustration by shrinking the real value of savings and disrupting the financial plans of individuals and firms.

Mediating Factors

We have thus far laid out the structural forces and precipitating events that have shaped the atmosphere for migration in Iran over the past half century. However, in addition to the migration drivers discussed above, there are other intervening factors that function as the infrastructure for migration, both figuratively and literally. They play an important role in creating aspirations for, and the actualization of, migration. Financial resources to cover the costs of migration, the presence and quality of means of transportation, and access to information about the migration process and the country of destination are among the most important mediating factors affecting migration decisions. Lack of such resources is one of the key reasons that the poor, particularly the poorest of the poor, constitute a very small share of migrants, despite having more economic incentives for migration than the middle class and wealthy individuals.[12]

The improvements in the availability, specificity, and reliability of information regarding the various steps of migration and its potential outcomes for the would-be migrants are profoundly transforming the migration landscape and culture in Iran. This is due to the increasing trends in the stock of current migrants (the cascade effect) and improved access to means of communication, particularly the internet. The rise in the share of the population living abroad (Figure 8.1) means that the current generation of would-be migrants in Iran has significantly larger networks of friends and family abroad, while the drastic rise in the penetration of internet and social media over the past few years has boosted routine interactions between migrants and their friends and family in Iran. These firsthand routine interactions with familiar persons help eliminate some of the uncertainties surrounding different facets of migration, hence increasing the likelihood of future migrations from the country.

Figure 8.7 illustrates trends in passengers on international flights leaving Iran (as a share of population) and the mobile internet penetration in the country as proxies for degree of direct exposure to information about other countries. As shown in this figure, the relative size of the outbound passengers from Iran increased from 0.3% of the population in 1980 to 6.0% in 2018. These passengers typically include Iranian tourists to other countries, foreign tourists to Iran, Iranian migrants returning abroad after visiting Iran, and new migrants leaving the country (which is only a small percentage of the outbound passengers). In the meantime, the rise in internet penetration, which occurred slowly during the 2000s before accelerating in the 2010s, helped break the state's de facto monopoly on the media and enabled people to learn about life and opportunities in other countries. The more frequent communications of recent years between Iranians inside the country and their growing networks of friends and family abroad have played an important role in shaping the culture of migration in Iran.

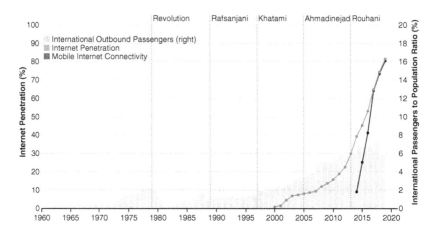

FIGURE 8.7. Iran's internet penetration and high-speed mobile broadband (left axis) and ratio of international passengers on outbound flights to population (right axis).

Sources: Iran's Statistical Yearbooks of 1965–2016, Statistical Center of Iran; ICT Statistics, International Telecommunication Union, accessed January–March 2020.

IMPLICATIONS AND OUTLOOK

Having explained the main trends and underlying drivers of migration, particularly those pertinent to the migration of highly educated and skilled persons, we now discuss the implications of brain drain and the potential role that the Iranian diaspora community could play in shaping the future of Iran. As mentioned earlier, while the government of Iran perceives migration of elites as a phenomenon which contributes positively to its political stability, due to public sensitivity surrounding the issue, it downplays the adverse effects of brain drain in its formal stance and rhetoric. The data presented in the previous sections indicate that, contrary to the regime's depiction, the current and forecasted trends of brain drain from Iran are, in fact, formidable. Over the past few decades, the governance deadlock and the decay of political and economic institutions have overshadowed Iran's brain-drain crisis. The state's dominance in the economy and the prevalence of corruption and lucrative opportunities for rent-seeking activities have, for decades, kept the return on education and entrepreneurship in Iran low. In turn, this low return on education and entrepreneurship, combined with the influx of graduates from low-quality higher education institutions (which were hastily created to temporarily curb unemployment), and the unmeritocratic practice of recruitment and promotion in government and state-owned enterprises, have significantly reduced the opportunity costs associated with migration, especially for the highly educated.

Over the past decade, Iran has struggled with the compounding effects of multiple profound crises that can only be addressed by the type and depth of reforms that are politically infeasible for the regime. It is therefore likely that all predisposing and proximate factors listed in Table 8.1 will remain in place or intensify in the foreseeable future. These structural issues will likely be augmented by various forms of shock (i.e., precipitating factors) which will in turn create an even larger desire for migration. However, if and when future political breakthroughs stop Iran's current downward spiral and pave the way for fundamental changes in governance, the diaspora will be able to help with the development of Iran through the following mechanisms:

- *Virtual and actual return of talent:* Professionals and highly skilled Iranian migrants can help fill the gap in knowledge and managerial skills by permanent, temporary, or virtual return to Iran. They can also facilitate the adoption of new technologies in Iran and help bring Iranian-produced goods and services into the global market. Academics among the Iranian diaspora can teach at Iranian universities and collaborate with their counterparts in the country to find solutions for Iran's challenges. However, the return of talent to Iran, actual or virtual, not only requires a welcoming atmosphere—free of hostility and ideological and gender discrimination—but also significant material and nonmaterial incentives, which will only become available when the economy begins to grow again. Despite the lack of economic opportunity in the private sector to motivate Iranian migrants to return home, in principle, the public sector could have still benefited from the experience and knowledge of the country's prominent migrants. However, the Islamic Republic's paranoid mindset about the intentions of the diaspora for contributing to causes inside Iran has deprived the country of reaping such benefits. From the other end, prominent migrants are also hesitant to collaborate with the Iranian government not only because of the regime's bad reputation and lack of legitimacy but also due to potential personal threats caused by internal conflicts in the regime. Under such circumstances, the majority of the rare cases of direct recruitment for the public sector from the diaspora were limited to those who had not been seriously critical about the regime's policies and simultaneously had an appetite for a political career within the present political structure of the Islamic Republic regime.

- *Financial investment:* Considering the decades of woefully insufficient and mis-allocated investment, Iran's market may become an excellent investment opportunity for wealthy individuals and financial managers among the diaspora. The inflow of capital from the diaspora can be in the form of foreign direct investment (FDI), venture capital, and equity. Such development will be contingent upon improvements in the rule of law, corruption, and the openness and transparency of the country's capital account and exchange rate policy.

- *Philanthropic contributions:* Given the financial success of many Iranian entrepreneurs and professionals among the diaspora community and their proven record of supporting Iranians causes (although mostly in their own country of residence), it is likely that their philanthropic contributions to Iran will expand dramatically once the current legal and political barriers are removed. In addition to the legal barriers in the United States and other countries to transferring money to Iran, many wealthy Iranians, even those who did not engage in political activities against the regime, do not risk visiting their home country for fear of being targeted for extortion by officials. Until such behavior by the regime changes, the philanthropic engagement of the diaspora will likely remain insignificant for the foreseeable future, despite the growing capacity and willingness of Iranian migrants to support causes in their home country.

- *Tourism:* In addition to short-term visits to Iran, the Iranian diaspora can help promote tourism to Iran and market goods associated with Iranian culture in their country of residence. As the real price of oil will likely decrease in the coming decades, tourism could potentially become one of Iran's most viable sources for earning foreign currency revenue needed for imports from other countries.

- *Remittances:* This type of contribution is primarily used for provision of basic needs for families of migrants, and thus is largely independent of the political situation. Historically, remittances sent by Iranian migrants have been small compared to those in other developing countries. For example, in recent years, migrants from India, China, Mexico, Nigeria, the Philippines, Egypt, Pakistan, Bangladesh, Morocco, Lebanon, Kyrgyzstan, Ghana, Kenya, and Haiti have sent significantly larger remittances back to their home countries than the Iranian migrants.[13] In fact, the amount of capital that Iranian migrants transfer out of the country has been consistently larger than the amount of remittances they send back.

As mentioned earlier, none of the above contributions from the Iranian diaspora will materialize without a major breakthrough in the political landscape of Iran to normalize and improve Iran's position in terms of international relations, the rule of law, corruption, macroeconomic stability, social policies, and human rights.

SUMMARY

In this chapter, we used data from various sources to shed light on different aspects of the migration landscape in contemporary Iran. The main quantitative findings of the chapter are as follows:

- By 2019, over 3.1 million Iranian-born people have emigrated from Iran, out of whom over 2.6 million (83%) have left the country since 1979.
- Nearly 1.0 million Iranians have applied for asylum since 1980, and about one-third of those requests have been granted.
- Around 700,000 individuals born in Iran have attended foreign universities. The number of Iranian students enrolled in foreign universities has steadily increased since the early 2000s and has reached about 130,000 by 2019.
- Based on global publication records, over 100,000 researchers of Iranian descent have worked in foreign universities and research institutions. Based on the head count, this figure corresponds to one-third of Iran's human capital in research.

Although the number of highly educated and skilled individuals who have already left Iran is high, the rate of brain drain from Iran will likely accelerate in the future given the increasing political uncertainties amid a downward-spiraling economy. In addition to their expansion in numbers, the achievements of Iranian migrants, both intellectually and materially, have made the Iranian diaspora into an emerging resource that can potentially help Iran break its low-growth logjam. In principle, this can take place through virtual and actual return, financial investments, philanthropy, tourism, and remittances. However, without fundamental changes in the political landscape, the prospect for significant contributions from the diaspora will remain bleak, while, in the meantime, the likely intensification of human capital flight from Iran will continue to deprive the country of one of its most valuable resources for future development.

9

RESEARCH AND DEVELOPMENT POLICY

IRAN'S HIGH-RANKING officials and state media frequently boast about a recent miracle that has happened in the country's scientific output (or scientific production, as it is often called). To what extent are these claims true? Which socioeconomic, political, and demographic factors might have contributed to this process? Besides quantity, how has the quality of scientific output in Iran evolved over time? How does Iran perform in this realm compared to other countries? And, what have been the positive implications and negative side effects of the state's policies for boosting research and innovation? This chapter aims to answer these questions.

To evaluate the quantity as well as quality of scientific production in Iran, we analyze large datasets obtained from different sources to shed light on the general picture and trends. In the rest of this chapter, we first provide an overview of the rising trends in the quantity of papers published by Iranian researchers. We put the results into context by discussing the direct and indirect implications of the demographic changes of the past decades, which have been amplified by the effects of government research policies and the increasing desire of students for

Based on S. Sadeh, M. Mirramezani, M. B. Mesgaran, A. Feizpour, and P. Azadi, "The Scientific Output of Iran: Quantity, Quality, and Corruption," Stanford Iran 2040 Project, 2019.

admission to foreign universities as a ticket for emigration. Further, we quantify the internationally coauthored papers of Iranian researchers and determine the extent to which researchers inside Iran collaborate with scholars abroad (mainly the Iranian diaspora). We then demonstrate how the quality of output by Iranian researchers varies across time and fields of study. We also make a comparative analysis of Iran's scientific output with other countries. Using available information on retracted papers, we conclude the chapter by discussing endemic plagiarism and other forms of scientific misconduct in the country; our firsthand investigative analysis of the so-called private graduate research consulting agencies, which offer a wide variety of services to graduate students, including thesis writing and paper production; and a more detailed analysis of the output of the country's hyperprolific researchers.

Herein, we show that, in addition to the demographic and social changes discussed earlier in the book, government policies on higher education and research have also affected Iran's academic landscape significantly. In particular, these policies have made faculty promotions and student graduations heavily contingent upon publication of papers in scientific journals[1]. More generally, in the current approach of the state to research, publication output seems to be considered equivalent to scientific and technological advancement, regardless of its quality and its organic role in the economy and society. Publication has therefore been treated as an end in itself. The heightened pressure for publication can damage the quality and credibility of science, giving rise to poor, irreproducible studies resulting from fraudulent or sloppy research. It also creates a delusion of "progress"—a fantasy of scientific accomplishments with very little real contribution to the body of scientific knowledge or to improvement in people's welfare. In a broader view, Iran's publication bubble fits into a wider range of sociopolitical behavior that is commonly referred to as *isomorphic mimicry*, that is, when policymakers in a developing country adopt the outward appearance of a successful process from advanced countries while hiding or overlooking the lack of the process's real function.

TRENDS IN SCIENTIFIC OUTPUT OF IRAN

We start our analysis by evaluating the quantity of scientific output of Iran in recent years. To this end, we analyzed the meta-data of all the papers published in the peer-reviewed journals indexed by Scopus, which

TABLE 9.1. Statistical summary of scientific publications by Iranian researchers between 1997 and 2018.

Papers Published by Iranian Researchers	Papers		Citations	
	Number (k)	Share (%)	Total (k)	Per Paper
All papers	437	100	4,400	10.1
Authors exclusively from Iran	350	80	3,150	9.0
With at least one international author	87	20	1,250	14.3
International corresponding author	28	6.5	550	19.3
Iranian (diaspora)	14	3.3	253	17.5
Non-Iranian	14	3.2	296	21.1
Published in journals hosted in Iran	53	12.2	197	3.7

is one of the largest databases of peer-reviewed papers.[2] Over the past two decades, Iranian researchers have published about 437,000 papers (Table 9.1), which places Iran as number 21 in the world's scientific publication output. Analysis of temporal changes in Iran's research output shows that the annual rate of publication has surged by fiftyfold over the past two decades (Figure 9.1)—outpacing the global trend in expansion of scientific publication, which has increased by no more than threefold over the same period. In 2018, Iran accounted for 2.6% of the world's scientific output, while two decades ago the country's contribution was as low as 0.1%. With this rapid growth rate of publication, Iran outpaces other fast-developing countries like China, South Korea, India, and Turkey.

Almost one-fifth of Iranian papers include at least one international collaborator. Although the share of multinational papers has substantially declined, the absolute number has always been on the rise (Figure 9.1). The internationally coauthored papers can originate from direct collaboration between research groups, a change in the affiliation of one of the coauthors during the research or publication process (e.g., a master's degree student starting a doctoral program abroad), and, to a lesser extent, participation by Iranian researchers in large multinational research projects. As discussed in chapter 8, the large wave of emigration by educated young adults over the past years and their establishment as researchers in foreign universities have certainly contributed to this trend of international collaborations.

Internationally coauthored papers have been written in collaboration with scientists from a wide range of countries (Figure 9.2). The United States (with over 20,000 papers) and Canada and the United Kingdom

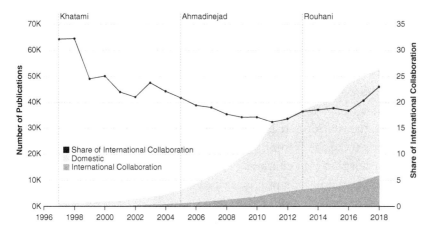

FIGURE 9.1. Number of publications by Iranian researchers (left axis) and share of international collaboration (right axis).

FIGURE 9.2. Map of international collaborations with Iranian researchers indicated by number of collaborative papers published between 1997 and 2018.

(each with about 10,000 papers) are the countries with the largest number of collaborative papers with Iranian researchers. A larger share of papers published in countries such as Canada, Malaysia, and Australia are in collaboration with Iranian authors compared to other countries, perhaps due to the presence of large numbers of highly educated Iranians in the these countries. In contrast, countries such as China and Japan, which are less popular destinations for emigration among Iranians and hence accommodate a rather small population of Iranian graduate students, have published fewer than expected collaborative papers with Iranian scholars.

Papers with international coauthors receive a disproportionate citation share of 25% while accounting for 17% of total publications. Most notably, the citation rate is highest when the corresponding author of a paper is part of the Iranian diaspora (17.5 citations per paper) or a non-Iranian scientist (21.1 citations per paper). In contrast, Scopus-indexed journals hosted in Iran published 12% of the papers but only acquired about 4% of total citations (Table 9.1).

The quantity and quality of publications also varied depending on the field of research (Figure 9.3). The largest share of papers were those in the fundamental sciences, such as chemistry, physics, biology, and math (41%), followed by medicine and health (22%), engineering (22%), agricultural, environmental, and veterinary sciences (10%), and social sciences (5%). We also calculated the weighted average ranking of journals in which papers of different fields were published as a proxy for the quality of publication in the field (Figure 9.4). With an average publication rank of 37, engineering outperforms the other major disciplines in publication

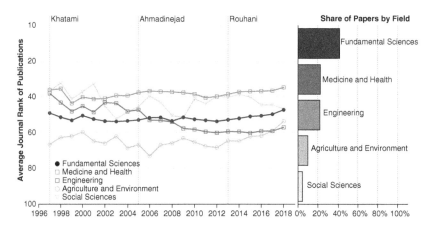

FIGURE 9.3. Trends in quality of papers published by Iranian researchers by field of study based on the normalized ranking of journals (left panel) and the distribution of papers published by Iranian scholars between 1997 and 2018 among different fields (right panel). A total of 437,000 papers were published over this period.

quality, followed by the social sciences, fundamental sciences, and agriculture and environmental science. While the weighted average ranks of journals for the other major fields have remained almost unchanged over time, the weighted average rank of publications in medicine and health shows a significant and consistent drop, falling from 38 to 58 in one decade (from 2004 to 2013).

We also analyzed how different research institutions contribute to scientific publications. A full list of universities with the largest contributions to Iran's scientific output, along with the number of their faculty members and normalized productivity (number of papers per faculty), are provided in Appendix D. The University of Tehran, Tehran University of Medical Sciences, and Islamic Azad University (all branches) have had the highest number of publications. However, other institutions like the Institute for Studies in Theoretical Physics and Mathematics (IPM), Sharif University of Technology, and Amirkabir University of Technology showed the highest faculty productivity, with an average of 7.4, 4.5, and 4.4 papers per faculty member (in 2018), respectively.

Research institutions can also be evaluated in terms of the average number of retractions per 10,000 papers, as a measure of scientific misconduct. Iran's institutions with the most publications since 1997 showed a large variance of retraction rates, but on average had a very high rate of about 13.3 retractions per 10,000 papers (Appendix D). In fact, Iranian publications in total have been retracted four times the global median, which has put Iran at the top of the list of countries with the most retractions.[3] The retraction list compiled by the Retractions Watch Database since 2004 reveals that the discovery of misconduct seems to be mostly the outcome of sporadic editorial investigations.[4] Since more reputable journals are more proactive in investigating misconduct, researchers who publish in them, mostly from elite and well-performing institutions, have disproportionately large rates of discovered misconduct. When a case of misconduct is identified, it is likely that other papers of the coauthors are also retroactively investigated. This, in turn, results in a situation in which a few authors are responsible for many of the retractions from any given institution. Nevertheless, our analysis of retractions reveals that misconduct is prevalent in all types of institutions in Iran: medical schools, technical schools, low-ranked universities, and even elite universities.

To better evaluate the quality of Iran's scientific output, we analyzed the degree of self-citation and share of Iranian papers published in, or

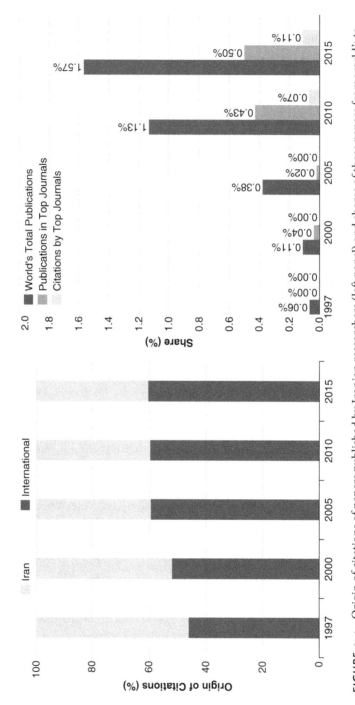

FIGURE 9.4. Origin of citations of papers published by Iranian researchers (left panel) and shares of these papers from world's total scientific output and top journals and share of the citations of these papers from top journals received in three consecutive years after publication.

cited by, the top journals—a total of 664 journals which are ranked first and second within each field in Scopus CiteScoreTM journal metrics.[5] For this analysis we excluded internationally coauthored papers. Analysis of the citations of Iranian publications indicates that a large portion of the citations are made by the coauthors or other researchers inside the country, although the country's rate of self-citation has declined from 54% in 1997 to 40% in 2015 (Figure 9.4).

Despite the rapid growth in number of publications, Iranian papers only make up 0.5% of papers in the top journals (Figure 9.4), meaning that the scientific output of the country is disproportionately published in lower quality journals. Even more striking is the share of citations that Iranian papers receive from other papers in top journals—only 0.1% of papers are referred to by these journals. Therefore, it can be concluded that Iran's scientific output has underperformed when it comes to contributing to the innovative and groundbreaking work that drives different fields.

In general, the number of citations that a country's papers receive has a strong correlation with its annual number of publications, although this typically reveals itself with a lag of a few years. In order to determine the current standing of Iran in the global research landscape, we analyzed Iran's rank by aggregate number of papers and aggregate external citations (which excludes a journal's self-citation) over time, as presented in Figure 9.5. In this figure, a gap between the two lines at each point in time can be seen as a surrogate for quality of papers in comparison to

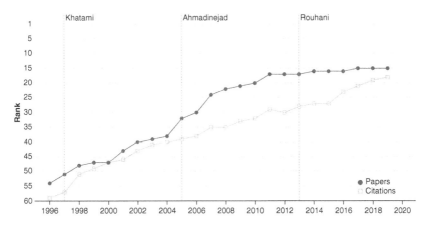

FIGURE 9.5. Global ranks of Iran by annual number of (citable) publications and external citations (i.e., journal self-citations excluded) between 1997 and 2019. *Sources:* SJR, Scientific Journal Rankings, Country Rankings, www.scimagojr.com.

other nations (although to a lesser extent, the distribution of publications among different fields also has an effect on the gap).

As can be seen, Iran has improved its ranking in both the number of papers and the number of citations. However, there has always been a gap between these two ranks with citations ranked as underperforming. More notably, this gap widened during the 2000s before stabilizing in the early 2010s and is more recently improving. It is unclear whether this is a new trend and Iran is going to rise in terms of the quality of research in the coming years or whether Iranian publications perform well in terms of citation just in the initial years after publication (e.g., due to excessive self-citation by authors).

MOTIVATIONS AND IMPLICATIONS

We have thus far demonstrated that the quantity of Iran's scientific output has skyrocketed in past decades at an impressive growth rate that is substantially above the world's average. We also evaluated trends in the quality of scientific papers from a number of different aspects and have shown that the growth in quantity has been achieved at serious costs: the spread and entrenchment of fraudulent activities and excessive focus on publishability rather than relevance to the needs of the country. In this section, we seek to explain the underpinnings of these developments and their implications. To this end, we examine the role of research expenditure and human capital as the main determinants of research output. The amount of a country's spending on research and development affects its research output and outcome through various channels: the size of the research community and the members' qualifications (relative to other sectors), provision of new and modern research equipment, and access to information (journals, conference attendance, etc.). Historically, research and development expenditures in Iran have been fluctuating around 0.5% of gross domestic product (GDP).[6] In real terms, the research expenditures of Iran have increased by a modest factor of about three over the past two decades—whereas the output, as shown earlier, has surged by a factor of about fifty. To put the current scientific productivity of Iran in a broader context, we conducted a cross-country comparison of the correlation between the GDP and the number of scientific publications in absolute and per capita terms. Iran's performance in both measures is currently about double the expected values based on the average performance of other countries (Figure 9.6).

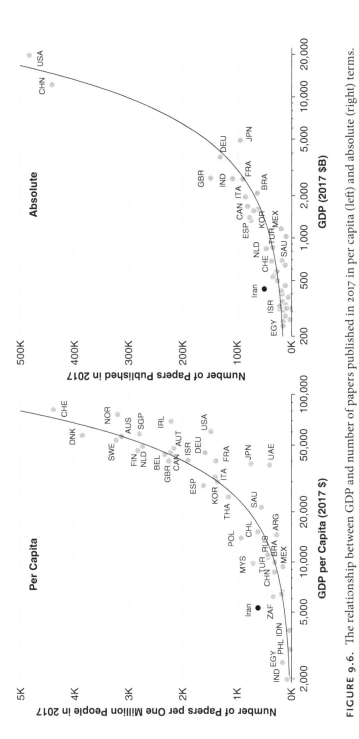

FIGURE 9.6. The relationship between GDP and number of papers published in 2017 in per capita (left) and absolute (right) terms. Note that horizontal axes are on log scale.

Sources: International Monetary Fund, World Economic Outlook; World Bank Open Data, World Bank Group, https://data.worldbank.org.

Having shown that the role of research and development expenditures cannot explain the trend of scientific output in Iran, we next focus on human factors as a potential driver for the surge in publications. In fact, as shown in chapter 3, due to the combined effects of Iran's demographic trends which led to an increase in the young population, and a concomitant rapid expansion of higher education, the number of people involved in research (e.g., graduate students) has risen drastically. This trend is very similar to the pattern of increase in the number of scientific publications (as shown before in Figure 9.1), hence arguing for human capital as the main contributor to the influx of academic papers.

The increase in human capital for research can be seen as a lagged consequence of the population boom of the 1980s. From 1975 to 1985, Iran's population grew dramatically at an annual rate of about 4%. As a result, Iran has seen a significant growth in its youth population over the past two decades. This was accompanied by the expansion of university capacity. The high demand for higher education, combined with the short-term and short-sighted policies of the state to defer the problem of unemployment, led to the mushrooming of universities. A notable example was the Islamic Azad University, which was established in 1982 and underwent a rapid expansion over the past decades to accommodate the demand for higher education. Unlike public schools and universities, Islamic Azad University was not free of charge (although run by government officials). This gave economic justification to the expansion of its branches all over the country which marked a new phase of commodification of higher education in Iran.

Based on data presented so far, several important conclusions can be drawn: first, Iran has an extremely high paper-per-dollar ratio, and second, the recent surge in number of publications has been primarily attributable to the size of the research community and policy mandates rather than a boost in research spending. From this argument it can be further inferred that, given the country's expected fiscal pressure in the mid- to long-term, which implies that research expenditures are unlikely to rise in the foreseeable future, any change in future scientific output (both in terms of quantity and quality) will continue to be mainly driven by the size and behavior of the research community. A forecast of the effective population of graduate students should, for example, provide a rough estimate of the trend of publications in the future.

While the increase in the number of graduate students who need to publish for various reasons (see below) can be considered as the main driver of the unconventional surge in the quantity of Iran's scientific output, lack of proper policies and prudent plans at the governance level can be identified as the main culprit for the research's lack of quality and irrelevance to the needs of the country and the prevalent academic corruption. As discussed before, the government has failed to invest proportionally in the enhancement of higher education, as for example evidenced by the decline in faculty-to-student ratio (see chapter 3). More generally, the policies mainly focus on the physical expansion of universities and higher education rather than creating fundamental capacity and ensuring quality. This is evident in the discourse of praising the number of publications without mentioning the impact or significance of those outputs.

This quantitative mentality has in fact dominated Iran's major policies on higher education, including the ones on graduation requirements for master's and doctoral students and academic appointment and promotion of professors.[7] However, the bylaws do not provide a meaningful way to measure the impact or contribution of a researcher's work in the real world. Therefore, when it comes to academic appointments in Iran, the researchers do not have an incentive for producing substantive research as long as their studies are published in an indexed journal. While master's degree students are encouraged to have a paper published in, or at least submitted to, an International Scientific Indexing (ISI) journal, doctoral students are required to have at least one work published in an ISI indexed journal, with more incentives for any additional publications. Therefore, higher education policies pertinent to graduation requirements and academic appointments form the incentives of the bulk of the research community in a predominantly quantitative manner, hence shaping the trend of quantitative increase in publications without much concern for the actual needs of the country.

With publication fever on the rise among the growing body of graduate students and researchers, a black market has infiltrated academia, giving rise to formation of a chain of shady businesses practicing a wide array of corrupt activities. Our firsthand investigation revealed that these agencies offer various types of services that cover a wide spectrum in terms of legality and ethics of research. For example, a few agencies that we approached denied the outright writing of papers from scratch but rather offered to "extract" a paper from a thesis that the student provides and to help with other aspects of publication such as translation of the manuscript, preparation of a cover letter, submission of papers to journals, and help in responding to reviewers' comments. Such agencies, therefore, capitalize on the fact that the inflated higher education system has failed to equip its students with the proper knowledge and skills required for scientific work and research.

Beyond "helping" with the research, many agencies in fact openly offered to "manufacture" an entire paper from scratch. This service is available in virtually any area of research that a customer demands, without even asking for any relevant data or other intellectual contributions. Particularly disturbing was our observation that the agencies have formed partnerships with predatory journals and dishonest editors, which in turn allows them to guarantee acceptance of papers in periods of time as short as a week. To solve the issue of a paper's impact, databases of journal metrics exist that provide fake information (e.g., impact factor) for the predatory journals supported by the agency. Based on the quotes we received, publishing a paper via these agencies, including the fees for the agency and the journal, would typically cost about $300–600. The emergence and growth of this academic black market in Iran are largely driven by commoditized academic research, distorted incentives, and overexploitation of quantitative metrics that measure quantity rather than quality and impact of the research. Iran needs to take major steps to improve the integrity and ethics of science before the legitimacy and image of the research community become even more damaged by the presence and dominance of such corrupt activities.

In addition to the contribution of the so-called research consulting companies which publicly offer their paper manufacturing services to university students, another suspicious phenomenon is the publication track record of some hyperprolific university professors who publish an unusual number of papers each year. In general, the process of publishing scientific papers includes several time-consuming steps: developing an idea that is worth publishing, conducting a literature review, performing experiments and surveys, collecting data and analysis, creating figures and tables, and writing the paper, then going through the editorial review process (at least once), addressing reviewers' comments, and proofreading the paper prior to publication. Other factors, such as the language barrier and teaching and administrative commitments, are known to be common impediments that hinder the research productivity of Iranian university professors. Given all these considerations, it is questionable how some university professors can, for example, publish twenty-plus papers in a single year, a phenomenon which we found not all that rare in Iran.

We focused on these hyperprolific researchers in order to obtain a more careful and thorough analysis of possible corrupt behaviors in academia.[8] This approach could be especially helpful as it narrows down the large list of potential researchers who cannot otherwise be scrutinized in detail, and hence guides the auditing selection process to those with a higher probability of conducting fraudulent activities. Since most of these researchers are well-rewarded based on the quantity of their publications (e.g., recipients of national and organizational research awards solely on the basis of number of publications), such an in-depth analysis of their research behavior and investigation of the quality of their publications can also send a strong signal to the rest of the community in cases of obvious and commonplace misconduct.

To analyze these selected researchers with an unusual number of publications, we used a simple audit selection criterion that takes into account the annual number of publications of a researcher (alternatively, one can use a selection criterion that takes into account the authors' year-over-year changes). We applied such a filter to the coauthors of all Iranian papers with minimum threshold parameters set to a total of twenty papers per year (Figure 9.7). This resulted in the selection of 441 unique authors from a total pool of over 72,000 researchers. We then compiled a list of authors of the Iranian papers on Scopus that include a note from the publisher indicating retraction (152 papers with 418 unique authors). A comparison of the above lists of authors revealed that, on a per author basis, the probability of being the (co-)author of a retracted paper is about five times higher among the hyperprolific researchers compared to randomly selected researchers (Figure 9.7). It is interesting to note that a large majority of the hyperprolific authors who published as many as twenty papers in 2018 (144 researchers) obtained their PhD (or other latest degree) from Iranian universities.

To gain further insight into the composition and types of these hyperprolific researchers, we also performed a qualitative in-depth inspection of their publications using their publication records on Scopus and Google Scholar.[9] We found that, on average, 19% of these authors' papers were published in Iranian journals, and 9% in predatory journals.

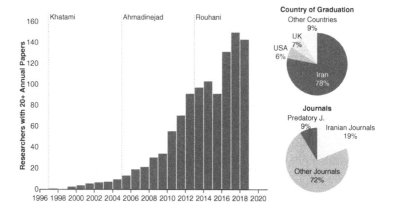

FIGURE 9.7. The left figure shows the number of authors whose (non-internationally collaborative) publications in Scopus were equal to or higher than twenty papers in a single year. The pie charts show the country of graduation of the 144 hyperprolific authors of 2018 (top) and the distribution of their papers (bottom), including those papers that were published prior to 2018.

Based on an informal review of the papers, citations, and other related information of a few dozen such authors, we inferred that these hyperprolific researchers belong to one of three groups. First is a group of distinguished researchers, often at one of the country's top universities, with cohesive publication records, a small share of self-citations, and a large number of external citations from high-quality journals (especially by researchers from developed countries). Second is a group of academics who concurrently hold important organizational or political positions. There is a reasonable amount of anecdotal evidence for lack of a meaningful contribution by these individuals to the many papers on which their names appear as coauthors while they are serving in office. It does not seem unreasonable to assume that favors given by the actual authors are returned by these top-ranked officials elsewhere. Third is a group of researchers who publish a large number of dishonest, and often very poor quality, papers that might entail various forms of misconduct such as data fabrication and falsification, plagiarism, fake reviews, and unethical and often reciprocal assignments of coauthorship status with their peers. Further work is needed to analyze these results more systematically and in more detail. Regardless, with this academic corruption prevailing even at the highest levels of government officials,[10] chances for the implementation of stricter measures and regulations against fraudulent misconduct appear small in the foreseeable future.

Despite the abovementioned common malpractices and the mass production of low-quality papers in the research market, many Iranian researchers are still incentivized by other means to publish quality research. As instability has grown inside Iran and economic prospects have become grim, researchers and students in Iran are looking outside the country for new opportunities. University students are increasingly considering emigration, and academic publication can help secure university admission and funding outside Iran. Iranian academics who are not looking for an opportunity to permanently leave also benefit from research experience abroad—for example, many are interested in sabbatical opportunities outside Iran. Additionally, many Iranians who find opportunities outside the country will continue to collaborate with their colleagues back home. As a result, there has been a growing trend in collaboration with researchers abroad. This growth in the number of internationally coauthored papers has occurred despite the state's paranoiac view on international collaborations and various forms of sanctions that have restricted Iranian scholars from accessing equipment and information from abroad. Absent these restrictions, the potential for collaboration could have been enormous, given the huge human capital of research inside Iran and the quality network of Iranian diaspora scholars in many of the world's top universities and research institutes.

SUMMARY

The state's productionist approach to scientific publication, with the direct and indirect influence from demographic and social changes, have collectively resulted in an unrivaled rise in the quantity of Iran's scientific output over the past two decades. Not being able to create enough jobs for the country's youth bulge, the state has implemented expansionist policies in higher education which have resulted in an increase in the number and capacities of graduate schools throughout the country. Often expressed in numerical terms, the state uses the country's scientific *production* as an underpinning of its propaganda to depict a developmental picture of itself. The overemphasis on quantitative measures of scientific productivity has given rise to a publication bubble with two undesirable consequences: inefficient use of the country's human resources and the growth and entrenchment of academic corruption.

Since Iranian researchers are heavily incentivized to publish in international research journals, often little to no attention is devoted to the actual intellectual and technological needs of the country. Instead, researchers almost solely focus on the publishability of their work. For example, very few papers (none in some areas) provide a holistic and visionary analysis of some of the formidable crises facing the country (e.g., water scarcity). Another factor that considerably undermines the analytical depth and cohesiveness of Iranian papers is the fact that an overwhelming majority of these papers are written by graduate students with minimal input from professors. Overall, the effective productivity of research in Iran, contrary to what is frequently claimed by the state, is too small if one wants to look beyond the numeric measures of output and evaluate outcomes and impacts.

In addition to creating an illusion of development by inflating the publication bubble, Iran's productionist approach to research is primarily responsible for the growth and entrenchment of various forms of misconduct that are spreading throughout the universities like wildfire. Sadly, officials seem indifferent to even the most obvious forms of fraudulent behavior, such as the so-called graduate student research consulting agencies that, over a mere week or two, generate fabricated papers and dissertations in virtually any field demanded. Since it overlooks punishment for these and other forms of fraudulent activities, Iran currently holds the top rank in the paper retraction rate in the world. If inaction against fraudulent publication activities persists, it will be likely that some of the credible and honest researchers will also become tempted to relax their strict research and ethical standards in favor of more publications in order to remain competitive for career promotions and research funds. New faculty recruitment can also be dominated by the type of applicant who managed to put together a paper-publishing machine, or joined an already existing one, during their doctoral education. Unless corrective actions are taken, the implications of the prevailing new paradigm of research will put the country in a vicious cycle that causes the research landscape to deprive itself of trustworthy research materials and researchers alike.

Conclusion

THE PATH FORWARD

PREVIOUS CHAPTERS OF THIS BOOK explained major trends in Iran's performance along different dimensions of development and discussed the root causes of why contemporary Iran has failed to have substantive economic and political development despite its tremendous potential. Many observers attribute this failure to factors such as culture, foreign interventions, class struggle, political factionalism, the oil curse, geography, bad economic policies, or simply lack of democracy. We, as discussed in the book, believe that the analysis of Iran's failure can be best explained through examining the quality of governance which provides a broader view of the dynamics of political and economic institutions and their interactions in a society which has been in transition from traditional to modern ways of life.

The future trajectory of development in Iran will vary greatly depending on the prevailing governance paradigm in the future. Table C.1 provides our view about the plausible direction of future changes in a number of important political, economic, and social indicators under three different scenarios: (1) business as usual, (2) reforms within the Islamic Republic framework (*Eslah-talaban*'s agenda) without fundamental changes in the political structure, and (3) a fundamental transformation of political institutions that leads to an improvement in the institutions of rule of law and democratic accountability. While there are many possibilities with regard to future events, these three broad scenarios can, to some extent, cover many of these possible events. For example, a coup by the IRGC can be seen as a version of the status quo (scenario 1) where the rule of law, civil society, and democracy are further weakened, and a pacted transition may be seen as a development which can potentially pave the way for improving the rule of law and democracy (scenario 3).

In our view, the continuation of business as usual will profoundly worsen all aspects of the socioeconomic landscape and turn Iran into a failed state with widespread poverty and perhaps even famine. While the rise of the reformist faction of the Islamic Republic can temporarily boost state credibility and give rise to minor improvements in some aspects of governance, their agenda lacks the vital elements that can potentially end the downward spiral in the economy and society. Under the transformational governance scenario, the priority is not on growth itself but rather on improving the rule of law, transparency, and democratic accountability which can foster growth in the subsequent steps. The type and depth of the changes to the political institutions needed to stimulate a new period of sustained economic growth cannot be achieved through the cosmetic changes that reformists are willing to offer or without changing the constitution. In our view, it is very naive to assume that marginal improvements in the technocratic capacity of the state, regardless of their success, can serve as the core of a successful strategy for breaking Iran's current development logjam.

Although democracy is an end in itself, lack of democratic institutions was not necessarily a decisive factor in hindering the economic development of Iran in earlier stages of development. After all, many of the fast-developing nations such as South Korea, Singapore, and more recently, China, began their period of sustained economic growth under an autocratic rule. Iran itself witnessed an impressive economic growth between 1960 and 1976 where the country did not have any substantive institutions of democratic accountability in general, and free and fair multiparty elections in particular. However, the path forward is entirely different. The economy is now far more complex, and the needs of different segments of society are much more diverse compared to half a century ago. This makes it difficult, if not impossible, to carry out a top-down modernization and development agenda without proper feedback for the performance of the government through meaningful elections and the presence of a strong and extensive civil society to give voice to different interests. Finally, if another self-proclaimed developmental regime emerges in the future that, similar to the Pahlavi and the Islamic Republic regimes, lacks institutions of democratic accountability (formal or de facto) to purge corrupt politicians, it would not take long for corruption to again paralyze the political system, as more opportunities will become available over time for ambitious people to become rich through politics rather than entrepreneurship.

In the decades to come, completion of Iran's demographic transition and closure of the golden window of opportunity, reduction in the role of oil in the economy, and adjustments to water scarcity through reducing agricultural production constitute important structural shifts which are not only inevitable but also irreversible. There are also a number of other critical trends such as brain drain and corruption which will likely persist well into the future regardless of short-term developments in economic and political environments.

Demographic changes will continue to play a major role for decades to come. While the fertility rate has been near the replacement level since the beginning of the twenty-first century, the population will nevertheless continue to grow due to its past momentum. In terms of age structure, the population will have a low dependency ratio until about 2040 which is conducive to economic growth. However, given the low economic participation and high unemployment rates of the past decades, this important one-time demographic window of opportunity will be entirely wasted if the status quo is continued into the future.

Furthermore, in the long run, the combined effects of recent technological advancements that lowered the cost of oil extraction from unconventional resources and the inevitable more forceful policies to reduce greenhouse gas emissions will cause a paradigm shift in the oil market from scarcity to abundance, hence, a lower relative price of oil vis-à-vis other goods. In addition, Iran's lack of sufficient investments in the upstream oil industry and the rising domestic demand for petroleum fuels will put downward pressure on future revenue from oil exports. Another important issue in the future of Iran is the country's struggle with water shortages. For decades, there have been large imbalances in Iran's water consumption and the sustainable levels of supply, causing a rapid depletion of the groundwater resources. As discussed earlier, Iran will inevitably have to increase food imports to ensure food security for its large and growing population even if it invests heavily in advanced agricultural technologies.

TABLE C.1. Projection of future directions of political, economic, and social developments under the business as usual scenario, reformists' agenda (*Eslahta-labi*), and transformational governance in the long run (++ = highly desirable, + = desirable, +/- = neutral, - = undesirable, -- = highly undesirable).

Dimension	Issue	Business as Usual	Reformists' Agenda	Transformational Governance
Political	State capacity	-	+/-	+/-
	Rule of law	--	-	+
	Democratic accountability	--	-	+
	Control of favoritism	-	-	+/-
	Control of clientelism	+/-	+/-	+/-
	Control of petty corruption	-	-	+/-
	International relations	--	+/-	++
	State legitimacy & credibility	--	+	+
Economic & Environmental	Economic growth	--	-	+
	Macroeconomic stability	-	+/-	+
	Poverty reduction	--	+/-	+
	Equality	--	-	+/-
	Control of capital flight	--	+/-	+
	Foreign investments	--	-	+
	Natural resource revenues	-	+/-	+/-
	Food security	-	-	+/-
	Control of air pollution	-	-	+/-
Social	Civil society	--	+/-	++
	Social capital	--	+/-	+
	Control of brain drain	--	--	+/-
	Control of crime	-	-	+/-
	Demographic structure	-	-	-
	Human rights	--	-	+
	Gender equality	+/-	+/-	+

In Iran's current situation, continuation of business as usual or giving false hopes of change under the reformists' (*Eslah-talaban*) failed agenda—which has proven to be a fool's paradise—will waste the potential to bring about substantive change and can result in loss of economic growth for another generation. Similarly, creating an economic policy wish list will be woefully inadequate to put the country in a virtuous development spiral. Instead, what can save Iran is a complete transformation of its political institutions.

The story of Iran's development is a lamentable one characterized by missed opportunities and wasted resources. Iran's decades of hibernation in its path of development has occurred during a historical epoch when many of its neighbors and other peers in the developing world made significant progress and lifted their nations out of poverty. However, this does not have to be the ultimate fate of an ancient nation. A country's future trajectory is influenced by its history but is not trapped by it. And Iran is no exception to this rule.

از این سموم که بر طرف بوستان بگذشت 　　 عجب که بوی گلی هست و رنگ نسترنی

به صبر کوش تو ای دل که حق رها نکند 　　 چنین عزیز نگینی به دست اهرمنی

APPENDIX A
GOVERNANCE INDICATORS

Several attempts have been made in recent decades to measure the quality of governance across time and countries. One such project, widely used in scholarly research and in development policy discussions, is the World Bank's Governance Indicators.[1] These indicators are produced by aggregating a large number of signals into six composite measures: government effectiveness, political stability and absence of violence, regulatory quality, control of corruption, rule of law[2], and voice and accountability.[3] Four of the World Bank governance indicators are related to the quality of state institutions (i.e., government effectiveness, political stability, regulatory quality[4], and control of corruption) and hence can be grouped together to represent the state, while the other two directly correspond to the other two sets of institutions, rule of law and accountability, in the framework discussed in chapter 1. Figure A.1 depicts the trends in Iran's governance indicators as reported by the World Bank since 1996. In our view, the only solid conclusions one can draw from these trends are those that are in line with conventional wisdom: (1) in relative terms, the quality of governance in Iran is significantly poorer than the world's mean; (2) no radical shifts have occurred in the state and rule-of-law institutions in recent decades; and (3) democratic accountability in relative terms has undergone a large decline over the last two decades. Overall, while these indicators can be useful for broad cross-country comparisons, they do not seem to provide the detailed information that is needed to study the evolution of institutions in Iran across time.

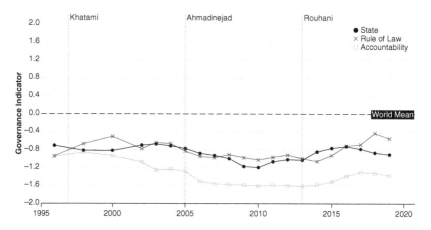

FIGURE A.1. Trends in the World Bank governance indicators of Iran between 1995 and 2019. The variables have a standard deviation of one and a zero mean (higher values indicate better outcomes).

Sources: Worldwide Governance Indicators (WGI) Project, World Bank, Washington DC.

APPENDIX B
WATER BALANCE DATA

TABLE B.1. Iran's water balance data.

Resource / Withdrawal	Parameter	Amount of Water (BCM)		
		2001	2016	Post-adaptation
Renewable Water Resources	TARWR	130	89	89
	Surface flow	92	63[a]	63[a]
	Groundwater recharge	38	26[a]	26[a]
Freshwater Withdrawal	Surface	42	40	23
	Groundwater	51	56	30[b]
	Total	93	96	53
Freshwater Use	Municipal	6	8	10
	Industrial	1	2	2
	Agriculture	86	86	41
	Total	93	96	53
Return Flow	From agriculture	26	27[a]	15[a]
	From industrial	1	1[a]	1[a]
	From municipal	2	2[a]	1[a]
	Total	29	30	17
	To surface	19	20[a]	11[a]
	To groundwater	10	10[a]	6[a]
	Groundwater recharge by return flows	7	7[a]	4[a]
Balance	Sustainable groundwater resources[c]	45	33	30
	Surface Outflow[d]	69	43	50
Stress Level	Withdrawal to TARWR ratio (%)	72	108	60

[a] Estimated by proportional adjustment of data from 2001.

[b] Assumed to be equal to sustainable groundwater resources.

[c] Sum of annual recharge of aquifers from renewable resources and return flow.

[d] Sum of renewable surface flow and return flow (to surface) minus surface withdrawal.

Sources: "Water Crisis and Feasibility Study of Connecting the Northern and Southern Waterbodies of the Country," 7th Edition, Plan and Budget Organization of Iran, 2018 (in Farsi); Water Resource Management and Sustainable Development, Iran Water Resource Management Company, Report No 7374 (http://wrbs.wrm.ir/) (in Farsi).

APPENDIX C
MIGRATION DATA

DATA AND METHODOLOGY

The migration and asylum statistics presented in this book were compiled from international agencies (e.g., United Nations Population Division,[1] United Nations High Commissioner for Refugees,[2] Eurostat,[3] OECD Statistics[4]) and national organizations (e.g., Iran,[5] the United States,[6] Canada,[7] Germany,[8] Australia,[9] the United Kingdom,[10] Denmark[11]). In rare cases where sufficient data were not available, we used figures reflected in the news or estimated by interpolation.

The statistics on Iranian international students were compiled using data from the Institute of International Education[12] and the national organizations listed above. To estimate the number of Iranian students who already resided in foreign countries prior to enrollment at universities (e.g., Iranian-born children who emigrated with their families), we used data on population age structure and educational attainment of Iranians as reported in the US census results.[13] This estimate was found using the share of Iranians in the United States with a bachelor's degree or higher, as reported in the American Community Survey, and applied to the stock of Iranian migrants over time. We also found the ratio of graduate to undergraduate students using data from the Institute of International Education and reference.[14]

To count the number of Iranian scholars inside the country and abroad, we first extracted all papers in the Scopus database with at least one author affiliated with an Iranian institution (nearly 600,000 papers).[15] We then compiled separate lists of unique first and last names from all authors whose affiliations were from Iran and ranked them based on the number of times each name appeared in the list (nearly 150,000 unique last names). After excluding obvious non-Iranian names, we obtained a final list of common Persian last names and their spelling variations (about 120,000). Subsequently, we searched each of these last names on the Scopus platform without restricting the affiliation country to Iran (about 830,000 unique individuals). We then searched the publication records of each of these authors using their unique author ID. Finally, for each country and year, we created a list of papers published by authors who were potentially Iranian (who could also be second-generation Iranians). In order to correct for overestimation caused by shared surnames between Iranians and other nations (mostly the Muslim countries), we compiled a list of 1,000 Persian first and last names that are almost exclusively used by Iranians. We then estimated the number of Iranian diaspora scholars in each country by comparing the share of these Iranian names among the authors identified in the previous step with an expected value calculated based on the prevalence of these names among the authors in Iran. It is also worth noting that these figures underestimate the total number of active scholars since not every scholar would publish a paper in a given year. Since the frequency of publication has increased over time, we expect that the degree of underestimation to be more pronounced in the earlier years. We also note that the number of asylum seekers in the United States includes both asylum-seekers who filed their claims inside the United States, and refugees who applied abroad.

ESTIMATION OF NET ANNUAL FLOW OF MIGRANTS

The net flow of migrants in a given year can be estimated from the difference between the inflow and outflow of international passengers. Figure C.1 shows Iran's net outbound passengers on international flights since 1960 and their running total. The net outflow of Iranian citizens who cross the borders by road has been about 470,000 since 1996 (Table C.1) which is much smaller compared with those who traveled by air. Using this method to estimate the annual flow and total stock of migrants offers a number of important benefits. First, contrary to immigration statistics reported by the host countries, the passenger traffic data have no time lag and almost immediately track the actual migration flows. For example, it typically takes five to ten years for an Iranian student who enters a foreign country as a student to obtain permanent residency or citizenship, and thus be counted in official immigrant statistics. Second, the passenger traffic data make up for missing or underreported data on the

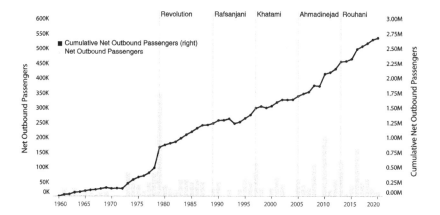

FIGURE C.1. Net outbound international passengers between 1960 and 2020 calculated as the number of air passengers on flights leaving Iran minus the air passengers entering Iran (left axis) and its running total since 1960 (right axis).

Sources: Iran's Statistical Yearbooks of 1965–2019, Statistical Center of Iran, Statistical Yearbooks of Air Transportation, Civil Aviation Organization of Iran.

TABLE C.1. Number of passengers entering and leaving the country by road (millions).

Year	Inflow	Outflow	Net Outflow	Year	Inflow	Outflow	Net Outflow
1996	0.21	0.23	0.019	2008	2.33	2.26	−0.07
1997	0.18	0.19	0.013	2009	2.87	2.84	−0.03
1998	0.18	0.20	0.020	2010	3.84	3.89	0.04
1999	0.26	0.29	0.036	2011	3.47	3.43	−0.04
2000	0.27	0.29	0.022	2012	2.65	2.68	0.02
2001	0.21	0.21	0.001	2013	3.18	3.30	0.12
2002	0.26	0.26	0.002	2014	2.98	3.32	0.34
2003	0.24	0.26	0.019	2015	3.63	3.27	−0.36
2004	0.32	0.37	0.056	2016	4.42	4.44	0.03
2005	0.39	0.43	0.042	2017	5.04	5.16	0.12
2006	1.52	1.62	0.11	2018	3.93	3.80	−0.12
2007	1.90	1.99	0.09	**Total**	**44.29**	**44.75**	**0.47**

Sources: Iran's Yearbook of Road Transportation, 1996–2018, Ministry of Road and Urban Development.

TABLE C.2. Statistics on the number of Iranian migrants and students in the US.

Year	Permanent Residence Total	Permanent Residence Refugee/ Asylees	Persons Naturalized	International Students Total Enrolled	International Students New Student Visas
1970	1825		416	6896	
1971	2411		501	8617	
1972	3059		569	10338	
1973	2998		578	12059	
1974	2608		562	13780	
1975	2337	36	601	20000	
1976	2700	52	567	23700	
1977	4261	78	838	36200	
1978	5861	15	1132	44800	
1979	8476	13	1217	51310	
1980	10410	124	1591	46500	
1981	11105	366	1677	35800	
1982	10314	701	1636	26200	3880
1983	11169	1450	1868	22000	4109
1984	13807	3544	2268	16640	3748
1985	16071	5420	3431	14000	4173
1986	16505	6022	4569	12100	3087
1987	14426	5559	4277	10200	1542
1988	15246	6895	4970	9000	997
1989	21243	8167	4485	7440	1027
1990	14905	8649	5973	6100	828
1991	9927	8515	10595	5000	709
1992	6995	3093	6787	4100	624
1993	8908	3875	7033	3800	534
1994	6998	2186	10041	2896	600
1995	9201	1245	11761	2587	522
1996	11084	1212	19278	2100	405
1997	9642	1447	11434	1969	370
1998	7883	754	10739	1660	372
1999	7203	1030	18268	1885	456
2000	8519	956	19251	1844	662
2001	10425	1364	13834	2216	861
2002	12960	4806	11773	2216	295
2003	7230	2023	10782	2258	272
2004	10434	3966	11781	2321	350
2005	13887	6480	11031	2251	470
2006	13947	6316	11363	2420	647
2007	10460	2570	10557	2795	801
2008	13852	3465	11813	3060	1048

(continued)

TABLE C.2. (*continued*)

Year	Permanent Residence		Persons Naturalized	International Students	
	Total	Refugee/ Asylees		Total Enrolled	New Student Visas
2009	18553	9804	12069	3533	1787
2010	14182	4735	9337	4731	1764
2011	14822	5386	9286	5626	2490
2012	12916	3430	9627	6982	3051
2013	12863	2481	11623	8744	3044
2014	11615	2521	9620	10194	3294
2015	13114	3756	10344	11338	3250
2016	13298	3111	9507	12269	2659
2017	13791	3656	8324	12783	2201
2018	10116	4441	8409	12142	1434
2019	5789		10232		1970

Sources: Statistical Yearbook of Immigration and Naturalization Service, Department of Justice, United States, 1978–2001; Yearbook of Immigration Statistics, Office of Immigration Statistics, Homeland Security, United States, 2002–2017.

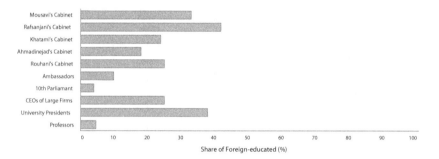

FIGURE C.2. Share of foreign-educated officials and business leaders in 2020.

number of Iranian immigrants in developing countries. Third, it allows for the exclusion of those Iranians who have been granted permanent residency permits or citizenship in a foreign country but primarily live in Iran (this situation is common among the parents of the first-generation migrants).

APPENDIX D
SCIENTIFIC OUTPUT DATA

DATA AND METHODOLOGY

The statistics about research publications were extracted from Scopus, which is one of the largest abstract and citation databases of peer-reviewed journals, currently covering about 71 million records, 23,700 journals, and 1.4 billion citations.[1] The articles included in the database encompass a wide range of topics, geographic areas, and languages. The time frame of the analysis spans from 1997 to 2018 except for the analysis of retracted papers, where papers published after 2004 are considered. We identified papers published by Iranian researchers by searching for papers with at least one author who was affiliated with an institution in the country. Books, book chapters, and conference proceedings were omitted from the analysis by limiting the search to articles (including those in press) and review papers. In order to find publications that were produced with international collaboration, we searched for papers that were affiliated with Iran and at least one other country. We used the correspondence address to determine whether a paper's corresponding author was in Iran. We estimated the extent of collaboration between researchers inside the country with the Iranian diaspora scholars by evaluating whether the names of foreign-affiliated authors were Persian. We categorized all papers into five major groups: (1) fundamental sciences (chemistry, physics and astronomy, materials science, biochemistry, genetics and molecular biology, mathematics, and computer science); (2) medicine and health (medicine, pharmacology, toxicology and pharmaceuticals, immunology and microbiology, neuroscience, health professions, nursing, and dentistry); (3) engineering (all fields of engineering, energy, and Earth and planetary sciences); (4) agriculture, environmental science and veterinary science; and (5) social sciences.

We used CiteScoreTM metrics (which is also a Scopus product) to assess how the quality of publications by Iranian researchers evolved over time.[2] To this end, we first ranked all journals within each subfield based on their impact factor (e.g., the engineering field constituted twenty-seven subfields such as mechanical engineering, electrical engineering, and bioengineering) and then normalized their ranks such that the ranks of all journals of a subfield range from 1 to 100 with 1 representing the best journal in the subfield. Then, using these normalized ranks along with the number of papers published by Iranian researchers in these journals, we calculated the average rank of the publications for each year and field. In conducting our analysis of misconduct, we used the Retractions Watch Database[3] published by the Center for Scientific Integrity,[4] which has compiled a total of nearly 20,000 cases of retracted papers since 2004. We note that the database does not include all cases of

TABLE D.1. Ranking of top twenty countries with the highest number of collaborations with Iran and countries with the most publication overall (excluding Iran).

Rank	Total Papers		Rank	Collaborative Papers with Iran	
1	United States	8327026	1	United States	20292
2	China	4427874	2	Canada	10123
3	United Kingdom	2412052	3	United Kingdom	9837
4	Germany	2175772	4	Germany	7435
5	Japan	1958849	5	Malaysia	7275
6	France	1521782	6	Australia	7065
7	Canada	1259550	7	Italy	5769
8	India	1252299	8	France	4879
9	Italy	1237354	9	Turkey	4301
10	Spain	1049979	10	China	4163
11	Australia	1007571	11	Spain	3924
12	South Korea	838972	12	India	3742
13	Russian	821894	13	South Korea	3094
14	Brazil	745033	14	Netherlands	2961
15	Netherlands	714173	15	Sweden	2852
16	Switzerland	526541	16	Switzerland	2722
17	Sweden	493638	17	Japan	2666
18	Poland	489430	18	Belgium	2376
19	Turkey	476948	19	Pakistan	2141
20	Taiwan	473335	20	Poland	2111

TABLE D.2. Number of published papers, faculty members, productivity per faculty, and retraction rate by research institute.

Research Institute	Total Papers 1997–2018	Publications in 2018	Faculty	Paper per Faculty (2018)	Retraction per 10,000 Papers
University of Tehran	48330	5062	2345	2.2	19
Tehran University of Medical Sciences	43742	4943	1518	3.3	10
Islamic Azad University (all branches)	38791	4699	39819	0.1	29
Sharif University of Technology	25974	2065	458	4.5	7
Amirkabir University of Technology	25940	2397	546	4.4	5
Tarbiat Modares University	24968	2524	724	3.5	8
Shahid Beheshti University of Medical Sciences	20008	3096	1266	2.5	10
Iran University of Science and Technology	19409	1867	475	3.9	21
Shiraz University	16612	1684	672	2.5	8
Isfahan University of Technology	15881	1724	482	3.6	7
Ferdowsi University of Mashhad	15507	1860	820	2.3	10
Shahid Beheshti University	14502	1556	800	2.0	8
University of Tabriz	14101	1738	743	2.3	10
Shiraz University of Medical Sciences	12638	1567	742	2.1	6
Isfahan University of Medical Sciences	12013	1380	668	2.1	14
K. N. Toosi University of Technology	10865	1018	324	3.1	12
Mashhad University of Medical Sciences	10546	1647	760	2.2	14
Tabriz University of Medical Sciences	10440	1577	716	2.2	17
Iran University of Medical Sciences	10379	1908	742	2.6	17
University of Isfahan	9476	1040	694	1.5	9
Payame Noor University	9470	1138	3647	0.3	8
The University of Guilan	7691	954	585	1.6	2
Shahid Bahonar University of Kerman	7472	822	645	1.3	14
Inst. for Studies in Theoretical Physics & Math.	7062	694	94	7.4	2
Razi University	6586	738	445	1.7	12
Urmia University	6124	820	482	1.7	39
Bu Ali Sina University	6099	613	428	1.4	4
Ahvaz Jundishapur University of Medical Sciences	5462	851	592	1.4	0
University of Mazandaran	5276	523	352	1.5	2
University of Kashan	5239	711	301	2.4	11
Baqiyatallah University of Medical Sciences	5209	671	301	2.2	61
Shahid Chamran University of Ahvaz	5089	581	579	1.0	11
Semnan University	4847	721	330	2.2	10
Kharazmi University	4846	479	487	1.0	0
Yazd University	4782	665	498	1.3	5
Mazandaran University of Medical Sciences	4608	581	330	1.8	2
Kerman University of Medical Sciences	4393	638	384	1.7	0

retracted papers, but to our knowledge, it is the largest source of information on this matter. A list of potentially predatory journals was obtained from references.[5] We also made several direct phone calls to some of the so-called research consulting agencies inquiring about the types of the services they offer and their associated costs (contact information for such agencies is readily available on the Web). We narrowed down our selection to those which appeared to be most professional.

NOTES

CHAPTER 1

1. Economic Time Series Database, The Central Bank of Iran, 2021, https://tsd.cbi.ir/.

2. Economic Time Series Database.

3. F. Fukuyama, "What Is Governance?" CGD Working Paper 314, Washington, DC: Center for Global Development, 2013.

4. B. Rothstein, "Understanding the Quality of Government in China: The Cadre Administration Hypothesis," CDDRL Working Paper 133, 2013.

5. Fukuyama, "What Is Governance?"; Rothstein, "Understanding the Quality of Government in China."

6. Institutions are defined as "stable, valued, recurring patterns of behavior that can be more or less complex, adaptable, autonomous, and coherent." F. Fukuyama, "The Patterns of History," *Journal of Democracy* 23, (2012); S. P. Huntington, *Political Order in Changing Societies* (New Haven, CT: Yale University Press, 1968).

7. "The ability of groups and individuals to make others act in the interest of those groups and individuals and to bring about specific outcomes." World Bank, "World Development Report 2017: Governance and the Law," 2017.

8. Fukuyama, "What Is Governance?"; F. Fukuyama, *State-Building: Governance and World Order in the 21st Century* (Ithaca, NY: Cornell University Press, 2004); F. Fukuyama, "The Patterns of History," *Journal of Democracy* 23 (2012); "World Development Report 2017."

9. Fukuyama, "What Is Governance?"; F. Fukuyama, *The Origins of Political Order: From Prehuman Times to the French Revolution* (New York: Farrar, Straus and Giroux, 2011); F. Fukuyama, *Political Order and Political Decay: From the Industrial Revolution to the Globalization of Democracy* (New York: Farrar, Straus and Giroux, 2014).

10. Huntington, *Political Order in Changing Societies*.

11. World Bank, *World Development Report 1997: The State in a Changing World* (New York: Oxford University Press, 1997).

12. Side effects (positive or negative) and consequences of an activity experienced by a third party who does not pay or receive compensation for that.

13. Taking more risks because someone else will bear the costs.

14. A transaction in which the seller or buyer has information about product quality that the other side does not have.

15. World Bank, *World Development Report 1997*.

16. World Bank. *World Development Report 1997*.

17. "The creation of new government institutions and the strengthening of existing ones." Fukuyama, *State-Building*.

18. "World Development Report 2017."

19. "World Development Report 2017"; F. Fukuyama, "Transitions to the Rule of Law," *Journal of Democracy* 21 (2010).

20. "World Development Report 2017"; Fukuyama, "Transitions to the Rule of Law."

21. Fukuyama, "Transitions to the Rule of Law."

22. "World Development Report 2017."

23. H. Bashiriyeh, "Cleavages in Iranian Politics since 1979," in *Politics and Culture in Contemporary Iran*, eds. A. Milani and L. Diamond (Boulder, CO: Lynne Rienner, 2015).

24. D. Kaufmann, A. Kraay, and M. Mastruzzi, "The Worldwide Governance Indicators: Methodology and Analytical Issues," *Hague Journal on the Rule of Law* 3 (2011).

25. Fukuyama, "The Patterns of History."

26. Fukuyama, "The Patterns of History"; S. I. Lindberg, A. Lührmann, and V. Mechkova, "From De-Jure to De-Facto: Mapping Dimensions and Sequences of Accountability," World Development Report Background Paper, World Bank, 2017.

27. Lindberg, Lührmann, and Mechkova, "From de-jure to de-facto."

28. Lindberg, Lührmann, and Mechkova.

29. Lindberg, Lührmann, and Mechkova.

30. A. Milani, "The Authoritarian Resurgence: Iran's Paradoxical Regime," *Journal of Democracy* 26 (2015).

31. Milani, "The Authoritarian Resurgence."

32. Huntington, *Political Order in Changing Societies*.

33. A. Milani and R. Pakzad, "Islamic Republic of Iran in an Age of Global Transitions: Challenges for a Theocratic Iran, Governance in Emerging New World," Governance in an Emerging New World 519, Hoover Institute, 2019.

34. Milani and Pakzad, "Islamic Republic of Iran in an Age of Global Transitions."

35. Huntington, *Political Order in Changing Societies*.

36. Fukuyama, *State-Building*.

37. B. Levy and F. Fukuyama, "Development Strategies Integrating Governance and Growth, Policy Research," Working Paper 5196, World Bank, 2010.

38. Fukuyama, *State-Building*; L. Pritchett and M. Woolcock. "When the Solution Is the Problem: Arraying the Disarray in Development," *World Development* 32 (2004).

39. J. E. Stiglitz, *Globalization and Its Discontents* (New York: W. W. Norton & Company, 2003).

40. Economic Modeling and Information Management Office, Ministry of Economic Affairs and Finance, databank.mefa.ir.

41. Economic Modeling and Information Management Office; Iranian Privatization Organization Performance Report in 1396 (in Farsi), 2017.

42. Iranian Privatization Organization Performance Report.

43. Economic Time Series Database.

44. Rothstein, "Understanding the Quality of Government in China."

45. A. Milani, *The Shah* (New York: St. Martin's Griffin, 2012).

46. T. Ginsburg and T. Moustafa, *Rule by Law: The Politics of Courts in Authoritarian Regimes* (Cambridge: Cambridge University Press, 2008).

47. "World Development Report 2017"; Fukuyama, *Political Order and Political Decay*; K. Basu and T. Cordella, *Institutions, Governance and the Control of Corruption* (London: Springer International Publishing, 2018).

48. Lindberg, Lührmann, and Mechkova, "From de-jure to de-facto."

49. Fukuyama, "The Patterns of History"; Lindberg, Lührmann, and Mechkova, "From de-jure to de-facto."

50. Milani, "The Authoritarian Resurgence."

51. Lindberg, Lührmann, and Mechkova, "From de-jure to de-facto."

52. S. Levitsky and L. A. Way, "Elections without Democracy: The Rise of Competitive Authoritarianism," *Journal of Democracy* 13 (2002); L. J. Diamond, "Thinking about Hybrid Regimes," *Journal of Democracy* 13 (2002).

53. Bashiriyeh, "Cleavages in Iranian Politics since 1979."

54. S. Rose-Ackerman, *Corruption and Government: Causes, Consequences, and Reform* (Cambridge: Cambridge University Press, 2010).

55. K. W. Deutsch, "Social Mobilization and Political Development," *American Political Science Review* 55 (1961).

56. Huntington, *Political Order in Changing Societies*.

57. Milani and Pakzad, "Islamic Republic of Iran in an Age of Global Transitions"; Deutsch, "Social Mobilization and Political Development"; L. J. Diamond, "Democracy in Decline: How Washington Can Reverse the Tide," *Foreign Affairs* 151 (2016).

58. J. Christiansen, "Four Stages of Social Movements," Research Starters, EBSCO Publishing Inc., 2009.

59. Fukuyama, *Political Order and Political Decay*; Huntington, *Political Order in Changing Societies*.

60. World Bank, Worldwide Governance Indicators (WGI) Project, https://datacatalog.worldbank.org/dataset/worldwide-governance-indicators; Transparency International, Corruption Perception Index: Global Scores, https://www.transparency.org.

61. Freedom House, "Freedom in the World 2020," https://freedomhouse.org.

62. Basu and Cordella, *Institutions, Governance and the Control of Corruption*.

63. P. Langseth and N. Christelis, eds. *UN Handbook on Practical Anti-Corruption Measures for Prosecutors and Investigators* (Vienna: UN Office on Drugs and Crime, 2004).

64. Basel Institute on Governance, "Basel AML Index 2017," https://baselgovernance.org/.

65. B. Rothstein, "Fighting Systemic Corruption: The Indirect Strategy," *Daedalus* 147, no. 3 (2018).

CHAPTER 2

1. I. Pool, "Demographic Dividends: Determinants of Development or Merely Windows of Opportunity?" *Ageing Horizons* , no. 7 (2007): 28–35.

2. Statistical Yearbooks (1966–2019) and Census Data (1956–2016), Statistical Center of Iran.

3. UN Population Division, United Nations Department of Economic and Social Affairs, https://www.un.org/development/desa/pd/, accessed June 2019.

4. Statistical Yearbooks and Census Data.

5. Statistical Yearbooks and Census Data.

6. Statistical Yearbooks and Census Data.

7. M.J. Abbasi-Shavazi, P. McDonald, and M. Hosseini-Chavoshi, *The Fertility Transition in Iran: Revolution and Reproduction*, (New York: Springer, 2009).

8. Statistical Yearbooks and Census Data.

9. M. J. Abbasi-Shavazi, "The Fertility Revolution in Iran," *Population et Sociétés* 373 (November 2001).

10. A. Aghajanian and A. Merhyar, "Fertility, Contraceptive Use and Family Planning Program Activity in the Islamic Republic of Iran," *International Family Planning Perspectives* 25 (1999).

11. F. Roudi, "Iran's Family Planning Program: Responding to a Nation's Need," Population Reference Bureau MENA Brief, June 2002.

12. Abbasi-Shavazi, McDonald, and Hosseini-Chavoshi, *The Fertility Transition in Iran.*

13. H. Malekafzali, "Population Control and Reproductive Health in the Islamic Republic of Iran," *Archives of Iranian Medicine* 7 (2004).

14. Malekafzali, "Population Control and Reproductive Health."

15. UN Population Division, United Nations Department of Economic and Social Affairs.

16. Statistical Yearbooks and Census Data.

17. P. McDonald, M. M. Hosseini-Chavoshi, M.J. Abbasi-Shavazi, and A. Rashidian, "An Assessment of Recent Iranian Fertility Trends Using Parity Progression Ratios," *Demographic Research* 32 (2015); M. Hosseini-Chavoshi, M.J. Abbasi-Shavazi, and P. McDonald, "Fertility, Marriage, and Family Planning in Iran: Implications for Future Policy," *Population Horizon* 13 (2016).

18. United Nations World Water Assessment Programme, *The United Nations World Water Development Report 2016: Water and Jobs* (Paris: UNESCO, 2016).

19. World Bank Open Data, The World Bank, https://data.worldbank.org/ ,accessed July 2017.

20. A. Aghajanian and V. Thompson, "Household Size and Structure in Iran: 1976–2006," *Open Family Studies Journal* 5 (2013).

21. Statistical Yearbooks (1966–2019) and Census Data (1956–2016), Statistical Center of Iran; UN Population Division, United Nations Department of Economic and Social Affairs, https://www.un.org/development/desa/pd/, accessed June 2019.

22. R. Lee and A. Mason, "What Is the Demographic Dividend?" *Finance and Development*, 43 (2006).

23. I. Pool, "Demographic Dividends."

CHAPTER 3

1. Statistical Yearbooks (1966–2019) and Census Data (1956–2016) Statistical Center of Iran; Statistical Yearbooks of the Ministry of Labor and Social Welfare (1999–2020), Ministry of Labor and Social Welfare, www.amarkar.ir; UN Population Division, United Nations Department of Economic and Social Affairs, https://www.un.org/development/desa/pd/.

2. Statistical Yearbooks and Census Data; Statistical Yearbooks of the Ministry of Labor and Social Welfare; UN Population Division; Statistics and Datasets, International Labor Organization (ILO), https://www.ilo.org/.

3. Statistics and Datasets, International Labor Organization (ILO).

4. Statistical Yearbooks of the Ministry of Labor and Social Welfare.

5. Statistics and Datasets, International Labor Organization (ILO).

6. Statistical Yearbooks and Census Data ; Statistical Yearbooks of the Ministry of Labor and Social Welfare.

7. Statistical Yearbooks and Census Data.

8. Statistical Yearbooks and Census Data.

9. Statistical Yearbooks and Census Data.

10. C. Goldin, "The U-Shaped Female Labor Force Function in Economic Development and Economic History," NBER Working Paper Series, Working Paper 4707, 1994.

11. Statistical Yearbooks and Census Data.; Statistical Yearbooks of the Ministry of Labor and Social Welfare; Institute for Research and Planning in Higher Education, Ministry of Science, Research, and Technology, irphe .ac.ir.

12. M. Toossi, "A Century of Change: The US Labor Force, 1950–2050," *Monthly Labor Review*, 2002.

13. Statistical Yearbooks and Census Data.

14. Statistics and Datasets, International Labor Organization (ILO).

15. Statistical Yearbooks of the Ministry of Labor and Social Welfare; Statistics and Datasets.

16. Statistical Yearbooks and Census Data.; Statistical Yearbooks of the Ministry of Labor and Social Welfare

17. Statistical Yearbooks of the Ministry of Labor and Social Welfare.

18. Statistical Yearbooks, Census Data, and Labor Statistics.

19. F. Sabahi, "Literacy Corps," *Encyclopædia Iranica*, 2004, https://www .iranicaonline.org.

20. United Nations Development Programme, Human Development Data (1990–2018), http://hdr.undp.org/en/data.

21. R .J. Barro, "Education and Economic Growth," in *The Contribution of Human and Social Capital to Sustained Economic Growth and Well-Being*, ed. J. F. Helliwell (OECD; 2001); E. Hanushek and L. Wößmann, "Education Quality and Economic Growth," World Bank Policy Research Working Paper 4122, Washington, DC: World Bank, 2007; E. Hanushek, "For Long-Term Economic Development, Only Skills Matter," *IZA World of Labor*, (2017); E. Hanushek, "Economic Growth in Developing Countries: The Role of Human Capital," *Economics of Education Review* 27 (2013).

22. Barro, "Education and Economic Growth"; Hanushek and Wößmann, "Education Quality and Economic Growth."

23. Economic Time Series Database and Other Statistics, The Central Bank of Iran, https://tsd.cbi.ir/ .

24. Trends in International Mathematics and Science Study (TIMSS), International Association for the Evaluation of Educational Achievement, 1995–2015, https://nces.ed.gov/timss/idetimss/; Programme for International Student Assessment (PISA), OECD, 2000–2018, https://www.oecd.org/pisa/.

25. Hanushek and Wößmann, "Education Quality and Economic Growth."

26. Statistical Yearbooks and Census Data, authors' estimates.

27. Statistical Yearbooks and Census Data; Institute for Research and Planning in Higher Education, Ministry of Science, Research, and Technology, irphe.ac.ir.

28. Statistical Yearbooks and Census Data.; Institute for Research and Planning in Higher Education, Ministry of Science, Research, and Technology, irphe.ac.ir.

29. The Human Capital Report 2016, World Economic Forum, https://weforum.org/ .

30. Institute for Research and Planning in Higher Education, Ministry of Science, Research, and Technology, irphe.ac.ir.

31. Statistical Yearbooks and Institute for Research and Planning in Higher Education, Ministry of Science, Research, and Technology, irphe.ac.ir.

CHAPTER 4

1. Calculated based on A. Khavarinejad, "Estimation of Gross Domestic Product of Iran," *Money and Economy* 5 (2009).

2. Estimated based on Khavarinejad, "Estimation of Gross Domestic Product of Iran."; H. Salehi Esfahaniand M. H. Pesaran, "The Iranian Economy in the Twentieth Century: A Global Perspective," *Iranian Studies* 42 (2009).

3. Salehi Esfahani and Pesaran, "The Iranian Economy in the Twentieth Century."

4. Economic Time Series Database and Other Statistics, The Central Bank of Iran, https://tsd.cbi.ir/ .

5. Economic Time Series Database.

6. Economic Time Series Database.

7. Economic Time Series Database; Statistical Yearbooks (1966–2019), Census Data (1956–2016), and Other Economic Statistics, Statistical Center of Iran.

8. Statistical Yearbooks, Census Data, and Other Economic Statistics.

9. Economic Time Series Database.

10. The Dutch disease is a term that refers to the adverse effects of appreciation of a currency, often due to a spike in the export of natural resources, on the competitiveness of other sectors, often manufacturing and agriculture.

11. A. Milani, *The Shah* (New York: St. Martin's Griffin, 2012); A. Amanat, *Iran: A Modern History* (New Haven, CT: Yale University Press, 2017); M. Parsa, *Social Origins of the Iranian Revolution* (New Brunswick, NJ: Rutgers University Press, 1989).

12. Statistical Yearbooks, Census Data, and Other Economic Statistics.

13. M. Bazargan, "Cuba, India, Iran," Document 15, Cultural Organization of Mehdi Bazargan, 2008.

14. J. Amuzegar, "The Iranian Economy before and after the Revolution," *Middle East Journal* 46 (1992).

15. Amuzegar, "The Iranian Economy before and after the Revolution."

16. Economic Time Series Database.

17. Brent Spot Price FOB, US Energy Information Administration, eia.gov.

18. Economic Time Series Database.

19. Statistical Yearbooks, Census Data , and Other Economic Statistics.

20. Statistical Yearbooks, Census Data, and Other Economic Statistics.

21. Statistical Yearbooks (1966–2018), Census Data (1956–2016), and Other Economic Statistics, Statistical Center of Iran; Statistical Yearbooks of the Ministry of Labor and Social Welfare.

22. Economic Time Series Database.

23. Economic Time Series Database and Other Statistics, The Central Bank of Iran (cbi.ir); Statistical Yearbooks, Census Data, and Other Economic Statistics.

24. Economic Time Series Database.

25. Statistical Yearbooks, Census Data, and Other Economic Statistics.

26. Statistical Yearbooks, Census Data, and Other Economic Statistics; Statistical Yearbooks of the Ministry of Labor and Social Welfare.

27. Economic Modeling and Information Management Office, Ministry of Economic Affairs and Finance, databank.mefa.ir; Iranian Privatization Organization Performance Report in 1396, (in Farsi), 2017.

28. Economic Time Series Database; Statistical Yearbooks, Census Data, and Other Economic Statistics; Statistical Yearbooks of the Ministry of Labor and Social Welfare, www.amarkar.ir.

29. F. Alvaredo, L. Assouad, and T. Piketty, "Measuring Inequality in the Middle East 1990–2016: The World's Most Unequal Region?" *Review of Income and Wealth* 65 (2019).

30. Alvaredo, Assouad, and Piketty, "Measuring Inequality in the Middle East 1990–2016."

31. Alvaredo, Assouad, and Piketty, "Measuring Inequality in the Middle East 1990–2016"; T. Piketty, *Capital in the Twenty-First Century* (Cambridge, MA: Harvard University Press, 2014).

32. The Central Bank of Iran, "Productivity in the Iranian Economy (1375–1395)," (in Farsi), 2018.

33. TFP is a measure of efficiency that corresponds to the portion of output growth that cannot be explained by changes in the amount of labor and capital inputs.

34. F. Mojaver, "Sources of Economic Growth and Stagnation in Iran," *Journal of International Trade and Economic Development* 18 (2009).

35. Amanat, *Iran: A Modern History.*

36. Economic Time Series Database.

37. Salehi Esfahani and Pesaran, "The Iranian Economy in the Twentieth Century."

38. That is, borrowing directly from the Central Bank the difference between the value of newly issued money and the costs to produced it.

39. Iran 2018 Article IV Consultation, International Monetary Fund, 2018, https://www.imf.org/ .

40. S. Dale and B. Fattouh, "Peak Oil Demand and Long-Run Oil Prices," BP, 2018.

CHAPTER 5

1. Monetary and Banking Act, 1960, Parliament Research Center, https://rc .majlis.ir.

2. Monetary and Banking Act, 1972, Parliament Research Center, https://rc .majlis.ir.

3. Jan Fredrik Qvigstad, *On Central Banking* (Cambridge: Cambridge University Press, 2016).

4. Economic Time Series Database, The Central Bank of Iran, https://tsd .cbi.ir/.

5. International Monetary Fund, DataMapper, https://imf.org/external/ datamapper/datasets.

6. Annual Report on Exchange Arrangements and Exchange Restrictions, IMF, 2016, https://www.imf.org/.

7. M. Hashem Pesaran, "The Iranian Foreign Exchange Policy and the Black Market for Dollars," *International Journal of Middle East Studies* 24 (1992); M. Bahmani-Oskooee, "History of the Rial and Foreign Exchange Policy in Iran," *Iranian Economic Review* 10 (2005).

8. Economic Time Series Database); Statistical Yearbooks (1966–2019), Statistics, Statistical Center of Iran.

9. E. Balls, J. Howat, and A. Stansbury, "Central Bank Independence Revisited: After the Financial Crisis, What Should a Model Central Bank Look Like?" M-RCBG Associate Working Paper Series, 67, Mossavar-Rahmani Center for Business & Government, Harvard Kennedy School, 2016.

10. G. E. Curtis and E. Hooglund, "Iran: A Country Study," Federal Research Division, Library of Congress, 2008.

11. Banks Nationalization Act, 1979, Parliament Research Center, https://rc .majlis.ir.

12. Law for the Administration of Banks, 1979, Parliament Research Center, https://rc.majlis.ir.

13. Curtis and Hooglund, "Iran: A Country Study."

14. For more details on the evolution of the banking system of Iran before the revolution, see H. Mehran, *The Goals and Policies of the Central Bank of Iran: 1960–1978*, 2nd ed. (Bethesda, MD: IBEX Publishers, 2015) (in Farsi).

15. Usury-free Banking Law, 1983, t Parliament Research Center, rc.majlis.ir.

16. M. M. Hussain, A. Shahmoradi, and R. Turk, "An Overview of Islamic Finance," *Journal of International Commerce, Economics and Policy* 7, no. 1 (2016).

17. S. H. Ashraf and A. A. Giashi, "Islamic Banking in Iran-Progress and Challenges," *Kuwait Chapter of Arabian Journal of Business and Management Review* 1 (2011).

18. Money and Banking Statistics, Macroeconomics Division, Plan and Budget Organization of Iran, https://mporg.ir.

19. N. Klein, "Non-Performing Loans in CESEE: Determinants and Impact on Macroeconomic Performance," Working Paper 13/72, International Monetary Fund, 2013, https://www.imf.org/.

20. D. Y. Liu, Y. C. Wu, C. H. Lin, and W. M. Lu, "The Effects of Nonperforming Loans on Dynamic Network Bank Performance," Discrete Dynamics in Nature and Society, 2017, .

21. G. Dell'Ariccia, E. Detragiache, and R. Rajan, "The Real Effect of Banking Crises," *Journal of Financial Intermediation* 17 (2008).

22. A. Demirgüç-Kunt and E. Detragiache, "The Determinants of Banking Crises in Developing and Developed Countries," *IMF Staff Papers* 45 (1998).

CHAPTER 6

1. BP, "Statistical Review of World Energy," London, June 2020.

2. Statistical Yearbooks (1966–2019), Statistical Center of Iran; Review of 26 Years of Iran's Energy Statistics, Ministry of Energy, Tehran 2015 (in Farsi); Iran's Energy Balance 1393, Ministry of Energy, Tehran, 2014, (in Farsi).

3. Statistical Yearbooks (1966–2019); Review of 26 Years of Iran's Energy Statistics; Iran's Energy Balance 1393.

4. World Development Indicators, World Bank, https://datatopics .worldbank.org/world-development-indicators/.

5. Monthly Oil Market Report, 2001–2021, OPEC, https://www.opec.org/.

6. Economic Time Series Database and Other Statistics, Central Bank of Iran, https://tsd.cbi.ir/.

7. J. P. C. Carey, "Iran and Control of Its Oil Resources," *Political Science Quarterly* 89, no. 1 (1974).

8. Carey, "Iran and Control of Its Oil Resources."

9. Statistical Yearbooks; Economic Time Series Database and Other Statistics; Carey, "Iran and Control of Its Oil Resources."

10. S. Dale and B. Fattouh, "Peak Oil Demand and Long-Run Oil Prices," BP, 2018.

11. BP, "Statistical Review of World Energy," https://www.bp.com/; Iran's Energy Balance 1393.

12. Statistical Yearbooks.

13. Dale and Fattouh, "Peak Oil Demand."

14. US Energy Information Administration, eia.gov.

15. "Oil 2020: Analysis and Forecast to 2025," International Energy Association, https://www.oecd-ilibrary.org/.

16. Carey, "Iran and Control of Its Oil Resources."

17. BP, "Statistical Review of World Energy."

18. M. Soltanieh, A. Zohrabian, M. J. Gholipour, and E. Kalnay, "A Review of Global Gas Flaring and Venting and Impact on the Environment: Case Study of Iran," *International Journal of Greenhouse Gas Control* 49 (2016).

19. Statistical Yearbooks;53 Years of Iran's Electricity Statistics 1346–1398, The Ministry of Energy, (in Farsi).

20. 53 Years of Iran's Electricity Statistics 1346–1398, The Ministry of Energy, (in Farsi).

21. World Development Indicators, World Bank, https://datatopics.worldbank.org/world-development-indicators/.

22. Statistical Yearbooks; 49 Years of Iran's Electricity Statistics 1346–1394.

23. Statistical Yearbooks.

24. US Energy Information Administration, eia.gov.

25. Lazard's Levelized Cost of Energy Analysis, Version 13.0, November 2019, https://www.lazard.com/.

26. Lazard's Levelized Cost of Energy Analysis.

27. P. Azadi, A. Nezam Sarmadi, A. Mahmoudzadeh, and T. Shirvani, "The Outlook for Natural Gas, Electricity, and Renewable Energy in Iran," Working Paper 3, Stanford Iran 2040 Project, Stanford University, April 2017.

CHAPTER 7

1. J. Clapp, "Food Self-Sufficiency and International Trade: A False Dichotomy," Food and Agriculture Organization of the United Nations, http://www.fao.org/.

2. Clapp, "Food Self-Sufficiency and International Trade."

3. Statistical Yearbooks (1966–2019), Statistical Center of Iran; Annual Agriculture Statistics, Vol. 1–3, Iranian Ministry of Agriculture (in Farsi); A Statistical Overview of Field Crops Harvested Area and Production in the Past 36 Years, Iranian Ministry of Agriculture, 2015 (in Farsi), https://maj.ir.

4. Annual Agriculture Statistics; A Statistical Overview of Field Crops Harvested Area and Production in the Past 36 Years, Iranian Ministry of Agriculture, 2015, (in Farsi).

5. Statistical Yearbooks.

6. Statistical Yearbooks.

7. Highlights of Census of Agriculture, USDA, 2012, https://www.nass.usda.gov/Publications/Highlights/index.php.

8. See an earlier version of this study for more detailed analysis and description of methods: Mohsen B. Mesgaran, Pooya Azadi, "A National Adaptation Plan for Water Scarcity in Iran," Working Paper 6, Stanford Iran 2040 Project, Stanford University, August 2018.

9. Mesgaran and Azadi, "A National Adaptation Plan for Water Scarcity in Iran."

10. G.W. Norton, J. Alwang, and W.A. Masters, *Economics of Agricultural Development: World Food Systems and Resource Use*, 3rd ed. (New York: Routledge, 2014).

11. Norton, Alwang, and Masters, *Economics of Agricultural Development: World Food Systems and Resource Use*.

12. Statistical Yearbooks; Annual Agriculture Statistics, Vol. 1–3; A Statistical Overview of Field Crops.

13. World Bank Commodities Price Forecast, World Bank Group, April 24, 2018, https://www.worldbank.org/en/research/commodity-markets.

14. A.C. Ruane, R. Goldberg, and J. Chryssanthacopoulos, "AgMIP Climate Forcing Datasets for Agricultural Modeling: Merged Products for Gap-Filling and Historical Climate Series Estimation," *Agricultural and Forest Meteorology* 200 (2015).

15. Water Crisis and Feasibility Study of Connecting the Northern and Southern Waterbodies of the Country, 7th ed., Plan and Budget Organization of Iran, 2018, https://www.mporg.ir (in Farsi).

16. Water Crisis and Feasibility Study.

17. Water Crisis and Feasibility Study.

18. The Millennium Development Goals Report, United Nations, 2015, https://www.un.org/millenniumgoals/.

19. For more information on Iran's water resources and consumptions as well as the impacts of environmental flow on the ecosystem services, see: Mesgaran and Azadi, "A National Adaptation Plan for Water Scarcity in Iran."

20. C. Perry, "Inquiry into Water Use Efficiency in Australian Agriculture," Water Conservation Technical Briefs, Submission 47, June 2012.

21. C. Perry, "Does Improved Irrigation Technology Save Water? A Review of the Evidence," Food and Agriculture Organization of the United Nations, 2017.

22. Perry, "Inquiry into Water Use Efficiency in Australian Agriculture"; Perry, "Does Improved Irrigation Technology Save Water?"

23. *Annual Agriculture Statistics.*

24. *Annual Agriculture Statistics.*

25. *Annual Agriculture Statistics.*

26. Map of the Status of Iran's Underground Water at Sub-basin Level, Ministry of Energy, 2017.

27. Mesgaran and Azadi, "A National Adaptation Plan for Water Scarcity in Iran."

28. Mesgaran and Azadi, "A National Adaptation Plan for Water Scarcity in Iran."

29. Mesgaran and Azadi, "A National Adaptation Plan for Water Scarcity in Iran."

30. Additional factors that can potentially affect the food-water nexus in the future but were omitted in the analysis (either due to the high uncertainties associated with them or their small effects), along with a brief assessment of their potential impacts on Iran's water situation, are available in Mesgaran and Azadi, "A National Adaptation Plan for Water Scarcity in Iran."

31. G. W. Norton, J. Alwang, W. A. Masters, *Economics of Agricultural Development.*

CHAPTER 8

1. M. Abdollahi, *Capitalism and Brain-Drain: A Dialectical Analysis of the Migration of Highly Qualified Manpower from Less Developed to More Developed Capitalist Countries, Iran and the U.S.* (Western Michigan University, 1979).

2. Abdollahi, *Capitalism and Brain-Drain*; National Science Foundation, "Doctorate Recipients from U.S. Universities 2017, Table 53, Doctorate recipients with temporary visas intending to stay in the United States after doctorate receipt, by country of citizenship: 2011–2017," December 2018.

3. Abdollahi, *Capitalism and Brain-Drain*; Open Door Data and Project Atlas, Institute of International Education, accessed January–March 2020.

4. Iranian-Americans' Contribution Project (IACP), iacp.org, accessed March 2020.

5. The Center for Recruitment of Faculty Members, Iran's Ministry of Science, Research, and Technology, https://mjazb.ir, accessed March 2020.

6. Lesbian, gay, bisexual, transgender, and queer individuals.

7. L. Mavris, "Human Smugglers and Social Networks: Transit Migration Through the States of Former Yugoslavia," Evaluation and Policy Analysis Unit, UNHCR, 2002, https://www.unhcr.org/.

8. N. V. Hear, O. Bakewell, and K. Long, "Push-Pull Plus: Reconsidering the Drivers of Migration," *Journal of Ethnic and Migration Studies* 44 (2018).

9. K. W. Deutsch, "Social Mobilization and Political Development," *American Political Science Review* 55 (1961).

10. A. Sanaei, "Incentives and Disincentives to Return Migration: The Case of Iranian Experts Living in the United States," *Majlis and Rahbord* 26 (2019), https://www.magiran.com/paper/1987635.

11. A. Amanat, *Iran: A Modern History* (New Haven, CT: Yale University Press, 2017).

12. A. V. Banerjee and E. Duflo, *Good Economics for Hard Times: Better Answers to Our Biggest Problems* (London: Penguin UK, 2019).

13. World Bank Open Data, World Bank Group, https://data.worldbank .org/, accessed January–March 2020.

CHAPTER 9

1. A. Taheri and M. Shams Bakhsh, Regulations for the Promotion of Faculty Members: Educational, Research, and Technology, Iran's Ministry of Science, Research, and Technology, 2016, (in Farsi); Regulations for Education in PhD Programs, Iran's Ministry of Science, Research, and Technology, 2016 (in Farsi); Requirements for Quality and Quantity of Publications for Completion of PhD Degree, Amirkabir University of Technology, 2015, (in Farsi).

2. Scopus Abstract and Citation Database, www.scopus.com.

3. J. Brainard and J. You, "Rethinking Retractions," *Science* 362 (2018).

4. Retraction Watch Database, http://retractiondatabase.org.

5. CiteScore Metrics, https://www.scopus.com/sources, accessed December 2018–January 2019.

6. Institute for Research and Planning in Higher Education, irphe.ac.ir.

7. Taheri and Shams Bakhsh, Regulations for the Promotion of Faculty Members; Regulations for Education in PhD Programs; Requirements for Quality and Quantity of Publications for Completion of PhD Degree.

8. A similar approach has been taken before. See: E. Wager, S. Singhvi, and S. Kleinert, "Too Much of a Good Thing? An Observational Study of Prolific Authors," *PeerJ* 3 (2015); J. P. Ioannidis, R. Klavans, and K. W. Boyack, "Thousands of Scientists Publish a Paper Every Five Days," *Nature* 561 (2018).

9. Google Scholar, https://scholar.google.com, accessed in December 2018– January 2019.

10. D. Butler, "Iranian Paper Sparks Sense of Déjà Vu," *Nature* 455 (2008); D. Butler, "Iranian Ministers in Plagiarism Row," *Nature* 461 (2009).

APPENDIX A

1. Worldwide Governance Indicators (WGI) Project. World Bank, https:// datacatalog.worldbank.org/dataset/worldwide-governance-indicators.

2. "The impersonal and systematic application of known rules to government actors and citizens alike." World Development Report: Governance and the Law, World Bank, https://www.worldbank.org/, 2017.

3. "The extent to which a country's citizens are able to participate in selecting their government, as well as freedom of expression, freedom of association, and a free media." D. Kaufmann, A. Kraay, and M. Mastruzzi, "The Worldwide Governance Indicators: Methodology and Analytical Issues," *Hague Journal on the Rule of Law* 3 (2011).

4. "The ability of the government to provide sound policies and regulations that enable and promote private sector development." Kaufmann, Kraay, and Mastruzzi, "The Worldwide Governance Indicators."

APPENDIX C

1. International Migrant Stock 1990–2019, United Nations Population Division., https://www.un.org/development/desa/pd/content/international-migrant-stock.

2. UNHCR Online Statistical Database, unhcr.org, accessed February 2020; UNHCR Statistical Yearbooks, 2004–2016, https://www.unhcr.org/statistical-yearbooks.html; Asylum Applications in Industrialized Countries: 1980–1999, Population Data Unit, UNHCR, 2001, https://www.unhcr.org/.

3. Eurostat Asylum Statistics, ec.europa.eu, accessed January–March 2020.

4. OECD International Migration Database and Labor Market Outcomes of Immigrants, OECD.org, accessed January–March 2020.

5. Statistical Yearbooks (1965–2019), The Statistical Center of Iran.

6. Statistical Yearbook of Immigration and Naturalization Service, Department of Justice, United States, 1978–2001; Yearbook of Immigration Statistics, Office of Immigration Statistics, Homeland Security, United States, 2002–2017, https://www.dhs.gov/immigration-statistics/yearbook.

7. Immigration Statistics, Department of Manpower and Immigration, Canada Immigration Division, 1966–1980; Admissions of Permanent Residents by Country of Citizenship, 1980–2016, Open Government, open.canada.ca, Government of Canada, accessed February 2020.

8. Länderreport 16 Iran–BAMF, Federal Office for Migration and Refugees, Germany, 2019.

9. Permanent additions to Australia's resident population, Australian Department of Home Affairs, accessed February 2020.

10. Immigration statistics, UK Home Office, accessed March 2020.

11. International Migration–Denmark, Report to OECD, 2017.

12. Open Door Data and Project Atlas, Institute of International Education, accessed January–March 2020; Education xxi. Education Abroad,

Encyclopædia Iranica, online edition, iranicaonline.org/articles/education-xxii
--education-abroad-1, accessed March 2020.

13. United States Census Bureau, census.gov, accessed February 2020.

14. M. Abdollahi, *Capitalism and Brain-Drain: A Dialectical Analysis of the Migration of Highly Qualified Manpower from Less Developed to More Developed Capitalist Countries, Iran and the U.S.* (Western Michigan University, 1979).

15. Scopus Abstract and Citation Database, www.scopus.com, accessed January 2020.

APPENDIX D

1. Scopus Abstract and Citation Database, www.scopus.com.

2. CiteScore Metrics, https://www.scopus.com/sources.

3. Retraction Watch Database, http://retractiondatabase.org.

4. Retraction Watch, The Center for Scientific Integrity, https://retractionwatch.com/the-center-for-scientific-integrity/.

5. J. Beall, "Beall's List: Potential, Possible, or Probable Predatory Scholarly Open-Access Publishers," https://beallslist.net/ (updated December 31, 2016); Blacklist Journals, Iran's Ministry of Science, Research, and Technology, 2018.

INDEX

Note: page numbers followed by *f* and *t* refer to figures and tables respectively. Those followed by n refer to notes, with note number.

Absolute Rule of the Jurist (*Velayat-e Faqih*), 31

accountability, 35–43; in constitution, 37; and control of corruption, 54; demand for, in prerevolution period (1970–1978), 13, 16*t*; effect on corruption, 36; effect on legitimacy, 35–36; effect on quality of governance, 35–36; effect on rule of law, 36; and establishment of meritocracy, 10, 36; as factor in effective governance, 7, 8*f*, 10–11; free media and, 10; of Iran's supreme leader, lack of, 11; moral, 10–11; social media and, 38–39; World Bank Governance Indicators on, in Iran *vs.* world mean, 229, 230*f*. *See also* bureaucracy, lack of accountability in; elections

accountability, diagonal (social): definition of, 11, 36; substantive (de facto) *vs.* procedural (de jure), 36–37, 37*t*; typical development process for, 37

accountability, horizontal: definition of, 11, 36; substantive (de facto) *vs.* procedural (de jure), 36–37, 37*t*; typical development process for, 37

accountability, lack of: and cycle of political decay, 48, 48*f*; in early stage of revolutionary state (1979–1988), 14, 16*t*; effects of, 55; as obstacle to reform,

26; in reconstruction and reforms period, 14, 16*t*; and spread of corruption, 40

accountability, procedural (de jure), 11; in vertical, diagonal, and horizontal dimensions, 36–38, 37*t*

accountability, substantive (de facto), 11; typical development process for, 37; in vertical, diagonal, and horizontal dimensions, 36–38, 37*t*

accountability, vertical: definition of, 11, 36; importance of political parties to, 37, 38–39; substantive (de facto) *vs.* procedural (de jure), 36–37, 37*t*, 38; typical development process for, 37

affordable housing program (*Maskan-e-Mehr*), poor design of, 21

Afghanistan, trade with Iran, 107, 115, 116*f*

agricultural land: areas of high groundwater stress, 180, 181*f*; areas of poor terrain and suitability, 180, 181*f*; degree of suitability for agriculture, 171–72, 172*f*; suitable land, percentage currently in use, 172, 172*f*

agricultural land, 1960–2019: farm size, 170, 171*f*; horticulture *vs.* rain-fed and irrigated land, 170, 171*f*; total harvested area, 170, 171*f* agricultural production: of fodders and vegetables, and heavy water use, 170; inefficiency of, 172; reduction in, potential dire consequences of, 172; and small farms, inefficiency of, 170–71

agricultural production, 1960–2019: by crop type, 169–70, 169*f*; of fodders and vegetables, increase in, 170; of wheat, lag in, 170

agriculture: electricity use, 1970–2020, 159*f*, 160, 165; food self-sufficiency as goal of, 167, 168, 186, 188; and food self-sufficiency *vs.* food security, 167–68, 188; in reconstruction and reforms period (1989–2004), 106; soil damage from, 172

agriculture, economic share of: in 1950s, 97; 1960–2020, 99, 100*f*; at beginning of 20th century, 97

agriculture, water use by: as focus of water crisis remediation plan, 178; increase with income per capita, 174; as large share of total water use, 166, 167; as unsustainable, 172

agriculture, water use reduction: consequences for farmers' employment, 167; consequences for food supply, 167; as only viable solution to water crisis, 167; strategies for, 167. *See also* water crisis remediation plan

Ahmadinejad, Mahmoud: and Central Bank financing of deficit, 129; and governance deadlock and economic stagnation period (2005–2020), 106; housing program, poor execution of, 107–8; illegitimacy of election of, in popular perception, 20; inflation under, 21; and legitimacy of state, damage to, 20–21; and period of governance deadlock and economic stagnation, 14, 16*t*, 20; as populist politician, 20–21; privatization under, 21, 28, 107–8; spending by, 21; tax collected under, as percentage of GDP, 25*f*

airline passengers, international outbound, 1960–2018, 201, 202*f*

Amir Kabir, 19

Anglo-Persian Oil Company, 147

Anglo-Soviet invasion of Iran (1941), and Reza Shah's abdication, 97

anti-imperialist stance of Iran, economic costs of, 18–19

artificial intelligence and automation, likely effects on Iran, 56, 122

Asian Contagion, 106

authoritarian regimes: legitimacy of, 16–17; and potential for unrest with social mobilization, 46

autocratic rule, and development, 224–25

balance of payments, 2011–2020, 120*t*

banking system: accounting system, inadequacy of, 139; and banking regulations, failure to enforce, 138; disconnecting from the international system, 139–40; financial depth, lack of change for decades, 141; and IFRS reporting requirements, failure to comply with, 139–40; necessary reforms, 26, 133–35, 140–41; and need for securitization of national debt, 133, 141. *See also* Central Bank of Iran (CBI)

banking system, domestic: and financing of budget deficits, 124–25, 128; as primary source of funds for businesses, 135; as relatively undeveloped, 135–36, 136*f*

banking system, financial instability of, 137–40; CBI's failure to address, 107, 139, 141; corruption and, 137, 139; and crisis, increasing potential for, 137, 139, 140; and crisis, likely effects of, 140; financial soundness indicators, 2005–2019, 137, 138*f*; low capital adequacy, 137–38, 139; masking of critical issues, 139; and negative net capital position, 139; real sector effects of, 140; sources of, 137–38

bank recapitalization and NPL reduction, 119, 120*t*, 121*f*

banks, commercial, 135–36; damage to functionality of, after revolution, 135; decline in lending capacity, 136; and Islamic finance system, 135; nationalization of, 135; number of, in 1978, 135; outstanding bank loans by sector, 1967–2020, 136, 137*f*; reduction in number, after revolution, 135; support from Central Bank, 139

banks, private, licensing of, under Khatami, 106

Banks Nationalization Act, 135

Basel AML index, 52

Basij, and clientelism, 50

Bazargan, Mehdi, 103

blackmail, 51*f*, 54

bonyads. See revolutionary foundations

brain drain: causes of, 43, 62, 75, 189; diaspora scholars, nations hosting, 193, 194*f*; diaspora scholars at foreign universities, 192–93, 193*f*; diaspora scholars publishing papers, 1970–2019, 192, 193*f*, 205; diaspora scholars returning to Iran, 192–93; effects of, 118; government position on, 189–90, 202; likely continuation of, 202–3, 205; patents published by Iranian-Americans, 192–93; percentage of Iranian scholars living abroad, 193

bribery, 51*f*, 52; and blackmail, 51*f*, 54

broad money: growth rate, 1965–2020, 127–28, 128*f*, 128*t*; ratio to monetary base, 1965–2020, 129–30, 130*f*; share of time deposits in, 1965–2020, 129–30, 130*f*

budget deficits: 2011–2021, 121*f*; causes of, 118; Central Bank's financing of, 27, 124–25, 128–29; as comparable to Soviet Union before collapse, 118–19; financing through seigniorage, 118, 124; and nonproductive spending, high level of, 133; and room for budget

cuts, 133; and tax revenue, low levels of, 133

bureaucracy, lack of accountability in: and active suppression of talented individuals, 42–43; and damage to state capacity, 42; need for establishment of meritocracy, 10, 36; and perpetuation of corruption, 40

bureaucracy, recruitment in: blocking of political rivals, 41; damage to social capital from, 43; exclusion of large segments of society from, 43; Islamic Republic's replacement of experienced bureaucrats with inexperienced supporters, 24; patronage and nepotism in, 41, 51*f*, 53; preference for ideological commitment over talent, 41–43

businesses, small and medium, role of financial sector in growth of, 123, 135

capital account: 1965–2020, 117, 117*f*; 2011–2020, 120*t*

capital adequacy ratio (CAR), 2005–2019, 137, 138*f*

capital flight: effects of, 118; in governance deadlock and economic stagnation period (2005–2020), 108, 117

capital formation rates: 1960–1969, 99; 1960–2020, 99, 100*f*; current, as negative, 118; in governance deadlock and economic stagnation period (2005–2020), 107; in reconstruction and reforms period (1989–2004), 106

capital investment shortfall, 119, 121*f*

CAR. *See* capital adequacy ratio

CBI. *See* Central Bank of Iran

Central Bank of Iran (CBI), 124–35; assigned missions outside traditional central bank roles, 124; and banking regulations, failure to enforce, 138, 141; buildup of debt to, 137; establishment of, 124; failure to reform, as political failure, 26; and financial instability of the banking system, failure to address,

Central Bank of Iran (*continued*)
107, 139, 141; and financing of budget
deficits, 27, 124–25, 128–29; and growth
in 1960–1969 period, 98; and inflation,
failure to control, 126–30; institutional
governance, issues in, 124, 125–26;
institutional governance, needed
reforms in, 134; insufficient autonomy
of, 27, 141; and interactions between
fiscal and monetary policy, 124–25;
and inversion of fiscal and monetary
policy roles, 133; Islamic finance
system and, 124, 125, 141; lack of independence, 125–26, 140; lack of proper
monetary instruments, 140, 141; lack
of transparency, 40, 126, 134–35; loss
of control over balance sheet, 124–25,
128–29; monetary policy, obstacles to
implementation of, 124–25; necessary
reforms, 26, 133–35, 140–41; objectives
of, 124; performance, evaluation of,
124–26, 140–41; performance, standard used to evaluate, 124–26, 140;
presidents' appointment of governors
based on political loyalty, 125–26; and
primary goals of central banks, 124;
role and responsibilities of, 124; and
sterilization of government-held foreign currency, 125, 128
Central Bank of Iran, and exchange rate:
failure to control, 130–33; multiple currency practices (MCP), 131, 132*f*; necessary reforms in, 134; use to control
inflation, 130, 132*f*
central banks: independence, transparency, and accountability as pillars of
good governance for, 125; price and
financial stability as primary goals of,
124
Chavez, Hugo, 21
China: accountability in, 38; autocratic
rule in, and development, 224; influence on Rafsanjani, 19, 105; Iran's ties
to, 18; key indicators of good gover-

nance *vs.* Iran, 5–6, 6*f*; trade with Iran,
107, 115, 116*f*
civil liberty, level in Iran, 49
civil society, suppression of: and lack of
class struggle, 111; and spread of corruption, 35, 49
class struggle, and Iranian economic performance, 110–11
clientelism in Iran: consequences of, 50;
and lack of accountability, 38; origins
of, 18; as type of corruption, 50, 51*f*
climate change: concern about, and drop
in demand for oil, 148–49, 151–52;
likely effects on Iran, 56
colleges and universities: associate degree
programs, number of students in, 92;
and cultural revolution, purging of
faculty in, 93, 199; and demand *vs.*
capacity, 89–90, 91*f*; faculty-to-student
ratio, 93; increase in students after late
1990s, reasons for, 89–90; institutions
producing largest numbers of publications, 211; number of published papers,
and retraction rate, 239*t*; number of
students, by field of study, 92, 92*f*;
number of students *vs.* nonstudents in
19–25 cohort, 90, 91*f*; patronage and
nepotism in faculty hiring, 41, 88, 93,
95; women as percentage of, 92. *See
also* higher education in Iran
colleges and universities, expansion
of capacity, 90, 216; and increased
number of publications, 216, 221;
and reduction of quality, 93, 202, 217,
221
conflicts of interests, in bureaucrats, 51*f*,
53
connection to outside world: internet
and, 44; lack of, and poor quality of
higher education, 19; satellite TV and,
44
constitution of Islamic Republic:
accountability in, 37; mix of democratic, theocratic, and autocratic elements

in, 17; recognition of political parties in, 37–38

corruption, 48–55, 51*f*; administrative, 50, 51*f*, 52–53; blackmail, 51*f*, 54; coercive, 50, 51*f*, 54; current high levels of, 118; and cycle of political decay, 48, 48*f*; definition of, 34, 49, 50; in diaspora community, 51*f*, 53; as driver of migration, 198, 202; elites' efforts to avoid exposure of, 40; as endemic, 50, 54; entrenchment of, 15; favoritism, 50, 51*f*, 53; and financial instability of banking system, 137, 139; government unwillingness to address, 52; investigation of, government fear of consequences of, 40; and judiciary's punishment of whistleblowers, 49; lack of rule of law and, 34–35; level in Iran (1995–2020), 49, 49*f*; nepotism, 41, 51*f*, 53; in non-elected parts of state, 50, 51*f*; petty, 49; public acceptance as norm, 34; and reform, blocking of, 118, 119–21, 122; *vs.* rent seeking, 50; and state capacity, damage to, 34, 40; and tax collection, 110; types of, 49, 50. *See also* scientific papers, and corruption in publication process

corruption, control of: accountability and, 36, 54; anti-corruption commission needed for, 54, 57; as collective action problem, 54–55; difficulty of, 54–55; elections and, 52; Iranian government's lack of interest in, 52; in Iran *vs.* peer countries, 6, 6*f*; transparency and, 54

corruption, political (grand), 49; as endemic, 54; increase over time, 54; types of, 50–51, 51*f*

corruption, spread of: factors contributing to, 34–35, 40; and rise of crime rate, 10, 15, 35, 36*f*

credit institutions, private: and financial crisis, 106; licensing of, under Khatami, 106

crime, increase in: destabilization of traditional social order and, 46–47; with spread of corruption, 10, 15, 35, 36*f*

crisis in Iran, current: austerity measures necessary to address, 45; causes and effects of, 1, 5, 15; as deepest since founding of Islamic Republic, 48, 118; as driver of migration, 198; and economic stresses, multiplication of, 112; global trends likely to exacerbate, 56; political decay underlying, 48, 48*f*; poor governance as cause of, 222; as potential catalyst for change, 1–2; rapid decline in legitimacy and, 23, 45; reforms needed to address, 56–57; as unprecedented, 1

cultural diffusion, effect of policies to prevent, 19

cultural police, corruption in, 51*f*, 54

cultural revolution (1980–1983), as driver of immigration, 199, 199*f*

currency: monetary base growth rate, 1965–2020, 127–28, 128*f*, 128*t*. *See also* broad money; monetary base (M_2 multiplier); money supply, growth of

currency depreciation, 130, 132*f*; as driver of migration, 200; economic effects of, 130; inflation and, 1960–2020, 127–28, 127*f*; sanctions and, 131–32

current account: 1965–2020, 117, 117*f*; 2011–2020, 120*t*

data on Iran: government manipulation of, 52; limited availability of, ix; politicization of, ix; for this study, sources of, 2, 59

debt, external, 2011–2020, 120*t*

democratic accountability: and accountability of public officials, 10–11; establishment of, as essential for future progress, 224–25; in Iran, *vs.* world mean, 229, 230*f* demography: average household size, 1956–2015, 69–70, 70f; births, 1960–2020, 59–60, 60f; child mortality rates, 1950–2020, 61, 61f, 75; data sources on, 59; deaths 1960–2020, 59, 60f; effects of changes in, 75; importance to development policy, 58; internal migration and, 59; life expectancy by sex, 1950–2020, 60–62, 61f, 75; male to female ratio (2016), 59; mortality, low, transition to, 57. See also fertility rates; population

Deng Xiaoping, influence on Rafsanjani, 19, 105

developing countries' state capacity, as insufficient for expected functions, 8

diaspora community: corruption in, 51f, 53; potential aid to Iran in the future, 203–5; reluctance to aid current regime, 203, 205; and remittances, 204; supporters of the Islamic Republic, location of, 53f

diet, and food demand, 173

divorces, number of, 1965–2020, 64, 65f

drug trafficking, government-sanctioned, 51f, 52

early stage of revolutionary state (1979–1988): and accountability, lack of, 14, 16t; administration's views on economy, 103; economic conditions in, 102–4, 121, 128t; economic contraction in, 13–14, 16t, 17, 44, 45t; economic policy, lack of, 103; economic self-sufficiency policies, effects of, 103, 104; employment ratio in, 97, 98f; evolution and interaction of governance components in, 13–14, 16f; and foreign reserves, decline of, 117; frequent changes of government in, 102; GDP growth in, 97, 98f, 99f, 102; income per capita in, 198; inflation in, 97, 98f; internal migration in, 102–3; Islamic Republic's economic mismanagement and, 102; job creation in, 102; nationalizations, effects of, 102, 103–4; oil export/revenue per capita in, 97, 98f, 101; and rule of law, undermining of, 14, 16t, 30–31; shares of sectors in outstanding bank loans, 137f; suppression of freedom in, 14; suppression of political opposition in, 17, 44; tax collected as percentage of GDP, 25f. See also legitimacy, in early stage of revolutionary state (1979–1988)

economically inactive population: definition of, 76; discouraged workers, percentage of, 77, 82; discouraged workers among women, 82; by gender and age, 1966–2016, 78–79, 78f; size, 1960–2020, 76–77, 77f

economic development, 43–45; contraction in early stage of revolutionary state (1979–1988), 13–14, 16t, 17, 44, 45t; effect of poor governance on, 55, 121; goals of, 43; in governance deadlock and economic stagnation period (2005–2020), 45, 45t; importance of well-developed financial sector to, 123; JCPOA agreement and, 22; jobless growth, periods of, 81, 81f; and lack of rule of law, effects of, 32–33; policy, importance of demography in, 58; in prerevolution period (1970–1978), 13, 16t, 43, 45t; in reconstruction and reforms period (1989–2004), 14, 44–45, 45t

economic forces in Iran, under-studied role of, 2

economic growth, 96–113; in 1960–1969 period, 98–99; capital inputs as predominant contribution to, 109; in early stage of revolutionary state (1979–1988), 102–4; in governance deadlock and economic stagnation period (2005–2020), 106–13; Islamic Republic's dysfunctional institutions and, 97; lack of, as driver of migration, 198, 200; periods of slump, 96;

periods of sustained growth, 96; political events shaping, 96–97; poor, class struggle and, 110–11; in prerevolution period (1970–1978), 99–102; in reconstruction and reforms period (1989–2004), 105–6; variance *vs.* other nations in recent decades, 97

economic growth, effect of education on: in Iran *vs.* other countries, 88, 89*f*; and quantity *vs.* quality of education, 88; scholarship on, 87–88

economic imbalances, current, 118–21; decisive action needed to resolve, 119; as driver of migration, 198; and economic indicators, 2011–2020, 120*t*; growth of deficits, interest payments and other imbalances, 2011–2021, 119, 120*t*, 121*f*; oil sanctions and, 119; and reform, corrupt interests blocking, 118, 119–21, 122

economic indicators, 2011–2020, 120*t*

economic opportunity, lack of, as driver of migration, 198, 200, 202–3

economic policy of Iran: lack of, in early stage of revolutionary state (1979–1988), 103; as trial and error process, 27

economic protests of 2017–2018, 47

economic protests of 2019, 47

economic reform: blocking of, by corrupt interests, 118, 119–21, 122; Islamic Revolutionary Guard Corps as obstacle to, 22–23; necessary banking system reforms, 26, 133–35, 140–41; as risk, with declining legitimacy, 55, 110, 144

economic self-sufficiency policies: effects of, 103, 104. *See also* food self-sufficiency

economy: future challenges for, 121–22; government control over, privatization and, 28; phases of growth and contraction, 1960–2020, 121; poor performance, as result of poor governance, 55, 121

education, 86–94; ideological purges of faculty and, 93, 199; ideological shaping of students as primary focus of, 88, 94; low return on, 202; mass education, introduction of, 87; poor quality, reasons for, 88, 89, 90*f*, 93, 95; primary and secondary, poor achievement test performance *vs.* other countries, 89, 90*f*, 95. *See also* colleges and universities; higher education in Iran

education, and literacy rates: 1970–2020, 46, 47*t*; current, 87; improvement in, 86–87, 94; *vs.* other countries, 1950–2020, 86, 87*f*

education, effect on economic growth: in Iran *vs.* other countries, 88, 89*f*; and quantity *vs.* quality of education, 88; scholarship on, 87–88

education levels: by age and gender, 2006–2026, 91, 91*f*; changes, 1970–2020, 46, 47*t*; improvements in mean years of schooling, 87, 94–95; improvements, cultural factors in, 89–90; improvements, demographic factors in, 89; low, reasons for, 86–87; policies to avoid cultural diffusion and, 19; and unemployment rate, 82; of women, 1965–2020, *vs.* labor force participation, 79, 80*f*

election of 2005, as rigged, in popular perception, 20

election of 2009: and emigration of Iranians, 194, 200; and reform, public loss of faith in, 21; as rigged, in popular perception, 20

election of 2013, Rouhani's victory in, 21

elections: anti-corruption function of, 52; in authoritarian states, to demonstrate legitimacy, 10; in Iran, corruption and manipulation of, 52

elections, and democratic accountability: and accountability of public officials, 10–11; establishment of, as essential for future progress, 224–25; in Iran, *vs.* world mean, 229, 230*f* electricity, 159–63; losses in transmission and distribution, 159, 165; prices, 1970–2020, 143, 144, 144*f*

electricity consumption: 1960–2019, 159, 159*f*; *vs.* added GDP value, 160, 165; *vs.* economic output, 160, 165; by major users, 1970–2020, 159–60, 159*f*, 165; per capita, *vs.* other countries, 160*f*

electricity demand: factors affecting, 159; growth in, 165; residential, increase in, 159*f*, 160

electricity generation: efficiency increases in, 161; fuels used for, 1970–2019, 160–61, 161*f*, 165; future needs, 162; future sources, options for, 162

embezzlement by bureaucrats, 51*f*, 52

employment: artificial intelligence and automation and, 56, 122; population growth and, 69

employment levels, oil revenues and, 81, 81*f*

employment ratio, 82; in 1960–1969 period, 97, 98*f*; in early stage of revolutionary state (1979–1988), 97, 98*f*; in governance deadlock and economic stagnation period (2005–2020), 97, 98*f*, 112; in prerevolution period (1970–1978), 97, 98*f*; in reconstruction and reforms period (1989–2004), 97, 98*f*

energy consumption: per capita, 1970–2020, 143, 143*f*; per unit of economic output, 1970–2020, 143, 143*f*

energy efficiency, since 1990, 143

energy market, global: changes in, likely effects on Iran, 56; and new technologies increasing oil supply, 148; and peak oil theory, 148–49, 152; and turn from fossil fuels, 148–49

energy market, and shift to oil abundance paradigm: causes of, 151–52; and diminished value of Iranian oil reserves, 122, 151–52; and limited leverage of Iran, 119

energy prices, 1970–2020, 143–44, 144*f*

energy sector: demand increases, 143, 143*f*; energy sources, 142–43; natural gas as most financially viable energy source, 161–62. *See also* electricity; natural gas; oil; renewable energy

energy subsidies, reform of, 107, 133, 140–41, 144

entrepreneurial capacity, nationalization and, 104

entrepreneurship, low return on, 202

environmental problems: as driver of migration, 198. *See also* climate change; water crisis

equality: as basis of legitimacy of Islamic Republic, 13, 17–18; destructive consequences of economically naive view of, 18

exchange rate: Central Bank's failure to control, 130–33; Central Bank's use to control inflation, 130, 132*f*; market exchange rate, 120*t*, 131, 132*f*; multiple currency practices (MCP), 131, 132*f*; necessary reforms in, 134; official exchange rate, 131, 132*f*; real exchange rate (RER), 131, 132*f*

exports: 2011–2020, 120*t*; *vs.* imports, 1960–2020, 113, 114*f*; oil *vs.* non-oil, 1960–2020, 113–14, 114*f*; political actions undermining, 113

external challenges of Iran, and current crisis, 15

external sector, 113–17; exports *vs.* imports, 1960–2020, 113, 114*f*; trading partners, changes in, 107, 115–17, 116*f*. *See also entries under* oil

extortion, 51*f*, 54

FATF. *See* Financial Action Task Force

favoritism, as type of corruption, 50, 51*f*, 53

fertility rates, 64–75; and average household size, 1956–2015, 70; changes, 1970–2020, 46, 47*t*; changes by age group, 1950–2010, 64–65, 66*f*; changes in marriage rates and, 64–66; contraceptive access and, 67–68; current, 67,

75; current pronatalist policy, effects of, 67–69, 68*f*; data on, inaccuracy of, 67–68; *vs.* GDP per capita, for Iran and select countries, 69, 70*f*; government policy, changes in, 66–67; low, transition to, 58; and population increase, 67–69, 69*f*; by province, 64; socioeconomic factors affecting, 64; stable, and projected population in 2025, 173

fertility rates, decline of: 1960–2020, *vs.* other countries, 69, 70*f*; 1980s–1990s, 64, 66*f*, 67, 75; and demographic window of opportunity, 5, 43, 58, 74–75, 74*f*; and increased time and money invested per child, 197; and population age pyramid, 71–73, 72*f*, 75; reasons for, 65–67; as success story, 69

Financial Action Task Force (FATF), 52

financial depth in Iran *vs.* other nations, 1965–2020, 135–36, 136*f*

financial sector, well-developed: and growth of small and medium enterprises, 123; importance for economic development, 123

financial shocks, as driver of migration, 200

financial soundness indicators (FSI), 2005–2019, 137, 138*f*

financial stability, as CBI goal, 134

five-year development plans, first, 14

Food and Agriculture Organization of the United Nations (FAO), 168

food demand, 173–75; 1960–2030, 175*f*; formula for calculation of, 173; income elasticity of, 173–74; projected level by 2025, 175; for specific foods, 1990 *vs.* 2015, 174–75, 174*f*

food imports, ratio to TARWR for Iran *vs.* other countries, 184, 185*f*

food security: definition of, 168; *vs.* food self-sufficiency, 167–68, 188; and future food demand, calculation of, 173; increase in, with international food trade, 184

food security policies, shortsightedness of, 19

food self-sufficiency: as counterproductive goal, 168, 186, 188; *vs.* food security, 167–68, 188; as goal of Iranian agriculture, 167

foreign currency reserves: 1865–2020, 117, 117*f*; 2011–2020, 120*t*; shrinking of, 119

foreign direct investment (FDI), failure to seize potential benefits of, 112–13

foreign nationals in Iran: likely undercounting of, 62, 83; number of, 62; origins of, 62, 83

fossil fuels, turn from: and drop in demand for oil, 148–49, 151–52; likely effects on Iran, 56

France, trade with Iran, 107

fraud by bureaucrats, 51*f*, 52

freedom: in Iran *vs.* peer countries, 6, 6*f*; Rouhani's promises to increase, 22; suppression of, in early stage of revolutionary state, 14

freedom, political, level in Iran, 49

Freedom House, 49

FSI. *See* financial soundness indicators

Fukuyama, F., 7, 8*f*

future of Iran: business as usual, disastrous consequences of, 224–26; democratic accountability as essential for, 224–25; reforms within Islamic Republic framework, as insufficient to affect change, 224, 226; successful, complete transformation of political institutions necessary for, 226–27; three scenarios for, 223–27, 226*t*. *See also* reform

gap hypothesis (Huntington), 46

gasoline prices: 1970–2020, 143–44, 144*f*; central setting of, 144

GDP: impact of water crisis remediation plan on, 183, 184, 184*f*; non-oil, 1960–2020, 81, 81*f*; share of oil in, 1969–2020, 149*f*

GDP growth: 1960–1969, 97, 98–99, 98*f*, 99*f*; 1960–2020, in oil and non-oil sectors, 98–99, 99*f*; 2011–2020, 120*t*; compounded effects of lag in, 6; in early stage of revolutionary state (1979–1988), 97, 98*f*, 99*f*, 102; in governance deadlock and economic stagnation period (2005–2020), 97, 98*f*, 106, 108; in Iran *vs.* peer countries, 5–6, 6*f*; by period, 43, 45*t*; in prerevolution period (1970–1978), 97, 98*f*, 101; in reconstruction and reforms period (1989–2004), 97, 98*f*, 105

GDP per capita: in 1950s, 97; in 2020, as similar to 2000 level, 118; at beginning of the 20th century, 97; in Iran, 88, 89*f*; *vs.* mean years of schooling, in Iran *vs.* other countries, 88, 89*f*; in Pahlavi regime, growth of, 97; World War II and, 97

geographical disadvantages, and poor economic performance, 111–12

Germany, trade with Iran, 107, 115, 116*f*

governance: definition of, 6–7; effect of accountability on quality of, 35–36; modern, goals of, 7–8; poor, as cause of current crisis, 55, 222; quality of, in Iran, factors influencing, 11; World Bank Governance Indicators of, 226–27, 229, 230*f*

governance, effective: interaction of factors in, 7, 12–13; key role in social and economic development, 6; lack of, as source of Iran's crises, 5; as product of state capacity, rule of law, and accountability, 7, 8*f*; *vs.* type of government, 7

governance, key indicators of: in Iran *vs.* peer countries, 5–6, 6*f*; in Iran *vs.* world mean, 229, 230*f*

governance deadlock and economic stagnation period (2005–2020): capital flight in, 108, 117; capital formation rates in, 107; capital inputs as predominant contribution to economic growth,

109; cash transfer scheme, 107; currency devaluation in, 106; and demographic window of opportunity, 106–7; dual economy in, 111; economic conditions in, 106–13, 121, 128*t*; economic development in, 45, 45*t*; and economic reform, risks of, with declining legitimacy, 110; and economic stresses, multiplication of, 112; employment ratio in, 97, 98*f*, 112; energy subsidies reforms, 107; evolution and interaction of governance components in, 15, 16*f*; and foreign direct investment (FDI), failure to seize potential benefits of, 112–13; GDP growth in, 97, 98*f*, 106, 108; government paralysis, causes of, 108; housing program, poor execution of, 107–8; imports in, 107; income and wealth inequality in, 109; income per capita in, 198; inflation in, 97, 98*f*, 106–7, 108, 110; legitimacy decline of, 15, 16*t*, 20, 45; and nuclear ambitions, economic effects of, 108; oil export/revenue per capita in, 97, 98*f*, 106; outstanding bank loans, by sector, 136, 137*f*; and petty bourgeoisie, expansion of, 111; privatization in, 107–8; social mobilization in, 15, 16*t*; start of, 20; total factor productivity in, 109–10, 111; and trading partners, change in, 107. *See also* banking system, financial instability of

government functions: minimum, intermediate, and activist levels of, 8, 8*f*; prioritizing of, 7–8; state capacity and, 8. *See also* bureaucracy

government institutions, types that constrain power, *vs.* types that use power, 7, 8*f*

government of Iran, 23–29; broad focus used to analyze, 11; as electoral autocracy, 38; heavy spending levels, 110; ill-advised interventions, consequences of, 8–9; Islamic Republic's radical changes to, 24; lack of transparency,

40; manipulation of public data, 52; power of supreme leader in, 11–12; ratio of expenditure to GDP, 23–24, 25f; repressive policies of, ineffectiveness in resolving root problems, 1; revolutionary-style approach (*jihadi*), effects of, 29, 30t; wide scope and low capacity of, 23–27, 24f, 55; World Bank Governance Indicators on, 229, 230f. *See also entries under* state; nongovernmental public organizations; parallel institutions created by the Islamic Republic

governments, size *vs.* capacity, 23–24, 24f

Green Movement: government suppression of, 47, 48; rise of, 47

Guardian Council: and Khatami's political reforms, 20; as nonelected part of state, 26; Supreme Leader's control of, 12

Hashemi Rafsanjani, Akbar, 14, 19, 25f, 105, 129

Herasat, and clientelism, 50

higher education in Iran: brain drain and, 93–94; as consumer staple in recent decades, 90; diaspora scholars publishing papers, 1970–2019, 192, 193f, 205; masters and PhD students, number of, 92; as means of easing pressure on weak job market, 90, 92; number holding degrees, 2006–2026, 91, 91f; percentage of students in foreign universities returning home, 192; poor quality of, self-imposed isolation and, 19; and research, productionist approach to, 94; STEM graduates, *vs.* other countries, 92; students in foreign universities, 1970–2018, 191–92, 191f, 205. *See also* colleges and universities; scientific papers published

hostage-taking, as ongoing practice by Islamic Republic, 113. *See also* United States embassy hostages

housing program under Ahmadinejad, poor execution of, 107–8

human capital, damage to, from chronic unemployment, 84

Huntington, Samuel, 7, 13, 17, 46

hydropower, use in electricity generation, 1970–2019, 161, 161f

IFRS. *See* International Financial Reporting System

imports: 2011–2020, 120t; *vs.* exports, 1960–2020, 113, 114f; regulations to control composition of, 131

import substitution policies: lack of industrial capacity for, 112; limited effect of, 114; naive rationale for, 103; regulations to support, 131

income, per capita: in advanced countries *vs.* Iran, 197; disparities in, as driver of migration, 197; and elasticity of demand for food, 173–74; and food basket composition, 174–75, 186; and food demand, 173–75, 175f; minimal growth in, 1979–2020, 5

income inequality, in governance deadlock and economic stagnation period (2005–2020), 109

independence, as basis of legitimacy Islamic Republic, 13, 17–19; economic costs of, 18–19; naive understanding of, 103

India: key indicators of good governance *vs.* Iran, 5–6, 6f; trade with Iran, 115, 116f

industrial policy in Iran: overriding of market signals in, 8; in reconstruction and reforms period (1989–2004), 14

industrial sector: electricity use, 1970–2020, 159f, 160; electricity use *vs.* added value, 160; and import substitution, failure of, 112

industry and mining, economic share, 1960–2020, 99, 100f

inequality: access to contraceptives, 68; high levels of, 101, 109; increase in, 84–85, 102, 121; inflation and, 126; water crisis and, 169. *See also* equality; poverty

inflation: in 1960–1969 period, 97, 98*f*; 2011–2020, 120*t*; under Ahmadinejad, 21; Central Bank's failure to control, 126–30; as chronic throughout history of Islamic Republic, 18; and currency depreciation, 1960–2020, 127–28, 127*f*; as driver of migration, 200; in early stage of revolutionary state (1979–1988), 97, 98*f*; in governance deadlock and economic stagnation period (2005–2020), 97, 98*f*, 106–7, 108, 110; growth of money supply and, 127–29, 127*f*, 128*f*, 182*t*; means of controlling, as well known, 26, 126–27; and national debt, 119; in prerevolution period (1970–1978), 97, 98*f*, 101–2, 127, 128*t*; as probably underestimated, 127; in reconstruction and reforms period (1989–2004), 97, 98*f*, 105; volatility of, 126

inflation, high: benefit to government and political elite, 133, 141; causes of, 110; as defining feature of the Islamic Republic, 110, 126–27, 140; economic consequences of, 18, 126–28, 127*f*, 128*f*, 128*t*, 141; government's minimal concern about, 133, 140

influence peddling, as type of corruption, 51*f*, 53

institutional autonomy, and diminished state capacity, 26–27

interest rates, high: and cash flow problems, 137, 138–39; and cost of borrowing, 139; necessity of offering, 139

International Financial Reporting System (IFRS), banks' failure to comply with, 139–40

International Monetary Fund, and Washington Consensus, 27, 105

international outbound airline passengers, 1960–2018, 201, 202*f*

International Scientific Indexing (ISI) journals, and publication standards in Iran, 217

internet: and availability of information on how to emigrate, 201, 202*f*; penetration, 1960–2018, 201, 202*f*

Iran-Iraq War: and budget deficits, 104; decision to end, 44; dire consequences for Iran, 14, 104; as driver of migration, 193–94, 199, 199*f*; and GDP decline, 102; impact on oil production, 145; and Iranian deaths, 59–60, 60*f*; Pahlavi era investments and, 104; slow recovery from, 44; and spread of corruption, 34–35; and state capacity, impact on, 24

Iran-Iraq War, end of: and public demand for economic improvement, 28, 104, 108; and rise of M_2 multiplier and share of time deposits, 129–30, 130*f*

Iraq, trade with Iran, 107, 115, 116*f*

IRGC. *See* Islamic Revolutionary Guard Corps

ISI. *See* International Scientific Indexing (ISI) journals

Islamic Advertisement Organization, and clientelism, 50

Islamic finance system: and banking system, 135, 141; and Central Bank of Iran, 124, 125; and suppression of financial markets, 125

Islamic Republic: diaspora community supporting, geographic distribution of, 53*f*; dysfunctional institutions, and sluggish economy, 97; establishment of, and migration of Iranians, 193–94; factors diminishing state capacity, 24–25; frequent changes of government in early years, 102; radical changes to governance system, 24; replacement of experienced bureaucrats with inexperienced supporters, 24. *See also* early stage of revolutionary state (1979–1988); governance deadlock and economic stagnation period (2005–2020); nationalizations under Islamic Republic; parallel institutions created by the Islamic Republic; reconstruction and reforms period (1989–2004)

Islamic Republican Party, 38

Islamic Republic legitimacy: equality as basis of, 13, 17–18; independence as basis of, 13, 17–19, 103. *See also* constitution of Islamic Republic

Islamic Revolutionary Guard Corps (IRGC): excessive autonomy of, 27; for-profit economic activities of, 22–23; lack of transparency, 40; as nonelected part of state, 26; as obstacle to economic reform, 22–23; as parallel institution, 25; privatization and, 28, 33; smuggling by, 52; tax exemptions of, 110

Italy, trade with Iran, 107

Japan, trade with Iran, 107, 115, 116*f*

JCPOA. *See* Joint Comprehensive Plan of Action

Jihad of Construction, 29

job creation: chronic shortage, reasons for, 84, 94; in early stage of revolutionary state (1979–1988), 102; in prerevolution period (1970–1978), 101; rate of growth, 82; in reconstruction and reforms period (1989–2004), 106

Joint Comprehensive Plan of Action (JCPOA): negotiation of, 15, 21; pressure on Iran to accept, 108, 149; and regime legitimacy, 22; US withdrawal from, 15, 22, 108, 119, 132, 145

judicial system: corruption in, 34, 51*f*, 54; failure to establish rule of law, 34; lack of independence from religious authorities, 31; as nonelected part of

state, 26; as political weapon, 31–33; punishment of corruption whistleblowers, 49; role in 1960–1969 period, 98

Khamenei, Ali: frequent changes of government prior to, 102; and JCPOA, 108; nuclear ambitions, economic effects of, 108; opposition to reform, 119–21; pronatalist policy, 67–68; and reconstruction and reforms period, 14, 105; and religious authorities' rule by law, 31

Khatami, Mohammad: administration of, as best hope of reform, 23; and Central Bank financing on deficit, 129; economy under, 106; electoral victory of, factors leading to, 19–20; important institutional developments under, 106; and reconstruction and reforms period, 105; taxes collected under, as percentage of GDP, 25*f*

Khatami, and reform movement, 47; causes of failure, 20; public loss of faith in, 21

Khomeini, Sayyid Ruhollah Musavi: economic self-sufficiency policies, effects of, 103, 104; and Governance of the Islamic Jurist, 31; and Iran-Iraq War, 44, 104, 108; and Islamic Republican Party, 38; lack of economic knowledge, 103; legitimacy of, based on religious authority, 30–31; rule by law under, 30–31

labor force, 76–86; damage to human capital from chronic unemployment, 84; definition of, 76; discouraged workers, percentage of, 77, 82; discouraged workers among women, 82; and employment ratio, 82; by gender and age, 1966–2016, 78–79, 78*f*; median age of workers, 1966–2016, 79; men's dominance of, 79–81, 80*f*, 82; migrant

labor force (*continued*)
  workers in, 83; and population growth, effect of, 78–79, 78*f*; profound changes in past half century, 76; ratio of workers to pensioners, 1965–2020, 86, 86*f*. *See also* economically inactive population; population, working age
labor force, by economic sector, 1960–2020, 76–77, 77*f*, 78; failure to industrialize and, 78; shift from agrarian economy and, 78
labor force, women in: by age, 1966–2016, 78–79, 78*f*; in developing countries, U-shaped trend in, 79, 93; and discouraged workers, 82; incentives for, 79; low participation rate, 79–81, 82, 93; *vs.* other countries, 79–81, 80*f*; small number, reasons for, 79–81, 82
labor force participation rate: 1960–2020, 77; in 2020, *vs.* other countries, 77; by age and gender, 1960–2020, 78–79, 78*f*; by gender, *vs.* other countries, 79–81, 80*f*; low, damage done by, 84, 94; variation by province, 83; for women, 79–81, 82, 93
labor market in Iran: factors affecting, 76; major trends, 1960–2020, 77–78
labor productivity: education and, 88; lack of increase in, 81, 81*f*, 95
Law for Administration of the Banks, 135
lawsuit cases, 35, 36*t*
leadership of Iran, lack of economic knowledge, 38
legal system in Iran: components in development of, 9–10; diminishing legitimacy of, and increase in crime and corruption, 10, 15, 35, 36*f*; Sharia and, 9–10
legitimacy, 16–23; Ahmadinejad's damage to, 20–21; of authoritarian regimes, 16–17; in early stage of revolutionary state (1979–1988), basis of, 13–14, 16*t*, 17–18, 19; effect of accountability on, 35–36; JCPOA and, 22; in prerevolution period (1970–1978), 16*t*, 17; in reconstruction and reforms period (1989–2004), 14, 16*t*, 19–20
legitimacy, decline of: and current crisis, 23, 118; and cycle of political decay, 48, 48*f*; effects of, 55; in governance deadlock and economic stagnation period (2005–2020), 15, 16*t*, 20, 45; and increasingly harsh response to protest, 47–48; and loss of faith in the legal system, 10, 15, 33–34, 35, 36*f*; and risk of economic reform, 55, 110, 144
literacy rates: 1970–2020, 46, 47*t*; current, 87; improvement in, 86–87, 94; *vs.* other countries, 1950–2020, 86, 87*f*
low-income households, 107

market exchange rate, 2011–2020, 120*t*
market failures: correction of, as goal of modern governance, 7; types of, 7
marriage: age at first marriage, 1976–2016, 64; number of, 1965–2020, 64, 65*f*; percentage of women ever married, by age, 1956–2019, 64, 65*f*, 66
MCP. *See* multiple currency practices
media: free, and accountability, 10; suppression of, and spread of corruption, 35, 40, 49
middle class, urban, rise in prerevolution period, 43–44
migration, drivers of, 195–201; mediating factors, 195, 196, 196*t*, 200–201; precipitating factors, 195, 196, 196*t*, 199–200, 199*f*, 203; predisposing factors, 195–97, 196*t*, 203; proximate factors, 195, 196, 196*t*, 198–99, 203; push-pull theory of, 195
migration, internal: demographic change and, 75; from rural to urban areas, 59, 60*f*, 63, 63*f*, 84
migration, international: countries hosting Iranian migrants, 190*f*, 191; data on, 189, 232–33; government position on, 189–90, 202; information on how

to emigrte and destinations as factor in, 201, 202*f*; large inflows and
outflows in past decades, 62; likely
continuation of, 202–3, 205; migrants
in US, 53, 191, 192, 193, 235*t*–36*t*;
migrants in US, high naturalization
rate, 191; migrant to population ratio,
1970–2020, 190–91, 191*f*; necessary
resources as factor in, 200–201; net
annual flow, estimation of, 233–36,
234*f*; number of new asylum seekers,
1980–2019, 193–95, 194*f*, 205; percentage of students in foreign universities
returning home, 192; reasons for, 191,
193–94; reversal of, real reform, 203;
by scholars, increasing incentives for,
221; students in foreign universities,
1970–2018, 191–92, 191*f*, 205; as symptom of discontent, 189–90; trends in,
1970–2020, 190–91, 191*f*, 205. *See also*
brain drain; scholars, diaspora
mineral resources, depletion of, without replacement by enduring assets,
118
minimum daily wage: in 2020, as below
poverty threshold, 84, 108–9; in 2020,
comparable to 1960s, 94; *vs.* China and
Turkey, 1960–2020, 84–85, 85*f*
Ministry of Agriculture, and Jihad of
Construction, 29
Mohammad Reza Shah, 30, 87, 98, 101
Monetary and Banking Acts (1960, 1972),
124
monetary base (M$_2$ multiplier): growth
rate, 1965–2020, 127–28, 128*f*, 128*t*;
ratio to broad money, 1965–2020,
129–30, 130*f*; shares of different components of, 128–29, 129*f*
monetary policy, 134, 140, 200
Money and Credit Council (MCC),
appointment based on political loyalty,
126
money-laundering, 51*f*, 52
money supply, growth of: causes of,

128–29; and inflation, 127–29, 127*f*,
128*f*, 182*t*
Mosaddegh, Mohammad, 97, 147
Mousavi, Mir-Hossein, 102
multiple currency practices (MCP), 131,
132*f*
Muslim Student Followers of the Imam's
Line (*aneshjouyan-e-peyro-khat-e-
imam*), and US embassy hostages, 24–25

NASA, AgMERRA Climate Forcing Dataset for Agricultural Modeling, 176,
176*f*
national debt: causes of, 118–19; inflation
and, 119; interest payments, 119, 120*t*,
121*f*; need for securitization of, 133,
141; as percentage of GDP, 2011–2021,
119, 121*f*
National Development Fund of Iran
(NDFI): and financing of budget deficits, 118, 124; lack of transparency, 40;
money put into, 132; purpose *vs.* actual
use, 132–33
National Iranian Oil Company (NIOC),
strikes at, 145
nationalization of the oil industry, 97, 147
nationalizations under Islamic Republic,
24; of banks, 135; effects of, 102, 103–4;
political support for, 32
natural gas, 153–59; as byproduct of oil
production, flaring of, 153, 157–59, 158*f*;
consumption levels, by use, 157, 158*f*;
as domestic energy source, 142, 143,
154, 155*f*, 156, 157, 158*f*, 164; imports of,
157; as most financially viable power
choice, 161–62; reinjection into mature
oil fields to increase yield, 155*f*, 157,
158*f*; use by petrochemical industry,
156, 164; use for transportation infrastructure, 156–57
natural gas, allocation of: as centrally
determined, 156, 164; priorities of uses,
157, 158*f*; as source of rent and patronage, 164

natural gas, in electricity generation, 165; 1970–2019, 160–61, 161f; future power needs and, 162

natural gas exports: domestic demand and, 164; as limited, 143; projects financed by, 153; *vs.* Qatar, 157; to Soviet Union, 153

natural gas infrastructure, development of, 153

natural gas liquids (NGLs): Iran's rank in production of, 146; as non-oil export in reported figures, 114; proven reserves, 149; reserve-to production ratio, 149; revenue from export of, 117

natural gas price: as centrally determined, 156; *vs.* global market prices, 156

natural gas production: 1970–2019, 155, 155f; 1970–2019, by use, 155f, 156; in 2020, 164; development of, 142, 153–54, 164; future of, 164; increase in, as unlikely, 155; *vs.* other countries, 154, 154f, 164; stability of, 155; value of, 164

natural gas reserves: discovery and development of, 153–54, 155; Iran's rank *vs.* other countries, 142, 154, 164; proven, 142, 154, 154f; as separate from oil reserves, 142, 153; South Pars/North Dome field, 113, 153, 155, 157, 159, 159f, 161; value of, 154

natural resources revenues, and inhibition of manufacturing, 94

NDFI. *See* National Development Fund of Iran

nepotism, 41, 51f, 53

1960–1969 period: capital formation rates in, 99, 100f; economic conditions in, 98–99, 121; employment ratio in, 97, 98f; GDP growth in, 97, 98–99, 98f, 99f; inflation in, 97, 98f; institutional prerequisites for growth in, 98; oil export/revenue per capita in, 97, 98f; social mobilization in, 98; technocratic

capacity and entrepreneurial activity in, 98

NIOC. *See* National Iranian Oil Company

nongovernmental public organizations: corruption in, 50, 51f; institutions comprising, 26; power of, and failure of reforms, 20; tax exemptions for, 110; tensions with elected part of state, 26. *See also* parallel institutions created by the Islamic Republic

non-income-generating assets, accumulation in banking system, 137–38

nonperforming loans (NPLs): accumulation in banking system, 137–38; hiding of, 138–39; ratio, 2005–2019, 137, 138f

NPLs. *See* nonperforming loans

nuclear power: direct and implied costs of, 161–62, 165; expansion of, as option for future power needs, 162; as percentage of power generation, 161, 165; use in electricity generation, 1970–2019, 161, 161f

nuclear program: economic effects of, 108–9; political function of, 21. *See also* Joint Comprehensive Plan of Action (JCPOA)

oil, 144–53; British embargo after nationalization, 97; as domestic energy source, 142; exploration, after revolution, 147

oil, domestic consumption: 1960–2020, 147; consumption of petroleum-derived products (2020), 147; real GDP per barrel, 147

oil exports: dramatic fluctuations, events causing, 113; *vs.* non-oil exports, 1960–2020, 113–14, 114f; nuclear deal and, 15

oil exports and revenue per capita: in 1960–1969 period, 97, 98f, 99; in early stage of revolutionary state (1979–1988), 97, 98f, 101; and foreign currency reserves, 117; in governance deadlock and economic stagnation period (2005–2020), 97, 98f, 106; in prerevolution period (1970–1978), 97, 98f; in reconstruction and reforms period (1989–2004), 97, 98f, 105

oil industry: economic share, 1960–2020, 99, 100f; economic share, in prerevolution period (1970–1978), 101; nationalization of, 97; revenues before and after nationalization, 147

oil market, global: climate change concerns, and drop in demand, 148–49, 151–52; new technologies increasing supply, 148, 152; and peak oil theory, 148–49, 152

oil market, and shift to oil abundance paradigm: causes of, 151–52; and diminished value of Iranian oil reserves, 122, 151–52

oil prices: decline, 2014–2015, 22, 108; decline, in Asian Contagion of 1997, 106; shift to oil abundance paradigm and, 122, 151–52

oil production: 1960–1969, 97, 99; 1960–2020, 144–45, 145f, 147–48; consortium agreements (1954, 1971) and, 144–45, 147, 148; cost per barrel, 151, 163–64; exports per capita, 1960–2020, 147, 149f; foreign investment in, 151; future, factors affecting, 152; growing need for more-expensive extraction technology, 151, 164; growth of, as unlikely, 112; increase, 1954–1972, 147; Iran's share of world market, 1975–2021, 145–47, 146f; low levels and national wealth, 153; low levels of, and stranded oil reserves, 152–53; number of wells, 1960–2020, 150, 150f; and peak oil theory, 148–49, 152; political disruptions affecting, 144–45, 147–48; potential duration of, 163; in prerevolution period (1970–1978), 101; production per well, 1960–2020, 150–51, 150f; sanctions and, 145, 148, 149, 152, 153; share of oil in GDP, 1969–2020, 149f

oil reserves: depletion levels, 1970–2030, 150–51, 150f; depletion without replacement by enduring assets, 118; diminished value of, with shift to oil abundance paradigm, 122, 151–52; likely stranding of, 152–53; proven, 142, 149; reserve-to production ratio, 149

oil revenues: 1979 to 2020, 5; after nationalization, 147; Ahmadinejad's spending and, 21; central role in economy, 142, 147; effect on state capacity, 25, 27; and elite attitudes toward entrepreneurship and rent-seeking, 147; and GDP 1960–2020, 98–99, 99f; Iran-Iraq War and, 104; and jobless growth, 81, 81f; large variations in, funds to counter, 132; and modernization in prerevolution period, 13; before nationalization, 147; oil sanctions and, 21, 22, 108, 119; as percentage of GDP, 163; as percentage of government revenues, 163; as primary source of foreign currency, 113; and ratio of government expenditure to GDP, 24, 27; reduced, economic effects of, 164; total, since 1979 revolution, 163; as unlikely to rise, 225. See also oil exports and revenue per capita

oil revenues, future: insufficiency to drive growth, 112; likely levels of, 152, 163

oil sanctions: economic effects of, 21, 22, 108, 119, 131–32, 200; impact on oil production, 145, 148, 149, 152, 153; as motive for emigration, 200; return in 2018, 108; and spread of corruption, 35

Oil Stabilization Fund of Iran (OSF), 106, 132

Oqaf (charitable endowments), tax exemptions of, 110

OSF. See Oil Stabilization Fund of Iran

Pahlavi regime, 13, 17, 97, 136, 137f. See also Mohammad Reza Shah; Reza Shah parallel institutions created by the Islamic Republic, 24; and government capacity, undermining of, 25–26; influence of, and corruption, 34–35; privatization and, 28. *See also* nongovernmental public organizations

patronage: relationships, development of, 9; and rent seeking, 50, 51*f*, 52

peak oil theory, 148–49, 152

peasants, migrant, political mobilization in prerevolution period, 43–44

pension crisis, 85–86; likely effects from, 86; and ratio of workers to pensioners, 1965–2020, 86, 86*f*

pension funds: managers' personal profits from, 85–86; takeover of state-owned enterprises, 85–86

periods in Iranian development: evolution and interaction of governance components in, 13–16, 16*f*; as ideal types, 15–16. *See also* early stage of revolutionary state (1979–1988); governance deadlock and economic stagnation period (2005–2020); 1960–1969 period; prerevolution period (1970–1978); reconstruction and reforms period (1989–2004)

petrochemical industry: basic products produced by, 156; growth of, 156; use of natural gas, 156, 164

police, corruption in, 51*f*, 54

political decay, 48, 48*f*

political parties: recognition in constitution, 37–38; suppression of, and spread of corruption, 35

political parties, stable programmatic, lack of: as obstacle to de facto accountability, 37, 38–39; as obstacle to reform, 26

poor and vulnerable, protection of, as goal of modern governance, 7

population, 59–62; 1950–2020, 59, 60*f*, 75; age dependency ratio, 75; age distribution by group, 1950–2050, 73, 73*f*, 75; age distribution *vs.* selected

countries (2020), 71, 72*f*; age pyramids, 1976–2026, 71, 72*f*, 75; distribution among cities, 63, 64*f*; elderly, rapid growth, 2020–2050, 73–74, 73*f*; and food demand, 173, 175*f*; immigration and, 62; life expectancy increases and, 60–61, 61*f*; percentage of foreign nationals, by province, 62; potentially massive redistribution of, with water crisis, 185; provincial distribution, 62–64, 62*f*; rural, in areas of groundwater stress, 185, 186*f*; working age population, 1950–2050, 73, 73*f*. *See also* labor force

population, urban *vs.* rural: 1956–2016, 63, 63*f*; 1960–2020, 59, 60*f*; by province, 63, 63*f*

population, working age: 1950–2050, 73, 73*f*; discouraged workers as percentage of, 77, 82; and employment ratio, 82; growth, 1960–2020, 94; percentage unemployed, underemployed, or discouraged, 77–78, 82, 118; rate of growth, 82

population dependency ratio, definition of, 76

population growth: 1991–2025, 173; annual growth rate, 173; and demand for natural gas, 154; and energy demand, 143; and expansion of universities, 90, 216; expansion policies, as unsustainable, 19; explosive growth of 1980–1985, 58, 59, 60*f*; and GDP decline in the early Islamic Republic, 102; and labor force, effect on, 78–79, 78*f*, 94; and water crisis, 186, 188

population growth, and demographic window of opportunity, 58, 74–75, 74*f*, 106; effects of failure to capitalize on, 122; failure to capitalize on, 5, 43, 75, 84, 88, 118

population growth rate: current, 59; effects of, 68–69, 75; fertility rates and, 67–69, 69*f*; by province, 62–63, 62*f*

poverty, high levels in 2021, 118, 121
precipitation, average annual: 1965–2019, 176, 177f; decline, 1980–2010, 176, 187; long-term, 176, 176f
prerevolution period (1970–1978): accountability, demand for, 13, 16t; and classical scenario of political decay in modernizing countries, 13, 17; economic conditions in, 99–102, 121, 128t; economic development in, 13, 16t, 43, 45t; economic growth, low quality of, 101; employment ratio in, 97, 98f; evolution and interaction of governance components in, 13, 16f; GDP growth in, 97, 98f, 101; income inequality in, 101; income per capita in, 198; inflation in, 97, 98f, 101–2, 127, 128t; internal migration in, 101; job creation in, 101; legitimacy, decline of, 16f, 17; oil exports and revenue per capita in, 97, 98f; oil production in, 101; oil revenues, modernization and, 13; outstanding bank loans, by sector, 136, 137f; peasants' political mobilization in, 43–44; rule of law as pro forma in, 30; social mobilization in, 13, 16t, 17, 43–44, 102; top-down modernization in, 13; tourism industry in, 101; and urban middle class, growth of, 43–44; working class social mobilization in, 17, 44
presidents of Iran: lack of economic knowledge, 38; patronage and, 52
price stability, as CBI goal, 134
prime ministers of Iran, lack of economic knowledge, 38
private credit to GDP ratio, 1970–2020, 128t
privatization in Iran: abuses during, Ahmadinejad and, 21; forces necessitating, 27; and government loss of control over economy, 28; groups benefiting from, 28–29; lack of rule of law and, 33; lack of transparency, 40; mismanagement of, 9, 27–29, 118; and transfer of assets to parastatal organizations, 33, 108; value of privatized assets, 28
property rights, lack of protections for, 32–33; effect of, 104
protests, violent crackdowns on: and decline of legitimacy, 47–48; as motive for emigration, 194, 200
public debt, 2011–2020, 120t
public investments, 105. See also capital formation rates

Qajar, Mozaffar ad-Din Shah, 97
quantitative approaches to evaluation governance, World Bank Governance Indicators, 229, 230f

Rafsanjani, Akbar. See Hashemi Rafsanjani, Akbar
Reaganism, 27
real exchange rate (RER), 131, 132f
reconstruction and reforms period (1989–2004): accountability, lack of, 14, 16t; agriculture in, 106; capital formation rates in, 106; economic conditions in, 105–6, 121, 128t; economic development in, 14, 44–45, 45t; employment ratio in, 97, 98f; evolution and interaction of governance components in, 14, 16f; failure of reforms, reasons for, 20; and foreign debt, growth of, 105; GDP growth in, 97, 98f, 105; income per capita in, 198; industrial policy in, 14; inflation in, 97, 98f, 105; job creation in, 106; legitimacy in, 14, 16t, 19–20; liberalizing economic reforms in, 105; oil export/revenue per capita in, 97, 98f, 105; and oil sanctions, effects of, 21, 22; outstanding bank loans, by sector, 136, 137f; risk-averse attitude in, 44–45; rule of law in, 14; social mobility in, 44; social mobilization in, 19–20

redistribution of wealth, destructive
consequences of economically naive
approach to, 18
reform: of Central Bank, necessary measures for, 133–35, 140–41; of Central
Bank, relative ease of, 26; current
government's resistance to, 23; demand
for, and legitimacy in reconstruction
and reforms period (1989–2004),
19–20; democratic accountability as
essential for, 224–25; and disastrous
consequences of business as usual,
224–26; within the Islamic Republic
framework, as insufficient, 224, 226;
needed reforms, 56–57; officials' lack
of incentives for, 140–41; one-dimensional, ineffectiveness, 56; path toward,
as currently unavailable, 56; successful,
complete transformation of institutions necessary for, 226–27; successful, diaspora community and, 203–4.
See also reconstruction and reforms
period (1989–2004)
reform, obstacles to, 26; blocking of,
by corrupt interests, 118, 119–21,
122; fear of unrest as, 110, 144, 203;
government's wide scope and low
capacity as, 23–24; lack of accountability as, 26; lack of political parties
as, 26; lack of social capital as, 40–41;
tensions between elected and nonelected parts of government as, 25–26,
40–41
reform movement: bureaucratization of,
in reconstruction and reforms period,
14; failure of, 14; rise and collapse of,
47
remittances from diaspora community,
204
renewable energy: and freeing of natural
gas for reallocation, 163; viability of,
162–63, 162f
rent seeking: *vs.* corruption, 50; patronage networks and, 50, 51f, 52

repression, social and political, as driver
of migration, 193–94, 197
RER. *See* real exchange rate
research and development spending, as
percentage of GDP, 214
retirement of baby boomers of 1975–1995,
and pension crisis, 85
Retractions Watch Database, 211
return on assets (ROA), 2005–2019, 137,
138f
revolutionary foundations (*bonyads*):
and clientelism, 50; lack of transparency, 40; as nonelected part of state,
26, 32; privatization and, 28, 32, 33; tax
exemptions of, 110, 140; as unregulated, 32
Revolution of 1979: as driver of migration, 199, 199f; effect on state capacity,
25; impact on oil production, 145, 147–
48; as replay of Qajar revolution, 13
Reza Shah: abdication, 97; and institution
of rule of law, 30; and mass education,
introduction of, 87
ROA. *See* return on assets
Rouhani, Hassan: avoidance of reforms,
22; and Central Bank financing on
deficit, 129; election, reasons for, 21;
and governance deadlock and economic stagnation period (2005–2020),
15, 106; and nuclear deal, 15, 21; and oil
sanctions, 108; promises of increased
freedoms, 22; tax collected under, as
percentage of GDP, 25f
rule of law, 29–35; control of state power
as main function of, 30; definition of,
9; as a factor in effective governance, 7,
8f, 9–10, 29; *vs.* rule by law, 30; shaping
of expectations and behaviors, 9; and
social contract, 9
rule of law in Iran: and cycle of political
decay, 48, 48f; effect of accountability
on, 36; *vs.* peer countries, 6, 6f; primitive stage of development, 30; process
of developing, 9, 30; as pro forma in

prerevolution period, 30; reconstruction and reforms period (1989–2004), 14; replacement by religious authorities' rule by law, 30–35; undermining of, in early stage of revolutionary state, 14, 16t, 30–31; World Bank Governance Indicators on, *vs.* world mean, 229, 230f

rule of law, establishment of: as essential for future progress, 224; as long-term process, 9, 29–30

rule of law, lack of: and conflicting sets of laws, 33; as driver of migration, 198; effects of, 32–33, 55; and endemic corruption, 34–35, 55; and public's lost respect for law, 33–34, 55

Russia, Iran's ties to, 18

scholars, diaspora: collaboration with colleagues still in Iran, 221; at foreign universities, 192–93, 193f; motives for emigration, 199, 221; nations hosting, 193, 194f; number publishing papers, 1970–2019, 192, 193f, 205; number returning to Iran, 192–93; percentage of Iranian scholars living abroad, 193; return to Iran, after real reform, 203. *See also* scientific papers

scholarship on Iran, limitations of, ix, x, 2

scientific papers, and corruption in publication process, 217–19, 221, 222

scientific papers, retraction rate: for Iranian institutions, as highest in world, 211, 222; for Iranian institutions, by institution, 239t; as measure of scientific misconduct, 211

scientific papers published: and black market, 217–18, 222; by graduate students, minimal faculty supervision of, 222; and isomorphic mimicry, 207; and journals guaranteeing publication for a fee, 218; prioritization of quantity over quality, 217; quality of, 94, 206–7, 210–13, 210f, 216–17, 221, 222; quantity

of, 94, 206–7, 214–17, 215f, 221, 222; as requirement for faculty promotion, 206; as requirement for graduate student graduation, 206; scholars with large number of, 218–20, 220f; *vs.* spending of research, 214–16

scientific papers published (1997 to 2018): data on, 207, 237–40, 239t; increase in, 87; number of citations of, 208, 208t; percentage in top journals, 211–13, 212f; as percentage of world's scientific output, 208; quantity of, 207–8, 208t, 209f; share by field, 210, 210f; universities producing largest numbers of, 211

scientific papers, citation of: as higher for papers with international collaborations, 208t, 210; number of, 208, 208t; percentage in top journals, 211–13, 212f; percentage of self-citations and citations by other Iranian scientists, 211–13, 212f; percentage *vs.* other countries, 213–14, 213f

scientific papers published with international collaborations: country of collaborator, 208–10, 209f, 238t; higher number of citations, 208t, 210; increase in, 221; number of, 208, 208f; share of, 208, 209f

Scopus, 207, 210, 213, 219, 220f, 232, 237, 238

secularization, increase in, 46

Sharia: and Iranian legal system, 9–10; secularization and, 46

small business, hostile environment for, 94

smuggling, 51f, 52

social capital, decline of, 5, 43; corrupt bureaucratic recruitment practices and, 43; corruption and, 34; and current crisis, 118; and inability to pursue reforms, 23, 26, 40–41

social contract, rule of law and, 9

social forces in Iran, under-studied role of, 2

social media, and accountability, 38–39

social mobility: in prerevolution period (1970–1978), 43; in reconstruction and reforms period (1989–2004), 44

social mobilization, 45–48; in 1960–1969 period, 98; definition of, 45–46; as driver of migration, 197; in governance deadlock and economic stagnation period (2005–2020), 15, 16*t*; indicators of, 46, 47*t*; and potential for unrest, 46; in prerevolution period (1970–1978), 13, 16*t*, 17, 43–44, 102; in reconstruction and reforms period (1989–2004), 19–20

social movements: four typical stages of, 47; government suppression of, 47–48; recent rise of, 47

social order, destabilization of, with social mobilization, 46–47

solar energy, potential for, 162–63, 162*f*

South Korea, trade with Iran, 115, 116*f*

Stanford Iran 2040 Project, ix–x

state capacity: bureaucracy's revolutionary-style approach and, 29, 30*t*; corruption's damage to, 34, 40; and cycle of political decay, 48, 48*f*; damage to, from bureaucracy's lack of meritocracy, 10, 36, 42, 52; definition of, 23; as factor in effective governance, 7–9, 8*f*; factors inhibiting, 25–26; institutional autonomy and, 26–27; Iran's wide scope and low capacity, 23–27, 24*f*; under Islamic Republic, factors diminishing, 24–25; obstacles to reform and, 26; oil revenues and, 25, 27; *vs.* state scope, 23

state capture. *See* corruption, political (grand)

state scope: definition of, 23; Iran's wide scope and low capacity, 23–27, 24*f*; privatization and, 28; *vs.* state capacity, 23

stock exchange, 105

student protests (1999), suppression of, and emigration, 194, 200

supreme leader: lack of accountability, 11; patronage and, 52; power in government of Iran, 11–12, 14

TARWR. *See* total actual renewable water resources

tax collection: corruption and, 110; inheritance tax, as small or zero, 110; low levels, and budget deficits, 133; low levels, causes of, 110; low levels, effects of, 118; necessary increase in, with reduced oil revenues, 164; as percentage of GDP, 25, 25*f*, 27; as percentage of GDP *vs.* other countries, 24, 24*f*

technological achievements, claims of, 21

technology, foreign, access to: in 1960–1969 period, 98; lack of, as damper on growth, 113; loss of, with turn to developing-world trading partners, 115–17

temperature, average annual, increase in, and water loss through evaporation, 176–77, 187

TFP. *See* total factor productivity

Thatcherism, 27

theft by bureaucrats, 51*f*, 52

total actual renewable water resources (TARWR), 177; current water use in excess of, 69, 177, 178*t*; decline of, 177; definition of, 177; ratio of food imports to, for Iran *vs.* other countries, 184, 185*f*; recommended water use as percentage of, 177

total factor productivity (TFP), in governance deadlock and economic stagnation period (2005–2020), 109–10, 111

tourism industry: political actions undermining, 113; potential revenue from, after real reform, 204; in prerevolution period (1970–1978), 101

transparency: and control of corruption, 54; establishment of, as essential for future progress, 224

transparency, Central Bank's lack of, 126;

benefits of restoring, 134–35; and public mistrust, 126; reasons for, 40

Transparency International, 49, 49f

Tudeh Party, ties to the Soviet Union, 38

Turkey: key indicators of good governance vs. Iran, 5–6, 6f; trade with Iran, 107, 115, 116f

Twelver Shia community, Khomeini as ranking authority in, 30–31

underemployment rate, 81–82

unemployment rate, 81–82; 1960–2020, 77; current, high level of, 118; disparities between rural and urban areas, 83; high, damage done by, 84, 94; variation by province, 82–83, 83f; variation with age, 82; variation with education level, 82; variation with gender, 82

United Kingdom, trade with Iran, 115, 116f

United Nations: and Iran-Iraq War, 104; water stress threshold defined by, 69

United States: Iranian migrants in, 53, 191, 192, 193, 235t–36t; Iranian migrants in, high naturalization rate, 191; legal barriers to transferring money to Iran, 204; oil production, 1974–2021, 146f; and oil technology advances, 148; and sanctions' reduction of Iranian oil exports, 149; trade with Iran, 115, 116f; withdrawal from JCPOA, 15, 22, 108, 119, 132, 145

United States embassy hostages: impact on Iran's international relations, 104; as justification for political oppression, 14; and non-oil export levels, 113; and oil sanctions, 148; and state capacity, impact on, 24–25

unrest, potential for: with economic austerity in time of declining legitimacy, 55, 110, 144; lack of rule of law and, 32; water crisis and, 169

unsustainable irrigated land (UIL), 180

urbanization: changes, 1970–2020, 46, 47t; as driver of migration, 197

wages: of unskilled labor in 2021, as comparable to level in 1960s, 84. See also minimum daily wage

Washington Consensus, 27, 105

water: dam capacity in service, 1960–2020, 168f; groundwater, 1960–2020, 168f; loss through evaporation, increased average annual temperature and, 176–77; reservoir dam capacity, 1960–2020, 168f; return flow from farms, contaminants in, 178

water consumption: four sectors consuming water, 166–67; as four times greater than water stress threshold, 166; industrial, high marginal benefits of, 167; municipal, as highest priority, 166–67; reduction of, as necessary to avoid water crisis, 166; water balance, 231t. See also agriculture, water use by

water crisis: adaptation to, 2011–2021, 119, 120t, 121f; causes of, 106, 186–87; drive for food self-sufficiency and, 19; as driver of migration, 198; expected population increase and, 69; population growth and, 186, 188; potential consequences of, 118, 169; potentially massive redistribution of population due to, 185; as rapidly growing problem, 112, 122, 166; renewable water per capita, as currently below water stress threshold, 69, 177, 178t; severity of, 118. See also agriculture, water use by

water crisis, addressing of: consumption regulation and, 166, 187; government actions so far, as counterproductive, 167, 186; high cost of delay, 166; improved water productivity and, 166, 187; necessity of strong action, 225; reduction of agricultural water use as only viable solution to, 167, 187; wastewater treatment and reuse and, 166, 187 water crisis remediation plan, 187–88; balancing of groundwater recharge and withdrawal, 178; desalination and, 187; effect on ratio of food import to GDP, 185; focus on reduction of agricultural water use, 178; government control of water use, necessity of, 187; potentially massive redistribution of population due to, 185; reductions in water use, 178*t*; research needed to finalize details of, 188; technological improvements and, 178; wastewater treatment and reuse, 178*t*

water crisis remediation plan, cost of, 183–85; *vs.* business as usual, 183–84, 184*f*; compensation to farmers and, 183, 187; food deficit, import to replace, 183–84, 184*f*, 188; impact on GDP, 183, 184, 184*f*

water crisis remediation plan, effect on agriculture output, 179–83, 182*t*; assumptions used in analysis, 177, 178*t*; steps used to evaluate, 180

water crisis remediation plan, greenhouse agriculture expansion in, 178*t*, 179; amount of water saved by, 179; cost of, 183

water crisis remediation plan, modern irrigation use in: amount of land suitable for, 179; amount of water saved by, 179; cost of, 183; expansion of, 178*t*, 187; and potential loss of saved water

to expand cropland, 178–79, 187; water savings from, 178–79

water crisis remediation plan, removal of irrigation from less-suitable land in, 179–80, 181*f*; agriculture output, effect on, 178, 179–83, 182*t*; rainfed farming in place of, 178, 180, 181*f*

wealth inequality, 109

White Revolution, 98

wind energy, 162–63, 162*f*

women: education levels, 1965–2020, *vs.* labor force participation, 79, 80*f*; unemployment rate, 82

women, in college or university: fields of study, 92–93; as percentage of students, 92

women in labor force: by age, 1966–2016, 78–79, 78*f*; in developing countries, U-shaped trend in, 79, 93; incentives for, 79; low participation rate, 93; *vs.* other countries, 79–81, 80*f*; small number, reasons for, 79–81, 82

women's rights movement: government suppression of, 48; rise of, 47

working class, social mobilization in pre-revolution period, 17, 44

World Bank: on accountability, typical development process for, 37; on corruption level in Iran, 49, 49*f*; and Washington Consensus, 27, 105

World Governance Indicators, on accountability, 10

World War II, and GDP per capita, 97

CPSIA information can be obtained
at www.ICGtesting.com
Printed in the USA
BVHW031953130422
634240BV00001B/7